The Politics of Style

Historical Materialism Book Series

The Historical Materialism Book Series is a major publishing initiative of the radical left. The capitalist crisis of the twenty-first century has been met by a resurgence of interest in critical Marxist theory. At the same time, the publishing institutions committed to Marxism have contracted markedly since the high point of the 1970s. The Historical Materialism Book Series is dedicated to addressing this situation by making available important works of Marxist theory. The aim of the series is to publish important theoretical contributions as the basis for vigorous intellectual debate and exchange on the left.

The peer-reviewed series publishes original monographs, translated texts, and reprints of classics across the bounds of academic disciplinary agendas and across the divisions of the left. The series is particularly concerned to encourage the internationalization of Marxist debate and aims to translate significant studies from beyond the English-speaking world.

For a full list of titles in the Historical Materialism Book Series
available in paperback from Haymarket Books, visit:
https://www.haymarketbooks.org/series_collections/1-historical-materialism

The Politics of Style

Towards a Marxist Poetics

Daniel Hartley

Haymarket Books
Chicago, IL

First published in 2016 by Brill Academic Publishers, The Netherlands
© 2017 Koninklijke Brill NV, Leiden, The Netherlands

Published in paperback in 2017 by
Haymarket Books
P.O. Box 180165
Chicago, IL 60618
773-583-7884
www.haymarketbooks.org

ISBN: 978-1-60846-828-7

Trade distribution:
In the US, Consortium Book Sales, www.cbsd.com
In Canada, Publishers Group Canada, www.pgcbooks.ca
In the UK, Turnaround Publisher Services, www.turnaround-uk.com
All other countries, Ingram Publisher Services International, ips_intlsales@
ingramcontent.com

Cover design by Jamie Kerry of Belle Étoile Studios and Ragina Johnson.

This book was published with the generous support of Lannan Foundation
and the Wallace Action Fund.

Printed in Canada by union labor.

10 9 8 7 6 5 4 3 2 1

Library of Congress Cataloging-in-Publication data is available.

For my parents:
Ken and Audrey Hartley

∵

Contents

Acknowledgements

This book is the fruition of a decade's reading and discussion. Its origins lie in my undergraduate years at Cardiff University, where one fateful winter afternoon I bought a copy of Terry Eagleton's *After Theory* from Blackwell's bookshop beneath the student union. An inauspicious book with which to begin one's journey into theory, perhaps, but one I shall never forget. My work owes much to Eagleton's prowess as a writer and populariser. My enthusiasm for Marxist theory was subsequently nurtured by many gifted academics at Cardiff. I would especially like to thank Richard Sugg, Roberta Magnani, Neil Badmington, Carl Phelpstead, Stephen Knight, Chris Norris and Barry Wilkins, each of whom taught me something different but invaluable, whether they were aware of it or not.

In my two years at the Universiteit van Amsterdam, I was lucky to become friends with Niall Martin, Rob Allen, Dan Hassler-Forrest, Andrew Kerr, Natalie Tal Harries, Sara Murawski, and many others whom I thank for the countless evenings of beer and discussion we shared together. It was also in Amsterdam that I met Gene Moore, one of the singularly most inspiring teachers I have ever had; the afternoons and evenings we spent debating the great modernist writers are amongst the finest memories of my time there. Likewise, Christoph Lindner was a great Master's thesis supervisor without whose pragmatic wisdom I may never have finished it. My biggest Amsterdam debt, however, is to Lucie Aschauer and Robert Barrett without whose enduring friendship the city would have been a far more melancholy place.

Most of the work on this book was enabled by a three-year doctoral scholarship awarded by the International Graduate Centre for the Study of Culture at Justus-Liebig-Universität Giessen (Germany). For this I thank the GCSC and especially the director, Prof. Dr. Ansgar Nünning. During my three years at the GCSC, I met many international scholars and made many friends, all of whom have influenced the present book in their own way. I would like to thank Julia Faisst, who taught me much about the hidden arts of thesis-writing, and who convinced me never to settle for a structure with which I was not truly satisfied. I would also like to thank my first doctoral supervisor Prof. Dr. Ingo Berensmeyer, who was always on hand for advice and whose intellectual enthusiasm spurred the project on. Prof. Dr. Greta Olson provided me with employment when my doctoral scholarship ended, for which I remain grateful; her professional and personal understanding has significantly eased the final stages of the writing process. Most of all, however, I would like to thank my dear friends Natalya Bekhta and Gero Guttzeit in whose warm and animated company I have spent countless hours discussing the ideas set forth in this book. Their intellectual generosity, patience and inimitable humour are the foundation on which this book was built. Natalya: this one's for the office.

Beyond Giessen, I would especially like to thank my second doctoral supervisor Peter D. Thomas. Peter's enviable erudition and his exactingly high standards of scholarship were coupled with a generosity of time and spirit that made him the ideal mentor. This book owes much to his guidance. Jean-Jacques Lecercle was kind enough to read a previous draft of the book and offered several important suggestions. I would also like to thank Hammam Aldouri, not only for his enduring friendship, but also for his constant willingness to share his truly intimidating philosophical expertise. Likewise, over the years Jernej Habjan has become an important friend and intellectual confidant; the conceptual rigour and originality of his work is that to which I aspire. I would also like to thank Madeleine LaRue, a virtuoso stylist and wonderful friend, who has provided regular encouragement, and Hugh McDonnell for his daily companionship. Lastly, I would like to acknowledge my debt to Terry Craven, whom I have now known for over a decade. Some of the ideas contained in this book have their roots in the intense discussions about poetry, politics and philosophy that we held in the cafés of Orléans ten years ago. Those days are long gone, but Terry's compassion, courage and intellectual honesty remain. He is a great friend.

Without the constant love and support of my partner Julia Kröger, I would never have finished this book or the thesis on which it is based. Her integrity, kindness, and her vision of what is truly important in life have sustained me. Julia: *sans toi, rien.*

Finally, I wish to thank my parents Ken and Audrey Hartley for their unconditional support – both emotional and material. Without the many sacrifices they have made, I could not have continued along the (treacherous) path of academia. This book is dedicated to them.

Introduction

In the discourse on style there is always more at stake than how one writes. What begins as a treatise on fine writing segues before long into a theory of literary innovation and, beyond that, into ruminations on the advent of historical novelty *tout court*. A seemingly innocent preference for one kind of writing over another quickly becomes embroiled in broader social judgments. Such connections between style and politics – broadly conceived – occur frequently in the work of three prominent Marxist literary critics: Raymond Williams, Terry Eagleton and Fredric Jameson. Yet what could possibly motivate three Marxists to attach such importance to the matter of style? Surely, one would have thought, there are more pressing political concerns than the shape of one's sentences? Economic crises, class struggle, the theory of surplus value: these are the common currency of the Marxist tradition. But syntax and word-choice? Where exactly do they fit in to the quest for world revolution?

Yet Fredric Jameson has described the issue of style as 'crucial' to the development of his overall project.[1] Likewise, Terry Eagleton, a self-described 'stylist'[2] who was first attracted to Jameson's work by the 'beauty of the style',[3] has made constant references to style as a central constitutive feature, not only of literary works, but also of critical texts more generally. Raymond Williams, who took a much more negative view of the matter (primarily because he associated it with absolutist decrees on what counts as 'good writing'), nonetheless developed a theory of style as 'social relation' which became an important component of his later conceptions of 'cultural materialism' and 'social formalism'. The first task of this book is thus to explain why it was that three Marxist critics came to see style – a primarily literary or artistic concept – as central to political criticism: that is, to delineate the historical and conceptual preconditions for the coming into being of a 'politics of style'.[4]

The second task is to study in more detail precisely what each thinker has written on style and to demonstrate how it figures in their overall intellectual and political projects – including an articulation of what their respective understandings of style imply about their conceptions of politics. Whilst this book in no way aspires to be an intellectual biography of each thinker, it

---

1 Interview in Buchanan 2006, p. 124.
2 Interview in Corredor 1997, p. 139.
3 Eagleton and Beaumont 2009, p. 114.
4 The phrase is borrowed from an important essay by Eagleton (1982) on Fredric Jameson: 'Fredric Jameson: The Politics of Style'.

will nonetheless develop a series of critical reconstructions of certain crucial aspects of their work.[5] The gist of these reconstructions is everywhere guided by the third and overriding task of the book: to develop a Marxist theory of style via an immanent critique of the work of Williams, Jameson and Eagleton, and to establish this theory as a foundational element of a Marxist poetics. In many ways this third task follows naturally from the second. For there are, inevitably, limitations in these theories of style and, in some cases, these limitations are mutually complementary. Thus, for example, Jameson's occasionally reductionist epic scope can be supplemented by the almost obsessively detailed critical rigour and mediatory concepts developed by Williams. In other cases, however, such a move is not possible. At this point, their work has provided a basis but I have turned to alternative sources to enhance it. Out of this process emerged my sense of the need for what I have come to call a 'Marxist poetics', whose theoretical foundations I attempt to sketch throughout this book. Ever cautious of such grandiose ambitions, however, the predominant focus of the present work is literary style alone. The reasons for this will become clear throughout the book; suffice it to say that one of the problems with these critics' work is that their respective sublations of literature into more expansive concepts – literacy or language (Williams), rhetoric (Eagleton), or generic 'symbolic acts' (Jameson) – occasionally subsumes the literary as such. By setting out from the literary, in full awareness of the historically and conceptually problematic nature of that term, I hope to overcome this contradiction and to shine new light on the problems at hand.

Why a poetics? Poetics is in many ways an ambiguous discourse. In the classical Greek technical handbooks, its task was to describe or delineate that which was rational within the process and product of *poiēsis* (Greek for 'making' or 'producing'). It hovered between the purely descriptive and the secretly or overtly prescriptive. Yet if in pre-modern times a poetics was the induction (or deduction) of specific rules or techniques of fine writing, in Romantic modernity this function became obsolete. With the drive for constant literary innovation and the gradual disintegration of the *Stiltrennung* ('separation of styles'), the rule-bound systems of classical poetics and rhetoric – including

---

5   Those who desire intellectual biographies or overviews should consult O'Connor 1989 and Higgins 1999 for Williams, Alderson 2004 and Smith 2008b for Eagleton, and Helmling 2001 and Buchanan 2006 for Jameson. On Williams's early life and thought, Dai Smith's (2008) biography is indispensable. Eagleton's (2001) memoir, whilst formally playful, is also useful in understanding his intellectual formation.

the tomes in which they were explicated – were gradually replaced by manifestos. The authority that was invested in pre-modern poetics and rhetorics
as systematisations of the codes of socially hegemonic discourses came to be
announced in the manifesto by fiat alone.[6] Literary manifestos combine bold
political pronouncements – precisely those things which had often been tacit
assumptions in pre-modern poetics – with complex reflections on literary and
artistic techniques. They are in many ways the poetics of an age which lacks
the relative social homogeneity of the ancient *polis* or republic (i.e., the social
and economic preconditions of the original poetic treatises and their authors,
who themselves constituted something akin to a class fraction). In that light,
a 'Marxist poetics' must look like nothing other than an attempt to square the
circle: the fusion of a predominantly pre-modern form with a critical discourse
(Marxism) whose roots can be traced back to nothing other than ... a manifesto![7]

'Marxist poetics' is thus the name for a historical and critical problem. It
designates that impossible Archimedean point at which the pre-modern is
explained from the vantage point of modernity, but at which the constant
innovations of modernity are viewed through the cool eyes of tradition. 'We
Marxists', wrote Trotsky, 'live in traditions, and we have not stopped being
revolutionists on account of it'.[8] Marxism is a discourse located at the intersection of the dual temporalities of innovation and tradition (both, as it happens, specifically modern temporalities), and a Marxist poetics reflects that:
championing stylistic innovation against those traditionalists who defend the
aesthetic status quo for the same reasons they defend the social inequalities
of the present, but stressing the importance of inherited styles against those
modernist ideologies of the clean 'break' with the past. A Marxist poetics, like
Marxist historiography more generally, attempts to articulate the epic purview
of the *longue durée* with the sudden explosion of the event.

---

6   A manifesto was originally 'a communication, authored by those in authority, by the state,
    the military, or the church, to let their subjects know their sovereign intentions and laws ...
    The revolutionary manifesto will break the conjunction on which this old manifesto rests
    and instead create a genre that must usurp an authority it does not yet possess, a genre that
    is more insecure and therefore more aggressive in its attempts to turn words into actions and
    demands into reality' (Puchner 2006, p. 12).
7   The Communist Manifesto of 1848.
8   Trotsky 2005, p. 115. Trotsky's remark comes in the context of a fascinating critique of what
    he sees as the Russian futurists' hollow attempts to break with the past – '[t]he futurist
    break with the past is, after all, a tempest in the closed-in world of the intelligentsia' (2005,
    p. 115).

This is to suggest that Marxist poetics has a quite specific relation to narrative. The rub of the issue comes in Aristotle's *Poetics* when tragedy is defined as an 'imitation of action' [*mimēsis praxeōs*] whose 'soul' is 'plot' [*muthos*].[9] It should come as no surprise that this emphasis on praxis lends itself to a Marxist rearticulation – it being Marx, after all, who called for the actualisation of philosophy through political praxis, and who viewed the world of ideas as a distorted mirror of social practices and relations.[10] Yet I wish to suggest that there is a more precise manner in which a Marxist poetics, based on the work of Williams, Eagleton and Jameson, owes a debt to this Aristotelian formulation. The crux is that 'Marxist poetics' has two senses. On the one hand, it designates Marxist literary theory broadly defined. On the other, it means that the very methods and modes of exposition which Marxist literary criticism employs have much in common with the operations of *mimēsis praxeōs* and *muthos* which Aristotle makes central to tragedy. Though there is no single methodology uniting the work of Williams, Eagleton and Jameson, all of them may be said to 'translate' literary practices and their products into – or 'reconstruct' them as – 'imitations of praxis' [*mimēsis praxeōs*]. Mimesis is understood here as the operation of imitation and conversion of the raw material of social experience, itself informed by human activity and social relations (embodied at the broadest level in the mode of production), into literary works – even where those works themselves deny all mimetic relation to social reality or are non-narrative in form. Marxist critics attempt to retrace the logic of this imitation and conversion via a method that employs what Aristotle calls *muthos*: the operation of organising events into a system or synthesis – i.e., *emplotment*. This is the process whereby the critic reconstructs the precise coordinates of the historical situation in which the work arose and to which it was a response, seeking that elusive point at which the 'inner' necessity of the work coincides with the 'external' necessity of the historical situation. From Williams's early insistence on a notion of culture as 'a

---

9   Aristotle 2000, 1449b, 1450a. These terms must be seen as dynamic operations imbued with processual vitality by the active 'making' [*poiēsis*] of which they are a part. I here follow Paul Ricoeur in viewing 'action' [*praxis*] as the 'correlate of the mimetic activity governed by the organization of the events (into a system)' (that is, by *muthos*, which Aristotle defines as 'the organization of the events' [*ē tōn pragmatōn sustasis*]) (Ricoeur 1984, p. 34). Likewise, I embrace Ricoeur's identification of 'narrative' with *muthos*, rather than the more limited modal form of *diēgēsis*. Cf. Ricoeur 1984, p. 36.

10   In *Valences of the Dialectic* Jameson (2009, pp. 475–612) has gone so far as to develop an entire historiography using the Aristotelian poetical categories of *peripeteia*, *anagnorisis* and *pathos*.

theory of relations between elements in a whole way of life' to Jameson's cumu-
lative life's work 'The Poetics of Social Forms',[11] Marxist theory aims to emplot
the relations between literary and social processes[12] – respecting the material
specificity of each whilst simultaneously seeking the point of their indifference.

Needless to say, the term 'narrative' is not intended to suggest that these
critics tell stories (literary fictions) about the making of stories. On the contrary,
the same caveat applies here as that of Paul Ricoeur concerning historical
discourse: 'historians are not simply narrators: they give reasons why they
consider a particular factor *rather than some other* to be the sufficient cause of
a given course of events'.[13] For Ricoeur, fictional narrators explain by narration
alone, by the quasi-logical and felt coherence of the emplotment, whereas
historians – and, in our case, Marxist critics – introduce logical argumentation
into their emplotments in order rationally to determine adequate causality. If
their methods sometimes draw on the very literary works they critique, they
are not, for all that, literature.

At this point, however, the reader may wonder why Marxist poetics is being
associated primarily with narrative (*muthos* and *diēgēsis*) when among the
greatest theorists of poetics must be counted the very poets themselves. From
Pound to Bernstein, Zukofsky to Forrest-Thomson, the connoisseurs of stylistic texture were often those poetic practitioners who theorised – sometimes
more, sometimes less accurately – what they and others actually wrote. It is
here that one of the curious features of literary history emerges: as a rule,
each literary theory is based on one genre or type of literature in particular. It is well known that the Russian formalists founded their theory of literature on poetry and short stories; when it came to the extended prose of
the novel, they foundered. Structuralist narratology, however, twinned at birth
with formalism, became one of the greatest sources of insight into the mech-
anics of the novel ever invented – yet it would have difficulty in coming to
terms with a poet such as John Ashbery.[14] Whilst this is certainly no reason
to reject such theories (why, after all, should a literary theory have to explain
all literature?), we should at least be aware that the present work does not
entirely escape this limitation; for all of its awareness of the debates on style

---

11   Williams 1963, pp. 11–12.
12   It should be stressed that such 'relations' are by no means limited to 'reflection'; they also
      include negation, subtraction, redoubling, and many others.
13   Ricoeur 1984, p. 186.
14   There have, however, been attempts to apply narratological theories to lyric poetry: cf.
      Hühn and Kiefer 2005.

in modern and postmodern poetry, and amongst inheritors and challengers of naturalist drama, its focus lies predominantly on prose fiction.

Nonetheless, if this book shares the bias innate to the principal literary theories of the past, it has the edge on them in one crucial sense: it is able to account for the rise and fall of specific literary categories themselves. What other theories lack is that meta-theoretical component which a Marxist poetics can offer. Many theories can explain the intricacies of narrative and many can articulate the nuances of style at the level of the individual phrase, but very few, if any, can compete with Jameson's explanation of the split which occurs in modernity between the level of narrative and the level of style as such. The discipline of stylistics dogmatically presupposes the pertinence of its principal category and object – style – whilst ignoring the factors that led to its prestige in the first place (namely, the demise of the rhetorical conventions of *elocutio*, socially and aesthetically regulated by the *Stiltrennung*, and the concomitant autonomisation of individual writerly styles along with social monadisation). This meta-theoretical component is surely of great value to any historically self-conscious poetics, since it can think the reasons for the genesis and decline of literary categories.

Even if the majority of this book focuses on prose, there is a fortuitous advantage in building a Marxist poetics on the basis of the writings of Williams, Eagleton and Jameson, for in a rough sense each theorist could be assigned to one of the three ancient modes – epic, drama and lyric – thus enabling a more polyvalent poetics than might otherwise have been possible.[15] Williams spent most of his working life as Professor of Drama at Cambridge University, so it comes as no surprise that some of his most useful concepts emerge from the study of a literary form designed for collective, often face-to-face appropriation. It is less easy to treat 'literature' as an apolitical corpus of privately read books when one has dealt constantly with the tacit and collective conventions which inform the production and reception of dramatic works. Eagleton, despite being an expert on the novel, has been more concerned than Williams and Jameson with what one might call the monological, textural aspects of style (here loosely affiliated with the lyric mode). Beyond his overt references to style, there is always at work in Eagleton, whether he be reading poetry, novels or plays, an acute sensitivity to stylistic nuance and its social and political implications. Finally, Jameson has always been overtly concerned with narrative (here associated with 'epic') – that is, with 'narrative as a socially symbolic

15   I call them 'modes' following Williams, who distinguishes between modes, types, genres and forms. For a useful tabulated explanation of the differences, see Jones 2004, p. 122.

act' (the subtitle to *The Political Unconscious*).[16] From his earliest work on Sartre to his more recent writings on Marx's *Capital*,[17] he has attempted to politicise and historicise narratology by investigating the historical conditions of possibility of specific forms.

These three broad approaches to the literary object cannot, of course, simply be 'combined' to produce some total theory of literature, but what they do provide is a series of mutual internal checks and limits. For example, Eagleton sometimes risks falling into a certain abstract celebration of linguistic autonomy, as if acts of textual or stylistic innovation were in and of themselves politically radical – and this despite his professed aversion to the postmodern reduction of radicalism to 'the terrors of tropology or the erotic skid of the signifier'.[18] To prevent such 'textualist' dilutions of the political, Williams's concepts of convention and formation act as checks by reminding us that politics is not located within the 'text', but is constituted via the human relationships in terms of which literary works are written and read (conventions) and the social positions and formations of those groups which produce literature (e.g., the Bloomsbury set, which, as Williams argued, was a class fraction of a newly professionalised bourgeoisie).[19] Taken together, a Marxist poetics avoids the two principal pitfalls of many non-Marxist theories of literature: it has a meta-theoretical component which can explain the historical causes of a given literary category's rise and (possible) demise, and, in principle, it avoids becoming an overly one-sided theory of literature.

There is one final methodological point to note. In *The Formal Method of Literary Scholarship*, Bakhtin and Medvedev made a crucial remark concerning all prior attempts to develop what they called a 'sociological poetics'. These attempts

> borrow everything concerned with literature in its specificity (terminology, definitions, descriptions of the structural peculiarities of literary phenomena, genres, styles, and their elements) from theoretical poetics, which worked out all of these basic concepts ... with the help of psychology (subjective, of course), esthetics (idealist), linguistics (mainly positivist, partly idealist), but with no help of any kind from the Marxist sociological method.[20]

---

16   I say 'overtly' because the 'covert' side of this interest is, of course, his obsession with 'style'.
17   Jameson 1984; Jameson 2011.
18   Eagleton 1982, p. 15.
19   Williams 2010, pp. 148–69.
20   Bakhtin and Medvedev 1978, p. 33.

The implication is that a sociological poetics should not uncritically 'borrow' non-sociological (broadly idealist) concepts only subsequently to contort Marxist theory to fit them. Rather, the work of a true sociological poetics must begin at the level of the specifics themselves: it must use the Marxist theory of history to generate the basic literary concepts with which it will work. These need not always be neologisms. Indeed, owing to the fact that Marxism did not begin life as a theory of literature, it is almost inevitable that many of the literary terms of a Marxist poetics will be inherited from other traditions. Nonetheless, these terms must undergo a process of immanent critique and be 'recalibrated' within a Marxist purview. Raymond Williams spent his entire career doing just that: he reworked older concepts, such as 'tragedy', 'form', 'convention' and 'genre' (not to mention 'culture') but also produced new ones: e.g., 'structure of feeling'. The aim of this book, then, is in many ways to perform just such a recalibration of a single term of literary analysis: style. By demonstrating the various ways in which style is *originally* social and political, prior to any secondary 'application' of sociological categories, we shall thereby avoid the trap of what we might call the 'methodological two-step': poetry first, politics after.

The first part of this book outlines four reasons why Raymond Williams, Terry Eagleton and Fredric Jameson were drawn to the concept of style in the first place: the internal contradictions of the concept of 'style' itself (whose themes of individual versus society, consciousness versus unconsciousness, and nature versus culture, made it germane to Marxist discourse), the epochal political conjuncture of what came to be known as 'Western Marxism', the anomalous terrain of British intellectual history, and the postwar debates within Marxist cultural theory more broadly. I then argue, in Chapter 2, that this interest in style was not an alien intrusion upon the Marxist tradition but had in fact been present from Marx's early writings, where it formed an integral element of his critique of the capitalist state, and has continued, as a subterranean current, until the present day. I conclude Part 1 by suggesting that any Marxist poetics would do well to study the work of that great moderniser of Aristotle, Paul Ricoeur, since his attempt to extend Aristotle's emphasis on plot as the imitation of human action lends itself to a Marxist rearticulation. I then criticise the various residual idealisms inherent to Ricoeur's notion of the 'threefold mimesis' and outline certain desiderata for a Marxist recalibration of his work.

Part 2 of the book then sets out to study in detail the understandings of literary style to be found in Williams, Eagleton and Jameson respectively. I attempt to show the centrality of style to the work of each critic, and to highlight its relation to the larger concerns of their oeuvres. Taking Williams's 1969 essay on English prose as a basis, in Chapter 4 I offer a first working definition of style in prose fiction. By exploring the emphasis Williams placed on stylistic discontinuities as linguistic indices of a writer's experience of a class-divided society, and by attempting to compensate for some of the weaknesses of Williams's approach to style (notably, his lack of a narratological theory of voice), it becomes clear that style is an inherently relational concept: it denotes not simply the verbal phrasing of an individual sentence, but rather a linguistic mode of social relation which, in prose fiction, is split into the three linguistic operations of instance, idiom and interpellation (terms taken from the work of the rhetorical narratologist Richard Walsh). If 'style' as a *singular* phenomenon has any real meaning, it is at the level of the overall lexical configuration of these linguistic operations.

In Chapter 5, I argue that Williams's implicit theory of style showed him to be a thinker for whom immanence is a central principle. I then give examples of this principle of immanence in his work as it relates to: keywords, language, forms and techniques, and what I have called his 'sociological perspectivism'. In the second half of the chapter, I show that Williams's reflections on language grew out of his lifelong work on naturalist drama. I also argue that his theory of style is inseparable from his development of the concept of the 'structure of feeling' – indeed, that the two are often taken by him to be synonymous. By following the various permutations and connotations of the concept of 'style' in Williams's work, I ultimately conclude that the meaning of 'politics' in the title of this book – *The Politics of Style* – must be understood in multiple ways, ranging from the most micrological shifts in transindividual subjectivity all the way to the capitalist state's distribution of the means of communication.

In Chapter 6, I evaluate what I call Terry Eagleton's political theology of style. I provide an overview of his early works of political theology and argue that his recent metaphysical turn and calls for a renewal of close reading both find their origins there. I tease out some of the problems with the overtly Catholic theory of language contained in that work and show how those problems persist in his writings to this day. I also suggest that, despite his consistent calls for attention to the stylistic texture of literary works, his is in fact the least satisfactory theory of style here on offer. This is primarily because his conception of style is spontaneously monological and singular as opposed to dialogical and relational. Nonetheless, I claim that the type of traditional close reading he advocates still has an integral role to play in any Marxist poetics.

In Chapter 7, I argue that, if we extend the logic of Lukács's *Theory of the Novel*, Fredric Jameson could be seen as the epic poet of postmodernity. I suggest that this is an ambiguous appellation insofar as it encompasses at once his gift for epic historical syntheses and his consequent tendency to underestimate the political efficacy of individual literary works. Indeed, I argue that he tends to downplay the importance of politics in favour of economics and its equivalent in the realm of historical temporality – stagist periodisation. In the second half of that chapter I reconstruct in some detail his theory of style as a linguistic symptom of modernity which arises out of the demise of pre-modern rhetoric and the narrative categories of experience, and which becomes synonymous with the bourgeois monadic subject who has lost all organic links to his or her public.

In Part 3 of the book, I develop a set of concepts for an overarching theory of style within the context of a Marxist poetics. These concepts develop out of both the immanent critique of the work of Paul Ricoeur performed in Chapter 3 and my assessment of the strengths and weaknesses of the respective theories of style evaluated in Part 2. It amounts to nothing less than a rewriting of Ricoeur's threefold mimesis from the perspective of style. Amongst the most significant conceptual innovations made in this section are: 'linguistic situation', denoting a hypothetical reconstruction of the state of language as a writer or set of writers would have experienced it, including its inner tensions and social stratifications; 'linguistic ideology', which is the linguistic situation as thought, ranging from spontaneous conception to self-reflexive theorisation; 'poetic shaping', which emphasises the compositional act as a productive and transformative one – thus ensuring that the implicit ideology of a style can never be reduced to the ideological content of the linguistic situation; and 'stylistic ideology', the specifically literary region of linguistic ideology, concerned primarily with the author's conception of the nature and aim of literary styles, as well as the self-conscious stylistic projects he or she develops.

I conclude with a summary of the main features of the Marxist theory of style here developed and some suggestions for future research in the field. It remains to be noted that there are, admittedly, more important things in life than style, but truly to understand style requires nothing less than grasping the dynamics of our collective life together.

"linguistic situation"

PART 1

Marxist Poetics in Context

..

CHAPTER 1

Why Marxism and Style?

What can explain the importance of what is, ostensibly at least, an aesthetic or literary concept to three inheritors and extenders of the Marxist tradition? The answer lies in a unique conjuncture of four factors: the multiple implications of the concept of 'style' itself, the historical and political fate of Marxism in the West, the intellectual context of literary studies in Britain and the US from the 1950s to the 1970s, and the debates on various types of criticism internal to the Marxist tradition. It is to the first of these that we shall now turn.

1   The Concept of Style

Style, one might say, is many things to many Frenchmen. For Sartre, it was a matter of metaphysics, for Barthes the hidden secret of the flesh. Buffon declared it was man himself, whereas Valéry once said it was the very devil. Camus spent much of his writing life trying to avoid it, but Flaubert pursued it with compulsion. Proust believed it was a source of timelessness, and spent many a *nuit blanche* arabesquing his way through Hades. Derrida, on the other hand, found it inseparable from the 'question of woman', whilst Stendhal, who asked of women something else entirely, saw it as a battlefield – the *ancien régime* on one side and the bourgeoisie on the other. What French writers mean by 'style', then, is probably not what most people mean by it.[1]

The point of this observation is simply to show that style is an inherently multiple concept, capable of connection to a large number of diverse issues. Part of the reason for this lies in the nature of the word 'style' itself. Originating in the Latin *stilus*,[2] the word initially denoted the stalk of a plant. Subsequently, via a metaphorical transference, it came to mean the sharpened instrument

---

1   Cf. Sartre 1947, Barthes 1953, Buffon and Clerc 1978, Rancière 1998, Proust 2003, Deleuze 2008, Derrida and Agosti 1978, Berthier and Bordas 2005.

2   Though cf. Aquilina 2014, p. 1: 'The Modern English spelling of "style", with a "y" instead of an "i", probably reflects the influence of the Greek word "stylos", that is, a pillar or column. The spelling is thus marked by what may seem like an error with the Indo-European root of the word "*-sti: to prick, hence sting, stimulus" being replaced by "sty" but which may also be interpreted as an association caused by the verticality of the pillar ("stylos" in Greek) resembling the shape of the Roman writing instrument ("stilus" in Latin)'.

used for inscribing letters on wax tablets, but with the associated sense of any pointed object used for engraving.[3] There are, then, two senses in which 'style' fuses nature and nurture in its very being. Firstly, it harbours within itself the transformation of a botanical organism into a human tool, nature writing itself into culture. Secondly, it contains a symbiosis between, on the one hand, the almost physiological uniqueness of the human hand and of the guiding motions peculiar to it, something practically instinctual, and, on the other, the technological instrument itself – the stylus – the very tool of writing. *Stilus*, then, is the acculturation of the botanical via the human, just as it is the cultural extension of the biological human body: humans act upon it and are acted upon by it. In that sense, style is not unlike the concept of culture *tout court*: it already contains within itself, sublated, the dialectical mediation between nature and nurture.[4] Culture implies, not the opposite of nature, but man's cultivation of it. Humans, at least as Marx sees them, only become truly human at the moment when they begin to produce their means of subsistence. If style is man himself, it is because it is neither wholly natural nor wholly unnatural.

There is another sense in which style is like culture: one either has it or one doesn't. On one reading this means that, like genius, it is supposedly something one is born with. On another, it is like a poltergeist that stalks the page and flits behind the backs of men, arrogantly singling out those worthiest of possession. 'Having style' in writing is the literary equivalent of sporting *haute couture*: a designer veil hovering mischievously between material fact and subjective ideal. For others, however, style is neither innate nor accidental, but can be learnt. Just as a Christian can become a good human by imitating Christ, so a teenage girl can become stylish by imitating models in glossy magazines, or – if her advisor happens to be Samuel Johnson – by steeping herself in the equable prose of Joseph Addison. Like class, then, style suggests at once an objective phenomenon and a highly charged category of value.

Even more problematic is that it seems to be neither fully conscious nor fully unconscious. Just as it is extremely difficult not to write with one's 'natural' handwriting, so style is often seen to be instinctual, immune to rational intervention. Yet at other times it is spoken of as something which can willingly be changed, an object of choice on the part of the writer or painter. The work of Roland Barthes, one of the most suggestive theorists of style of the twentieth century, suffers from precisely this confusion. One moment, he describes

---

3 Gauger 1995.
4 '[I]t is less a matter of deconstructing the opposition between culture and nature than of recognizing that the term 'culture' is already such a deconstruction' (Eagleton 2000, p. 2).

style as if it were beyond all deliberation, a totally unconscious, involuntary, and therefore necessarily apolitical affair; the next, it becomes that which one can consciously aim to avoid, its dissolution being the political goal *par excellence*.[5]

In some sense, this is simply a modern replay of the duality inherent to the *stilus* itself: its simultaneous capacity to engrave and to erase.[6] In a prefiguration of the Freudian psychic economy, what one end of the pen writes the other unwrites, constantly threatening to condemn all utterance to the determinate chaos of the palimpsest. Yet, if it *undoes* writing, it also enables it. Speech is limited to its immediate geography and to a simplicity coextensive with the boundaries of the mnemonic, but writing enables a potentially global transmission and a hypotactic complexity unthinkable to preliterate cultures. Viewed from this angle, style is the fault line between the material and the spiritual, *Welt* and *Geist*.

Taken to the extreme, it is also the dividing line between the human and the non-human. To claim that David Cameron possesses a rare, charismatic style may well be untrue, but it is not nonsensical. Yet to compliment the wind for its effortless stylishness would make no sense at all. Which would seem to suggest that at some point 'style' managed to cover up its origins. It began life as part of the plant-world and ended up turning its back on all that was not man. It is the etymological equivalent of the *nouveau riche* – that social group historically renowned for its proactive concealment of its lowly origins.

Indeed, there is much of the *arriviste* at work in the word 'style'. For the *arriviste* is one who has fought her way into the ranks of the higher class, hauling herself up the social ladder by stamping on the heads and hands of those below her. Once there, she strives to blend in, to imitate the hegemonic mode of parlance, ridding herself of all linguistic tics which would betray her lowly origins. It is here that 'style' in the sense of 'deviation from a linguistic norm' comes to assume its most overt political nuance. On the one hand, it denotes that which sets the individual at odds with society, the latter being understood as that body of speakers and writers who share certain linguistic conventions and the former as she who manipulates them in unusual ways, or even attempts to break with them completely. On the other hand, however, there can also exist a hegemonic 'style', set by a particular social group, to which individuals feel they must submit. 'Style' in the modern sense of 'fashion' portrays this paradox most clearly: one must conform to the latest trend at the

---

5   For more on this ambiguity, see Chapter 7.
6   This paragraph is inspired by certain phrases in Chapter 9 of Gauger 1995.

same time as displaying one's irrepressible individuality. It is no coincidence that the rise of 'style' as a dominant literary and social category was coeval with the ascendance of the bourgeoisie, a class renowned for its egotistical individualism coupled with a strict social conventionality.

The conceptual history of what has come to be known as 'style' in the literary sense paints a similar picture. We must thus be very careful not to confuse the individualist conception of style just outlined with its pre-modern predecessors; there are, of course, certain overlaps (all classical approximations of what we now call 'style', for example, involve some sense of verbal shaping and phrasing) but their ideological functions and degrees of elaboration are profoundly variable. Originating in the classical system of rhetoric, 'style' was known as *lexis* in Greek or *elocutio* in Latin and constituted the third (and relatively minor) element of the rhetorical pentad: *inventio, dispositio, elocutio, memoria, actio* (or *pronuntiatio*).[7] It was not just *what* you said that was important – though this was central – but *how* you said it. Yet, with the breakdown of the classical Greek *polis* and, later, of the Roman state, rhetoric lost its natural habitat.[8] By the time of the rise of the novel, which was coeval with the rise of the bourgeoisie,[9] communally accepted norms of fine speaking and writing were on the wane, precisely because they relied upon the social hegemony of the aristocratic class the bourgeoisie was now replacing. The rise of style, conceived as a way of writing unique to a particular individual, one who does not aspire to submit to collective conventions of composition, was thus coextensive with the rise of the bourgeois individual as such. In reconstructing a history of 'style', then, one must take account of the profound shift which occurs from *lexis* and *elocutio* to 'style': it is nothing less than a linguistic index of the emergence of capitalist modernity.

In all these ways, then, style can be seen to involve issues which have traditionally exercised Marxists: the relation of nature and culture (which harks back to the young Marx's claim that history as such constitutes man's natural history), aesthetic value (which is one aspect of social valuation in general), consciousness and unconsciousness (clearly linked to debates on the nature and function of ideology), production and technology (staples of classical Marxism), individual and society (or, rather, the Marxist claim that the

---

7   Chapter 2 includes a detailed analysis of the nature of *lexis* in Aristotle's *Rhetoric*.

8   For a less brutally abbreviated account of this process, see Kennedy 1999, Vickers 1988 and Curtius 1990.

9   This is also an exceptionally foreshortened perspective. See the classic account of this relationship in Watt 1957. For a more recent, and philosophically more sophisticated, version, see McKeon 2002.

'individual' is itself a social category), and, finally, hegemony (as developed most sophisticatedly in the work of Antonio Gramsci). Seen in this light, it becomes clear just why Marxists might have suggestive things to say on the matter of style, ones not immediately evident at first sight. Yet, even if we admit that style is, after all, an unexpectedly germane concept for Marxist thought, that concept still has to have found its way onto the Marxist radar. To do so, a situation would have to have arisen in which it became possible for an aesthetic term to become invested with unexpected political potential. It is just such a historical situation that formed the basis of what has since become known – not without its problems – as 'Western Marxism'.

2   Epochal Political Conjuncture: Western Marxism and Beyond

Marx and Engels were pioneers: they developed an economic theory of capitalism and its overthrow, all the while divorced – usually by political exile – from any single national mass political movement.[10] The second generation (Labriola, Mehring, Kautsky, Plekhanov) – the first 'Marxists' – came of age in a period of relative quiet following the defeat of the Paris Commune; their task would be to systematise and popularise the writings of Marx and Engels, transforming them into a coherent worldview which could then be communicated to the masses. The third generation, however, which included Lenin, Luxemburg, Trotsky and Bukharin, came of age during the period of inter-imperial rivalries. Their writings reflect both an attempt to develop Marxism in new directions (e.g., a theory of politics and of empire) and the sheer urgency of their symbiosis with mass political movements. They enjoyed a unity of theory and practice in a period of ascendancy for the working class.

'Western Marxism', however, is characterised first and foremost by its origins in a period of political defeat. The fate of the world revolution after 1917 hinged on the success of subsequent Europe-wide working-class revolutions, with the industrial and technological wealth of the West being crucial to the success and endurance of the Russians – not least since the nation was now being decimated by civil war. But this was not to be: one after another, the united imperial forces mercilessly put down the insurrections: the German

---

10   The following summary of Western Marxism relies largely upon Anderson 1976. For an alternative assessment of the Western Marxist tradition, see Jacoby 1981. Arguably the best critique of Anderson's thesis is Wolfgang Fritz Haug's important essay, 'Westlicher Marxismus?' (Haug 1987, pp. 234–59).

(Berlin, Munich), Hungarian, and Italian (the general strike in Turin) revolutions. Socialism was penned back within one country and fascism was on the rise. According to Perry Anderson's thesis, this single overriding fact of political defeat had a fatal result: Marxist theory became structurally divorced from the mass political movements of which it was supposed to be the consciousness. Whether because of political expulsion (Karl Korsch), withdrawal from active politics (Lukács) or outright imprisonment and death (Gramsci), leading Marxist thinkers of their generation were cut off from the lifeblood of Marxist thought.

The other major feature of this structural divorce – and, for our purposes, perhaps the most significant – was the flight of Marxism into the academy. The Frankfurt School was the most emblematic example: Horkheimer was never a member of a working-class political party; Marcuse was only briefly involved with one in his youth; Adorno had no personal ties whatsoever to socialist political life. Even when intellectuals remained within a national Communist Party, as did Louis Althusser, its monolithic Stalinism proved impervious to thought. According to Anderson's thesis, then, the major works of Western Marxism 'were, without exception, produced in situations of political isolation and despair'.[11] The problem with this argument, however, is that, as Wolfgang Fritz Haug has shown,[12] the flow was not all one-way: if 'Western Marxism' (a term whose homogeneity Haug rightly questions) involved a flight into the academy, there also existed a movement *out of* the university, via Critical Theory, back into political life – not the least form of which was the explosive student movement. Moreover, Anderson seems to presuppose that the academy itself lacks any material efficacy, whereas Haug rightly sees it as an 'independent force of production [*eigenständige Produktivkraft*]'.[13] Nonetheless, even if we reject Anderson's Platonic ideal of 'Western Marxism', we can at least concur that the role of the academy in the production of Marxist thought became more prevalent during this period.

These extrinsic factors had direct repercussions on the intrinsic nature of the works produced. Since Marx's 'Theses on Feuerbach', the whole drive of Marxism had been to overcome philosophy by praxis, but now it was driven back to its German philosophical roots. The ranks of 'Western Marxism' consisted almost entirely of philosophers, and their philosophies of choice were, according to Anderson, reversions to bourgeois or idealist thought – Hegel's at

---

11   Anderson 1976, p. 42.
12   Haug 1987, pp. 236–8.
13   Haug 1987, p. 248.

the helm. This was also the period in which aesthetics, which until that point had always played an important but relatively unacknowledged role in Marxist theory (unacknowledged also by Anderson himself), became a central topic: Lukács on literature, Adorno on music, Benjamin on cinema and photography. The newfound centrality of aesthetics was a direct consequence of the structural dislocation of Marxism and of its distance from immediate mass political movements. Anderson even goes so far as to claim, crucially, that the very *styles* in which Western Marxists wrote were symptomatic of this distance: 'in Lukács, a cumbersome and abstruse diction, freighted with academicism; in Gramsci, a painful and cryptic fragmentation, imposed by prison; in Benjamin, a gnomic brevity and indirection; in Della Volpe, an impenetrable syntax and circular self-reference; in Sartre, a hermetic and unrelenting maze of neologisms; in Althusser, a sybilline rhetoric of elusion'.[14] All of them resulted from 'the gulf for nearly fifty years between socialist thought and the soil of popular revolution'.[15]

On Anderson's reading, then, the historical conditions of possibility for the emergence of what Raymond Williams called 'academic theory', in which 'the question of "communism" or one of its variants did not *necessarily* arise',[16] was the following: political defeat, the structural divorce of Marxist theory from mass political movements, and a concomitant rise of a concern with the aesthetic. Despite the many problems with this thesis (Haug's objections being the most significant), it is certainly true that the phenomena Anderson describes under the rubric 'Western Marxism' constituted some of the major historical preconditions for Marxists to come to think of style, an aesthetic concept, as having *political* import. It was not, of course, the only possible precondition: after all, Trotsky's *Literature and Revolution* (1924), written in the heat of battle, is nothing if not a bestiary of styles and their political insinuations. The difference here, though, is that Trotsky's work positively hums with the urgency of a man defending the revolution against attack. Here is someone attempting to construct a socialist culture from the ground up, rooting out all traces of a now obsolete form of consciousness. The work of the British and American Marxists, by contrast, by and large lacks this sense of urgency: it is a discourse ill-at-ease with the academy, but nonetheless resigned to it. Unlike Anderson, however, I do not read this as a sign of outright political defeat, but rather as a transmogrification of the contemporary political terrain.

---

14   Anderson 1976, p. 54.
15   Anderson 1976, p. 55.
16   Williams 2010, p. 237.

The role of Terry Eagleton and Fredric Jameson was thus largely that of mediators: bringing together the findings of the 'Western Marxists' and introducing them to a British and American public. This coincided with a geographical shift of no little significance: 'Today [1983] the *predominant* centres of intellectual production seem to lie in the English-speaking world, rather than in Germanic or Latin Europe'.[17] This was the explosion of what became known as 'Theory'. To understand why it caused such a stir, we must first grasp the political and intellectual co-ordinates of literary studies in the British and American universities at that time.

3   Intellectual Context: the British Anomaly

Already in 1968 Perry Anderson highlighted the unique structural position of literary criticism as a discipline within the British national culture.[18] On the continent, where the bourgeoisie had openly battled the aristocracy for hegemony, and where emergent revolutionary traditions had produced totalising Marxist discourses, ones which take as their object the totality of society as such, the bourgeoisie (so Anderson) had produced its great intellectual counter-reaction: classical sociology. But in Britain, where the bourgeoisie had reached a historic compromise with the aristocracy, and which had no flourishing Marxist culture (indeed, had known nothing of Marxism until the 1930s), no sociology had been forced to emerge. British empiricism reigned supreme, from philosophy to jurisprudence:

> The peculiar destiny of the nineteenth century industrial bourgeoisie in Britain is the secret of this twin default [the lack of a Marxist or sociological tradition]. The class which accomplished the titanic technological explosion of the Industrial Revolution never achieved a political or social revolution in England. It was checked by a prior capitalist class, the agrarian aristocracy which had matured in the eighteenth century, and

---

17   Anderson 1983, p. 24.
18   This explanation is based on Anderson 1968. The arguments set forth in that essay were part of an overarching theory of the development of British capitalism, many of which were formed in tandem with Tom Nairn. The arguments became known as the 'Nairn-Anderson Theses' and were vigorously debated in the pages of the *New Left Review* and the *Socialist Register*. They were disputed most vehemently by E.P. Thompson (1995), whose *The Poverty of Theory: An Orrery of Errors* is a compendium of the fiery polemics he penned against Anderson's essays and against Althusserianism more generally.

controlled a State formed in its image. There was no insuperable contradiction between the modes of production of the two classes. The industrial bourgeoisie, traumatized by the French Revolution and fearful of the
nascent working-class movement, never took the risk of a confrontation
with the dominant aristocracy. It never evicted the latter from its hegemonic control of the political order, and eventually fused with it in a new,
composite ruling bloc in mid-century.[19]

Those immortal dates – 1789, 1830, 1848, 1871 – had no place on the British cal-
endar. Until the early twentieth century, British intellectuals formed an intellectual aristocracy, 'related by family to their class, not by profession to their
estate'.[20] After the thirty-year upheavals (1914–45) across the European continent, however, the composition of the intelligentsia would change. Unlike its
continental counterparts, ravaged by war, occupation, revolution and counter-
revolution, the British Isles went relatively unscathed throughout the troubles.
It became a haven for émigrés fleeing the carnage; moreover, these émigrés
constituted a quite specific social group. They formed what Anderson calls the
'White' counter-revolutionary emigration, and consisted of thinkers – Wittgenstein, Malinowski, Namier, Popper, Berlin, Gombrich, etc. – who saw in England
the opposite of 'the permanent instability of their own societies': 'tradition,
continuity and orderly empire'.[21] On arrival, they discovered a national culture
congenial to their conservatism and an academy ripe for the injection of new
intellectual life – the very intellectual life, as it happens, that had been born of
the political struggles they came to Britain to avoid.

The upshot was their intellectual domination of Britain. Totality remained
an outcast, knocking on familiar doors that simply would not open. There was
no alternative: according to Anderson, it had to seek refuge elsewhere. By this
time, Britain was master of a third of the world, and what better place to safely
confront one's fundamental questions about the totality of human life than at
gun-point in the colonies?

Colonial administration had an inherent need of cogent, objective information on the peoples over which it ruled. The miniature scale of prim-

---

19   Anderson 1968, p. 12.
20   Anderson 1968, p. 16. Cf. Collini 2006.
21   Anderson 1968, p. 18. The 'Red' Emigration quite naturally avoided these parochial climes:
      the Frankfurt School went to the USA via France, Lukács went to Russia, Brecht to Scand-
      inavia and then to America. 'It did not opt for England, because of a basic cultural and
      political incompatibility' (ibid.).

itive societies, moreover, made them exceptionally propitious for macro-
analysis ... British anthropology was thus able both to assist British imperialism, and to develop a genuine theory – something sociology in Britain
was never able to do.[22]

Nonetheless, on the domestic front, totality did find a single, solitary outlet in
the unlikeliest of places: literary criticism. F.R. Leavis claimed English was the
'chief of the humanities': 'no other country', responds Anderson, 'has ever produced a critical discipline with these pretensions'.[23] Where France could boast
a highly technical literary criticism and a moral and ontological philosophy –
the average continental distribution – Britain was the precise opposite: its
philosophy grew analytic and its literary criticism metaphysical. How did this
occur? Anderson suggests its unique ambitions lay in the fact that Leavis, alone
of the thinkers his essay surveys, was 'deeply affected by Marxism';[24] indeed, in
1963 Leavis himself admitted that Marxism had been *Scrutiny*'s 'doctrinal challenge', the spur for the ever-widening gyre of its attentions.[25] Yet, because he
was acquainted only with its less intellectually strenuous avatars, Leavis came
to associate Marxism with the very society it condemned, thus adding to his
sense of being surrounded on all sides by decline and inhumanity. Without
an alternative theory of the social totality, however, he was incapable of transcending a general cultural pessimism and nostalgia for a long-lost 'organic
community'. It was only Raymond Williams, schooled in the Leavisite mode at
Cambridge, who would inherit Leavis's total scope and use it to produce what
Anderson calls 'the one serious work of socialist theory in Britain' – *The Long
Revolution* (1961).

    This is an incredibly powerful explanation of British national culture, but
as with all of Anderson's seductive syntheses one must enter major caveats.
Stefan Collini has argued that Anderson's explanation 'overestimates the *historical role* of theories' and is 'framed too exclusively in terms of the Big Names';[26]
that is, Anderson is attempting to articulate a Marxist history of British intellectual life in terms more suitable to a 'Great Man' theory of history. More
damning still is Lawrence Goldman's comparison of the fates of the (British)
Social Science Association (s.s.a.) with those of the American Social Science
Association, modelled on the s.s.a., and the German *Verein für Sozialpolitik*

22   Anderson 1968, pp. 47–8.
23   Anderson 1968, p. 50.
24   Anderson 1968, p. 53.
25   Cited in Anderson 1968, p. 54.
26   Collini 2006, p. 180; emphasis in the original.

(which would become synonymous with the names of Weber, Simmel, Sombart and Tönnies).[27] Where the S.S.A. was practically effective in realising or making realisable legislative reform, the A.S.S.A. and the Verein both failed as reformist organisations on account of a growing political ineffectivity produced by changing historical circumstances. In the case of the Verein, this was a result of what became known as the 'Second *Reichsgründung*': Bismarck's change of economic policy and political alliances in the late 1870s, which put a stop to the German liberalism that had been in the ascendant during the process of unification, and also put paid to the influence of liberal pressure groups, including the Verein. Consequently, both the Verein and the A.S.S.A. migrated into the academy, where they eventually flourished and became *informally* politically influential. Thus, where Anderson sees sociology as at once a form of totalising attack on the *ancien régime* – which, crucially, is implicitly part of a *successful* bourgeois revolution (it being precisely this which the English lacked) – and an intellectual counter-revolution against Marxism,[28] Goldman argues that 'a close analysis of the Verein and the A.S.S.A. would suggest the opposite – that sociology, if it expressed the *ambitions* of the liberal middle class, was a product of, and compensation for, its political failure'.[29] Anthony Giddens goes a step further: capitalist industrialisation in Germany 'proceeded without the occurrence of a "successful" bourgeois revolution, and in the framework of a process of political centralization secured by Prussian military imperialism',[30] and it was precisely this process that sapped the influence of the Verein on the German state. Once again, then, Anderson's synthetic history of British culture can be shown to be deeply problematic. To put it provocatively, one might say that where Anderson sees sociology as the outcome of 'successful' bourgeois revolutions, Goldman's account invites the conclusion that sociology was born of 'passive revolution' or 'revolution from above'.[31] Sociology did not emerge from

---

27 Goldman 1987.

28 'Sociology ... was itself largely (not exclusively) a response to a previous totalizing system.
— It notoriously emerged as a bourgeois counter-reaction to Marxism on the continent. All of Weber's work on economy and society forms an immense, oblique contestation of the Marxism which had conquered the working-class movement in imperial Germany; his political hostility to that movement was undying. Pareto sought to combat the primitive
— 'mob-rule' of socialism by writing a violent attack on Marx; Durkheim sought to domesticate it within the reformist perspectives of French positivism. A profound fear of the masses and premonition of social disintegration haunts the work of all three' (Anderson 1968, p. 8).

29 Goldman 1987, p. 169.

30 Giddens 1972, p. 28.

31 For an account of Gramsci's theory of passive revolution, see Thomas 2009.

the victorious bourgeoisie so much as from a politically weak, 'progressive' class fraction of the bourgeoisie whose exile into the academy paradoxically enabled its elaboration of sophisticated and totalising theories. Its total scope was born of opposition, not only to the landed aristocracy and the rising working-class movements, but also to large sectors of the bourgeoisie itself.[32]

As for the unusual status of English literary criticism, however, it is Francis Mulhern's study of the journal *Scrutiny* that will allow us to supplement Anderson's account. Mulhern shows that *Scrutiny*'s 'field of action was, unalterably, that of the classical sociologists'.[33] Both *Scrutiny* and classical sociology took as their objects of study 'the community of customs, values and beliefs'.[34] Like classical sociology, it harboured a fundamentally dualist conception of society 'that united a technicist conception of "civilization" ... with a complementary idealist conception of "culture"'.[35] What set it apart from its continental counterparts, however, was its residual Romanticism, its focus on literary criticism, and its militant tone.[36] What can explain these attributes, why did they emerge as and when they did, and what induced the unusual totalising scope of English literary criticism? These are questions Anderson never satisfactorily broaches. The answer, however, is that Cambridge elected to introduce a new English course in 1917 at precisely the moment that the cultural contradictions of a crumbling Victorian social order, triggered by Britain's global economic decline and exacerbated by the First World War, were reaching their climax; this coincided with a dramatic shift in the social composition of the national intelligentsia. The new course, 'English Literature, Life and Thought', was introduced by Hector Chadwick (Professor of Anglo-Saxon) because he foresaw – rightly – that peace would bring a new generation of, and a vast numerical increase in, students – the great majority of whom, for the first time in British history, hailed from petit-bourgeois origins. Moreover, precisely because

---

32   This view is borne out by Wolfgang Mommsen's account of the relation between politics and scholarship in the work of Max Weber (Mommsen 1989, pp. 3–23) and Göran Therborn's analysis of Durkheim's relation to the Third Republic (Therborn 1976, p. 262 ff.). Both Weber and Durkheim were critics of the landed aristocracy, both saw the socialist revolutionary movement as a threat to (national) society, yet both were also critics – within strict limits and often for different reasons – of the excesses of their respective nations' liberal bourgeoisie (though in Weber's case, this criticism did not stretch to Germany's desire for global imperial hegemony, which he wholeheartedly supported).

33   Mulhern 1979, p. 311.

34   Mulhern 1979, p. 310.

35   Mulhern 1979, p. 311.

36   Mulhern 1979, pp. 311–12.

of the immense increase in student numbers, Chadwick knew he could not rely on the modest complement of the Cambridge English faculty to teach them. He recruited Mansfield Forbes (historian), E.M.W. Tillyard (classicist), and I.A. Richards (trained in Mental and Moral Sciences), who themselves hired freelance teachers likewise drawn from heterogeneous disciplines. 'In the unstructured, indefinitely bounded space opened up by the Tripos reform', writes Mulhern, 'the contradictory social and cultural forces of the twenties met and mingled freely, giving rise to a debate of unprecedented breadth and rigour'.[37] These, then, were the material conditions for the emergence of an unusually totalising literary criticism: its *internal* disciplinary heterogeneity coupled with an institutional informality, which, once consolidated into the formation of *Scrutiny*,[38] concentrated its threefold *external* opposition to the gentleman-amateurs of Cambridge, Marxist thought, and 'industrial society' in general.

It should now be clear why literary critical pronouncements in such a context had a quite different valence to their continental counterparts. An argument about literature in Britain was always, almost inescapably, an argument about the whole of human life. This was the conjuncture which produced a body of British writings (in our case, by Raymond Williams and Terry Eagleton) whose curious politicisation of literature puzzles certain continental observers to this day. Still, even this does not entirely explain why style in particular should become a locus of political interest. This can, I think, be explained by the intramural situation of the Cambridge English faculty just outlined. In virulently opposing – on both literary and class grounds – the aristocratic gentlemen-amateurs who had preceded them, the new Cambridge English critics insisted on analytic and systematic rigour in the practice of criticism. One way of achieving this was the promotion of detailed, analytical inspection of specific passages of literature. This mode of reading was first pioneered by I.A. Richards, most notably in *Practical Criticism* (1929), though it later became synonymous with Leavis and the 'Cambridge School' more generally. Richards, writing in the wake of the catastrophe of the First World War, which he associated with dogmatism and propaganda, believed that investigating meaning was imperative: 'the need was for precision, for clear-cut separations of kinds

---

37 Mulhern 1979, p. 22.
38 Note that *Scrutiny* was actually a result of the new English course having been institutionalised in 1926, which had paradoxically weakened its initial 'critical revolution' and forced to the peripheries young postgraduate student pioneers such as Leavis. Cf. Mulhern 1979, p. 28ff.

of language-use and awareness of their different grounds of legitimacy'.[39] Viewing literary criticism as a form of social psychology, and poetry as a potential 'League of Nations for the moral ordering of the impulses',[40] his emphasis on close textual analysis was thus inseparable from his inheritance of what Williams would name the 'culture and society' tradition of nineteenth-century thought. It was this politically overdetermined mode of reading which became 'the nub of the study of English both in Cambridge and more generally'.[41]

It is often observed that one of the goals of such 'close reading', as it became known, 'was to do more than insist on due attentiveness to the text. It inescapably suggest[ed] an attention to *this* rather than to something else: to the "words on the page" rather than to the contexts which produced and surround them'.[42] Moreover, it is also commonly recognised that Leavis invested practical criticism with an exaggerated importance: nothing less than enabling Western civilisation to avert its impending demise. What is less remarked upon, however, is the way in which practical criticism produces a quite specific textual object: a short excerpt of prose or poetry, rather than a work in its entirety. Given such short passages, often consisting of no more than a few sentences, it is logical that the category of style suggests itself as a concept of analysis in a way that it might not have done, had the object of criticism been more expansive. By the time Williams arrived at Cambridge Leavis was still a Faculty outsider ('utter defeat at Cambridge', he would later remark)[43] but his ideas about literature were becoming increasingly hegemonic – not least in British classrooms thanks to the large number of his students who later became teachers. Any Marxist criticism that wished to dethrone Leavisite close reading would thus have to pass by way of the excerpt. The intellectual battle-lines were drawn: for Marxist theory to win hegemony, it would not be enough simply to expose the concealed political presuppositions of Richards and Leavis; it would have to be able to account for the styles of textual extracts in a more supple and convincing manner than the practical critics themselves. Williams and Eagleton would go on to attempt to do just that, exposing the conservative nostalgia of their critical predecessors whilst inheriting and evolving the method of close reading.

On the other side of the Atlantic matters were somewhat different. There is no space here to chart the rise of the New Critics, the increasing postwar

---

39   Heath 1994, p. 25.
40   Cited in Heath 1994, p. 26.
41   Heath 1994, p. 26.
42   Eagleton 1996b, p. 38.
43   Cited in Heath 1994, p. 31.

democratisation of the American universities, or other such important factors in the formation of literary and cultural studies in the United States. We must simply remark upon an important structural anomaly which informed Fredric Jameson's professional situation. American English Literature departments at that time were dominated by the New Critics and their courses of study often advanced only as far as Tennyson.[44] But Jameson was formed in French departments, 'where people were reading the most advanced contemporary texts all the time and where, very importantly, politics were not subject to Anglo-American censorship'.[45] Thus, there existed what one might call a situation of uneven development within the humanities: French departments, in Jameson's view, were geared towards an understanding of literature as political in a way that English departments categorically were not, and they enabled a critical comprehension of the *present*. This unique situation was then supplemented by Jameson's doctoral study under Erich Auerbach at Yale, which effectively formed him in style studies: 'the relationship of the individual text and the style and the words and so forth, to movements and historical contexts was a great deal closer and more intimate than the purely aesthetic appreciations of most English departments'.[46] If the French departments equipped Jameson with a contemporary purview, style studies connected him to the residual pre-war practice of philology. The politico-literary approaches of the former fused with the stylistic analyses of the latter: together, they produced Jameson's political understanding of style.

4   Internal Debates: Types of Marxist Criticism

These relatively external intellectual and political factors combined with important debates *within* the Marxist critical tradition. In general, there have been four types of Marxist criticism, all of which are present to some degree in any Marxist analysis, but one of which will usually predominate: anthropological, political, ideological and economic.[47] Anthropological criticism, a broadly Second International affair, examined the relation between art and social evolution, or what the early Marx – after Hegel – called 'species-being' [*Gattung-swesen*]; political criticism refers to those cultural writings by figures such as

---

44   'Interview', in Buchanan 2006, pp. 122–3.
45   Ibid.
46   'Interview' in Buchanan 2006, p. 123.
47   I take these classifications from Eagleton 1996a, pp. 1–15. Like Eagleton, I also wish to stress the essentially schematic nature of these terms.

Lenin and Trotsky during the tumult of the Russian Revolution; ideological criticism, essentially coextensive with the literary analyses of Western Marxism, focuses on the ideology of form, the way in which 'the material history which produces a work of art [is] somehow inscribed in its very texture and structure, in the shape of its sentences';[48] finally, economic criticism, which cannot be clearly periodised, deals with the material modes of cultural production. Given what we have seen regarding the roles of Eagleton and Jameson as intellectual mediators of the 'Western Marxist' tradition to an Anglo-American public, and given, too, the unique institutional circumstances in which they found themselves, it is no great surprise that their work aligns more or less readily with the ideological aspect of Marxist criticism. They inherited from 'Western Marxism' an acute sensitivity to literary form and its ideological significance, and they did so because it fused alarmingly well with the very *non*-Marxist discourses in which they had been trained: practical criticism and stylistics.

With 'Western Marxism' was born an insistence on the double optic which has come to define British and American Marxist literary theory: 'seeking on the one hand to take the full pressure of a cultural artefact while striving at the same time to displace it into its enabling material conditions and set it within a complex field of social power' –[49] and all of this with a view to 'possess[ing] the work more deeply'.[50] This dual perspective has its origins in an outright intellectual and political rejection of the doctrine of socialist realism, one of whose defining features was an indifference to form and style and a fixation on monolingual, 'transparent' content.[51] It was in their recognition that form was, on the contrary, precisely the locus of some of the most tenacious residues of previous or politically opposed forms of social consciousness that the 'Western Marxists' developed some of their most crucial contributions to Marxist criticism. In this context, then, style itself became a formal mediator between vulgar sociologism and apolitical formalism, between socialist-realist indifference to form and a formalist evacuation of content. It was also the link between the otherwise alien heritages of 'Western Marxism' and practical criticism.

In all these ways, then, it is clear why a superficially aesthetic or literary concept – style – has become the focus of such unexpected concern to three Marxist thinkers. A unique conjuncture of intellectual and political factors overdetermined the concept with a significance entirely disproportionate to

---

48   Eagleton 1996a, p. 11.
49   Eagleton 1996a, p. 7.
50   Eagleton 1975, p. 13.
51   For a detailed and subtle account of socialist realism, see Robin 1986.

its typical modicum of literary-critical relevance. Yet, unbeknownst to many, the concept of style has in fact played a recurring, subterranean role in the Marxist tradition from the early writings of Marx onwards. Whilst Williams, Eagleton and Jameson were certainly not always aware of this tradition, it is worth reconstructing it at some length so as to reveal the constant presence of literary and aesthetic concerns at the heart of Marxist political and economic thought. Moreover, it will serve as a basic introduction to the two dominant ideologies of style in Western literary discourse: Aristotle's collective, relational theory of style and its modern, individualist counterpart. This will provide some important historical contextualisation for the various theories of style encountered in Part 2.

CHAPTER 2

From State Censorship to the Poetry of the Future: Style in the Marxist Tradition

Marx was concerned with style from his earliest writings on Prussian press censorship all the way to his later historiographical essays. Likewise, much 'cultural Marxism' of the twentieth century inherited this problematic and, in its turn, used the problem of style to think the relationship between Marxism and culture more generally. This chapter will attempt a critical reconstruction of these reflections as they originate in the writings of Marx. As with any analysis dealing with style, however, it is of the utmost theoretical importance to distinguish between actual stylistic practices on the one hand and ideologies of style on the other: this chapter is concerned primarily with the latter.[1]

1 An Overview of Marx's Early Writings

It is necessary to begin by setting out the general framework of Marx's early writings, since this will provide the theoretical context for his comments on style and censorship.[2] What Marx seems to call for in these early texts is for human beings to become what they properly are. What we are in the young Marx's eyes is productive, rational, social animals.[3] These four attributes ('animality', taken from the subject 'animal', being the fourth) form the basis of human labour. This differs from mere animal activity in that it is universal (as opposed to unilateral), consciously undertaken (as opposed to instinctively performed), free (in that it can become an end-in-itself) and world-fashioning (in the sense that man's natural history is a dialectical pole of human history

---

1   For those seeking an analysis of Marx's own written style, see Silva 1971 and Prawer 1978. On the distinction between stylistic practices and stylistic ideologies, see Chapter 8, section 2.2. of the present work.

2   The best selection of these early writings in English remains Marx 1975c.

3   Note the Aristotelian analogues of these terms: *poiēsis* (production), *zōon logon echon* (animal 'having' language/ discourse) and *zōon politikon* (political animal). Nonetheless, it is also quite possible to see Marx's conception of praxis and species-being as completely at odds with Aristotle's understanding of a fixed human essence. See, for example, Margolis 1992.

as such).[4] For Marx, labour is the constitutive life-activity of man, life-activity being what is determinate of a given genus.[5] This means that man is a *Gattung-swesen*, a species-being, not only in the sense that all humans belong natur-alistically to the same genus,[6] but also in the sense that what is universal to all human beings is precisely universality itself.[7] Human labour is both intern-ally and externally universal: it can be applied to any object at all (such that man 'makes the whole of nature his inorganic body')[8] and it is oriented to the human species as a whole, for it produces goods that in principle any human being could use.[9]

As it stands, however, man is currently unable to realise his own *Gattung-swesen*: he theoretically *is* a species-being, but is unable to activate this the-ory in practice. According to Marx, what prevents this realisation is aliena-tion, a situation in which some (implicitly undesirable) third party intervenes between man and his essence as human. Joseph Margolis summarises this well: 'man is alienated [for Marx] insofar as he fails to grasp that his own nature

---

4 Adapted from Chitty 2009, p. 133.

5 It goes without saying that Marx's early, predominantly anthropological theory of human labour is a controversial one. It has given rise to two interconnected debates among its interpreters: the first concerns a so-called 'break' which occurs between the early and the mature Marx, from an initial anthropological focus on 'human nature' to a purely relational conception in which 'human nature' is rearticulated as the structural ensemble of social relations. The main progenitor of this line of thought was, of course, Louis Althusser: cf. Althusser 2005. The second issue concerns Marx's theory of labour itself. Moishe Postone identifies two opposing interpretations which have produced 'two fundamentally different modes of critical analysis: a critique of capitalism *from the standpoint* of labor, on the one hand, and a critique *of* labor, on the other' (Postone 1993, p. 5). The former assumes that labour is transhistorical whereas the latter identifies labour under capitalism as historically specific. In the first, labour is the *subject* of the critique of capitalist society, whilst in the latter it is the *object*. More recently, Jason Read has argued that both interpretations miss the point: 'The opposition between these two critical strategies generally assumes that labor itself is one-sided, thus forgetting the duality of labor. An examination of the relationship between abstract and living labor makes possible a criticism in which labor is both the object, in the sense that it is a criticism of the apparatuses and structures that constitute abstract labor, and the subject, in the sense that it places the potentiality of labor at the center of this critique' (Read 2003, p. 77).

6 This is one of the aspects of Feuerbach's thought which Marx criticises in the sixth thesis on Feuerbach: 'Essence, therefore, can be comprehended only as "genus", as an internal, dumb generality which *naturally* unites the many individuals' (Marx 1975c, p. 423).

7 Chitty 2009, p. 128.

8 Marx 1975c, p. 328.

9 Chitty 2011, p. 485.

and the world's (the world in which his labor – his praxis – is effective) are the *products of his praxis*, through history'.[10] The exemplary form of alienation is religion (since God is the ultimate mediator between man and his essence),[11] but economic expropriation is also crucial (especially in the form of the commodity, which masks the social relations of its production). For our purposes, however, the most significant form of alienation discussed in the early writings is political.[12] The very existence of a political state, Marx claims, is already a sign of a cleavage between civil and political society: 'the sphere in which man behaves as a communal being [*Gemeinwesen*] is degraded to a level below the sphere in which he behaves as a partial being ... it is man as *bourgeois*, i.e. as a member of civil society, and not man as citizen who is taken as the *real* and *authentic* man'.[13] The consequence of this is a disjunction between sensuous content and abstract political form, between 'man in his sensuous, individual and *immediate* existence' and 'man as an *allegorical, moral* person'.[14] The aesthetic logic of this argument – 'aesthetics' here denoting that bourgeois discourse primarily concerned with the artistic resolution of the rift between concrete and abstract, content and form – should not be overlooked: the form of the state hangs loosely on the body politic like a badly fitting toga. True human emancipation, which Marx will come to know as 'communism', would entail the return of man's essence unto himself, the destruction of the mediator, and the reharmonising of form and content: 'Only when real, individual man resumes the abstract citizen into himself and as an individual man has become a *species-being* in his empirical life, his individual work and his relationships ... only then will human emancipation be completed'.[15] In this light, one might say (perhaps controversially) that if Marx's eleventh thesis on Feuerbach called for the realisation of philosophy in praxis, then 'On the Jewish Question' equates man's becoming species-being with the practical realisation of the bourgeois discourse of aesthetics.[16]

---

10   Margolis 1992, p. 337.
11   Cf. Feuerbach 1989, p. 153: 'God is the concept of the species as an individual ... he is the species-concept, the species-essence conceived immediately as an existence, a singular being [*Einzelwesen*]'.
12   This is obviously not to say that religious and economic alienation are not indirectly political.
13   Marx 1975c, p. 231.
14   Marx 1975c, p. 234.
15   Ibid.
16   See Eagleton 1990, pp. 196–233. For Eagleton the entire discourse of aesthetics 'seeks to resolve in an imaginary way the problem of why, under certain historical conditions,

Central to Marx's analyses here – especially in his *Critique of Hegel's Doctrine of the State* (1843), which prepared the theoretical ground for 'On the Jewish Question' – is a theory of the modern state: 'The abstraction of the *state as such* was not born until the modern world because the abstraction of private life was not created until modern times. The abstraction of the *political state* is a modern product'.[17] He contrasts the modern situation with that of the Middle Ages, in which 'the life of the people was identical with the life of the state [i.e., political life]'.[18] As Lucio Colletti observes, '[p]olitics [in the Middle Ages] adhered so closely to the economic structure that socio-economic distinctions (serf and lord) were also political distinctions (subject and sovereign)'.[19] Likewise, Marx also contrasts the modern state with the Greek *polis* in which 'the political state as such was the only true content of their [the citizens'] lives and their aspirations'.[20] According to the young Marx, then, it is only in modernity that the political realm becomes abstracted from the life of the people as a particular reality over and above their daily existence.

This shift – from the substantial unity of the spheres of economics and politics to their mutual separation – had profound consequences for the understanding of style itself. In the comparatist spirit of the young Marx – one he himself inherited from the young Hegel – I now wish to set those modern theories of style which informed Marx's early writings on press censorship (namely, Buffon's and Fichte's) against one of the best-known ancient conceptions of style: book three of Aristotle's *Rhetoric*.[21] In doing so, I hope to mirror the logic of the young Marx's comparisons of ancient Greece with their modern counterparts. By contrasting Aristotle's theory of style with those of Buffon, Fichte and the early Marx, we shall be in a better position, not only to assess what Marxism might be able to offer stylistics more generally, but also to argue that Marx's aesthetic thought was not a convenient add-on to his political and economic formulations, but a serious, constitutive element thereof.

---

human bodily activity generates a set of "rational" forms by which the body itself is then confiscated' (Eagleton 1990, p. 207).

17   Marx 1975c, p. 90.

18   Ibid.

19   'Introduction' to Marx 1975c, p. 34.

20   Marx 1975c, p. 91.

21   By which I mean his tendency to locate the *differentia specifica* of a historical phenomenon – in this case the modern state – by comparing it with its equivalents in previous historical epochs. More precisely, he compares total social configurations: how the *polis* functioned within the social totality of classical Greece versus how the state functions within the social totality of capitalist modernity.

2   Style in Aristotle's *Rhetoric*

The first difficulty in discussing 'style' in Aristotle's *Rhetoric* lies in how one
interprets the Greek word *lexis*. It can be variously translated as 'style', 'elocution' or 'diction', though its meaning also covers the more general 'way of saying
something' and 'how thought is expressed in words, sentences and a speech
as a whole'.[22] In terms of discursive levels, *lexis* covers word-choice, sentence-
phrasing and discourse as such. This ambivalence in the exact domain of style
mirrors the ambivalence of Aristotle's attitude towards it. In an ideal world,
he argues, it would be unnecessary even to consider *lexis*, since 'to contend by
means of the facts themselves is just, with the result that everything except
demonstration is incidental'.[23] At the same time, he begrudgingly admits that
it is not enough to have a supply of things to say, but is also necessary to say it in
the right way,[24] and that *lexis* has 'some small necessary place in all teaching'.[25]

Despite these oscillations, Aristotle insists that there exists a 'virtue' or 'excellence' of style [*lexeōs aretē*]. Initially, this is defined as ' "to be clear" [*saphē*]
... and neither flat nor above the dignity of the subject, but appropriate [*prepon*]'.[26] This is soon expanded into the general formula of virtuous *lexis*: 'Thus,
it is clear that if one composes well there will be an unfamiliar quality and it
escapes notice and will be clear'.[27] It is worth unpacking each of these aspects,

---

22   Ricoeur 2003, p. 384, n. 13; see also Kennedy in Aristotle 2007, p. 193. When referring
      to Kennedy's translation of Aristotle's *On Rhetoric*, I shall cite page numbers and/ or
      footnotes when referring to commentary by Kennedy, but shall conform to the standard
      Bekker pagination system for references to Aristotle's text itself.

23   Aristotle 2007, 1404a. Cf. *Topics* 1.1: 'Things are true and primary when they are persuasive
      through themselves, not through other things; for in the case of scientific principles there
      is no need to seek the answer to *why* but each of the first principles is persuasive in and
      by itself' (Aristotle 2007, 100b18).

24   Aristotle 2007, 1403b.

25   Aristotle 2007, 1404a.

26   Aristotle 2007, 1404b. Unless otherwise indicated, square brackets within quotations con-
      taining original Greek terms are Kennedy's.

27   Aristotle 2007, 1404b. Later theorists of style, Theophrastus chief amongst them, divided
      these attributes of the single virtuous style into distinct virtues, but Aristotle recognises
      only one single *lexeōs aretē* which Doreen C. Innes describes as 'an interdependent pack-
      age of three items – clarity, propriety, and ornamentation' (Innes 1985, p. 255). As it hap-
      pens, there are actually five 'items': she omits 'concealment' and 'correctness'. Nonetheless,
      the important point is that she recognises the interdependence of moments within the
      single virtuous style. It is also worth noting that, although Theophrastus recognises four
      separate virtues of style (correctness or *hellēnismos*, clarity, appropriateness and orna-

since they prove important in determining the internal function of *lexis* within the *Rhetoric* and, more broadly, in understanding the precise relation between *lexis* and *polis*. Clarity, we are informed, is produced by the use of nouns and verbs 'in their prevailing [*kyrios*] meaning'.[28] Virtuous style also includes 'unfamiliarity': 'To deviate [from prevailing usage] makes language seem more elevated; for people feel the same in regard to word usage as they do in regard to strangers compared with citizens. As a result, one should make the language unfamiliar; for people are admirers of what is far off, and what is marvellous is sweet'.[29] There is a clear relation, then, between *kyrios*, or 'prevailing', 'lordly' meaning and the political boundaries of the *polis* as such. The precise nature of this relation is analogical: non-*kyrios* usage is to *kyrios* usage as the stranger [*xenos*] is to the fellow-citizen [*politēs*]. In other words, at this point in the third book of the *Rhetoric*, the relation between *lexis* and *polis* can be described as metaphorical, analogy being the fourth type of metaphor recognised by Aristotle.[30]

This relation is developed in what is perhaps the most influential attribute of the virtuous style, 'propriety' or 'appropriateness' [*to prepon*]. Altogether, I discern six subdivisions of this attribute: word-choice must be appropriate to subject matter;[31] the speaker must be appropriate to the spoken,[32] which is then further subdivided into *lexis* as appropriate to genus and *lexis* as appropriate to 'moral state' or habit [*hexis*];[33] finally, *lexis* must be appropriate to the particular genus of rhetoric in which it is put to use (i.e., deliberative, forensic or epideictic).[34] There are thus two fundamental and interlocking logics at work within the *to prepon*. Firstly, there is a political logic: the *actual* conventions of inclusion and exclusion appropriate to the *polis* regulate the internal con-

---

mentation), this difference from Aristotle is relatively insignificant since it is an *exclusive* list. That is, all four must always be present for style to be virtuous. The difference only becomes important in later theories of style, such as Cicero's, which make the distinction between necessary virtues (clarity and correctness) and unnecessary ones. See Innes 1985, p. 256.

28   Aristotle 2007, 1404b. The word *kyrios*, not insignificantly, has overtones of lordliness and authority.
29   Aristotle 2007, 1404b.
30   'Metaphor is the application to one thing of a name belonging to another thing; the transference may be from one genus to the species, from the species to the genus, or from one species to another, or it may be a matter of analogy' (Aristotle 2000, 1457b).
31   Aristotle 2007, 1404b.
32   Ibid.
33   Aristotle 2007, 1408a.
34   Aristotle 2007, 1413b.

ventions of public discourse. Secondly, there is an ethical logic: the *to prepon*
is Aristotle's doctrine of the mean applied to *lexis*.[35] Public speech must activate the shared conventions of the *polis* if it is to be persuasive. This means that
the distribution of the means of communication in rhetoric must reflect those
of everyday political life.[36] It would, for example, be 'inappropriate' 'even in
poetry' for a slave to use fine language,[37] just as it would be ridiculous for an
old man to wear clothes which are fashionable with the young.[38] Within this
thick web of conventions and ingrained expectations, the *to prepon* is the linguistic equivalent of 'simply what is done'. In other words, one of the animating
criteria of virtuous style is conformity to the rules, written and unwritten, of
social propriety within the *polis*. The conventions of fine speaking are intrinsic
to the conventions determining political inclusion.

This should come as no surprise. It is a quite obvious consequence of the
social organisation of the Greek *polis*. The word *politikos*, as Aristotle uses it,

> covers both what we mean by *political* and what we mean by *social* and
> does not discriminate between them. The reason for this is obvious. In the
> small-scale Greek city-state, the institutions of the πόλις are both those in
> which policy and the means to execute it are determined and those in
> which the face-to-face relationships of social life find their home. In the
> assembly a citizen meets his friends; with his friends he will be among
> fellow members of the assembly.[39]

It is well known that the list of virtues in Aristotle's *Ethics* is one appropriate
to the prevailing gentleman's code of Greek society. Likewise, the rules for
virtuous *lexis* go hand in hand with the presupposition of the social unity of
the *polis*. It is precisely because verbal eccentricity is analogous to the geo-
politically exotic that it has to be smuggled in under the radar.[40] The successful

---

35   Cf. Innes 1985, p. 260. This separation of the two logics is merely analytical. Ethics is, to
      Aristotle, a sub-branch of politics: 'the Good of man must be the end of the science of
      Politics' (Aristotle 1934, 1094a).
36   This use of 'distribution' is inspired by Jacques Rancière's notion of the 'distribution of the
      sensible': 'I call the distribution of the sensible the system of self-evident facts of sense-
      perception that simultaneously discloses the existence of something in common and the
      delimitations that define the respective parts and positions within it' (Rancière 2004, p. 12).
37   Aristotle 2007, 1404b.
38   Aristotle 2007, 1405a.
39   MacIntyre 2002, p. 55.
40   Style is virtuous, ironically, when it thieves, deceives or conceals (Aristotle 2007, 1404b,

rhetorical speaker is one who has learnt to activate old convictions so as to bring about new ones. Style, as a form of linguistic social relation, is one of the instruments through which he does so.

Two things should by now be obvious: firstly, classical theories of style are linguistic extensions of the broader logic of the social form to which they are immanent; secondly, classical theories of style are *relational* and *communal*: the key is for individual speakers to relate to their peers via the collective conventions of fine speaking to which they must conform.

3   The Young Marx on Style and Censorship

It is against this dual backdrop – that of Marx's early writings on the state and the communal conventions of style in the Greek *polis* – that we should read the first newspaper article Marx ever wrote, 'Comments on the Latest Prussian Censorship Instruction' (1842). At the time, Friedrich Wilhelm IV had begun his reign by ostensibly relaxing censorship laws, only to find himself subsequently incapable of controlling the liberal dissent he thereby unleashed.[41] To counteract this wave of agitation, he promulgated new censorship instructions, effectively clamping down on his own liberalisations. One of the decrees of the new censorship instructions was that 'censorship should not prevent serious and modest investigation of truth'.[42] Marx responded to this restriction on the very styles of journalistic writing with an argument which goes to the heart of his simultaneously aesthetic and political opposition to censorship:

> [T]ruth is general, it does not belong to me alone, it belongs to all, it owns me, I do not own it. My property is the *form*, which is my spiritual individuality. *Le style c'est l'homme.* Yes, indeed! The law permits me to write, only I must write in a style that is not *mine*! I may show my spiritual countenance, but I must first set it in the *prescribed folds*! What man of

---

1405a): it must veil its unfamiliarity in familiarity and appear to be that which it is not. And it must do so or else the shared conventions of the *polis*, both social and linguistic, cannot be effectively activated, thereby rendering null and void the three 'entechnic' modes of rhetorical proof [*pisteis*]: if the *lexis* is too 'strange', the *ēthos* of the speaker is no longer 'worthy of credence' (1356a); if too excessive, it is impossible to infiltrate and manipulate the *pathos* of one's fellow-citizens; and if it overshoots the arguments [*logoi*] then it tails off into comedy.

41   I am basing this account on Rose 1978, pp. 15–32.

42   This is a quotation from the original censorship instruction, cited in Marx 1975b, p. 111.

honour will not blush at this presumption and not prefer to hide his head under the toga? Under the toga at least one has an inkling of a Jupiter's head. The prescribed folds mean nothing but *bonne mine à mauvais jeu*.[43]

[[D]ie Wahrheit ist allgemein, sie gehört nicht mir, sie gehört Allen, sie hat mich, ich habe sie nicht. Mein Eigenthum ist die *Form*, sie ist meine geistige Individualität. Le style c'est l'homme. Und wie! Das Gesetz gestattet, daß ich schreiben soll, nur soll ich einen anderen als *meinen* Styl schreiben! Ich darf das Gesicht meines Geistes zeigen, aber ich muß es vorher in *vorgeschriebene Falten* legen! Welcher Mann von Ehre wird nicht erröthen über diese Zumuthung und nicht lieber sein Haupt unter der Toga verbergen? Wenigstens läßt die Toga einen Jupiterkopf ahnen. Die vorgeschriebenen Falten heißen nichts als: bonne mine à mauvais jeu.][44]

We have come a long way from the communal stylistic conventions of the Greek *polis*. At first glance, it would be easy to read this passage as indicative of Marx's early Romanticism: the outrage of the poet-radical at an attempt to curb the individual creative genius, to set it in prescribed folds – the fury of a Prometheus bound. There is certainly something in that reading, but a closer analysis reveals a coherent theory of style that links, not only to the central aspects of Marx's early writings outlined above, but also to late eighteenth- and early nineteenth-century theories of authorship and copyright.

Firstly, he claims that truth is universal; it is only the *form* which is my individual property, my spiritual individuality. Next follows a series of conceptual and idiomatic puns on style as an individual's spiritual face, countenance or visage – in other words, style as the physiognomy of an individual writer, indicative of his inner being. What the state is trying to do, Marx suggests, is to force the writer to screw his face into an alien pose. The German here is *vorgeschriebene Falten*, which literally means 'prescribed folds', but which, in the idiomatic phrase *mein Gesicht in Falten legen*, has another primary sense of 'frowning pensively', drawing as it does on the meaning of *Falte* as 'wrinkle'. At this point, Marx claims that it would be better to hide one's head beneath a toga than contort one's spiritual countenance into a state-decreed rictus. The issue of style and censorship reproduces on a smaller scale the larger problem of the political state as such: the state enforces the merely *abstract* universality of the legal person onto the authentic, sensuous individual. A more human form

---

43   Marx 1975b, p. 112.
44   Marx 1975a, p. 100.

of association – one in keeping with the inherent sociality of man's species-being – would enable a type of individual stylistic expression whose limits were self-willed rather than externally imposed. That is to say, Marx does not seem to be calling for some spontaneous Romantic formlessness, but rather for a form of collective aesthetic self-regulation: a stylistic concrete universal. According to Hegel, a concrete universal is one which 'particularises itself and in this particular, this becoming finite, yet remains infinitely within itself';[45] yet, for Marx – as we saw in the explication of 'On the Jewish Question' – it is yet to be realised. He saw the battle for the emancipation of stylistic practice as at one with the battle for human emancipation as such.

Already, then, a stark contrast exists between Aristotle's presuppositions about style and those of Marx: where the former presupposes relational, communal conventions of fine speaking which are internally stratified in line with the politico-economic distinctions of the *polis*, Marx assumes that style is something purely non-relational and individual. Yet this sits uneasily with his implicit desire for what I have called a stylistic concrete universal: this latter would presumably constitute the sublation of the Aristotelian and the modern conceptions of style respectively. Where for Aristotle the *polis* functioned *in and through lexis*, for Marx the modern state is *opposed* to individual styles: the solution would thus be to combine the collective and relational nature of style in the *polis* with the individual expressivity which style has come to assume in modernity. But this solution could only be realised – if we accept the logic of the early Marx – by total human emancipation, that is, the overcoming of the separation of the political state from civil society. In the next section, I shall place Marx's remarks in the context of two eighteenth-century theories of style as a way of deepening our sense of this shift from pre-modern to modern ideologies of style.

4 Marx After Buffon and Fichte

In the passage cited above, Marx (mis)quotes Buffon's well-known phrase, *Le style est l'homme même* [(the) style is (the) man himself]. This dictum is usually taken to mean that style reflects personality, but in fact its meaning is somewhat different.[46] It occurred in the context of Buffon's inaugural 1753 address to the French Academy. Buffon informed his fellow *immortels* that

---

45   Cited in Chitty 2011, p. 480.

46   M.H. Abrams has noted this misunderstanding: Abrams 1953, p. 373, n. 13.

facts, knowledge and discoveries were external to man, the common property of all. They were, he said, appropriable, liable to transportation and alteration:

> Only those works which are well written will pass into posterity ... if they are written without taste, without nobility and without genius, they will perish, because knowledge, facts and discoveries are easily appropriable; they travel and even gain from being put to work by more skilful hands. These things are outside of man; style is man himself. Thus, style cannot be appropriated, nor transported, nor altered: if it is elevated, noble, sublime, the author will be equally admired in all ages; because truth alone is durable, even eternal.[47]

> [Les ouvrages bien écrits seront les seuls qui passeront à la postérité ... s'ils sont écrits sans goût, sans noblesse et sans génie, ils périront, parce que les connaissances, les faits et les découvertes s'enlèvent aisément, se transportent et gagnent même à être mises en oeuvre par des mains plus habiles. Ces choses sont hors de l'homme, le style est l'homme même: le style ne peut donc ni s'enlever, ni se transporter, ni s'altérer: s'il est élevé, noble, sublime, l'auteur sera également admiré dans tous les temps; car il n'y a que la vérité qui soit durable et même éternelle.][48]

Style, then, as opposed to knowledge, facts and discoveries, is immutable, immovable and immortal. Style is the man himself; it is, one might say, his property, the proper of man: it cannot be expropriated, it never changes and it never differs.

In 1753, however, these philosophical pronouncements on style had not yet been codified into law. It was only Fichte's intervention into late eighteenth-century German copyright disputes that enabled this to happen. At the time, piracy was rife, and there was still no unified pan-Germanic legal system or rationale to deal with it.[49] The very notion of the author as legal proprietor was still in the process of being born. It was in the context of these simultaneously economic and aesthetic debates that in 1793 Fichte wrote his essay, 'Proof of the Illegality of Reprinting'. He begins by distinguishing between the physical [körperlich] and intellectual [geistig] aspects of a book.[50] The physical refers to the printed paper. The intellectual can be further subdivided into its material

47   My own translation of the French passage cited directly below.
48   Buffon 1853, p. 330.
49   For the historical background I rely heavily on Woodmansee 1984.
50   Mayeda 2008, pp. 173–4. Mayeda's commentary includes a full translation of Fichte's

[*materielle*] aspect – the ideas communicated, or the ideational content – and its formal aspect – the *style* in which these ideas are presented. By defining rightful ownership as when the expropriation of a thing by others is physically impossible, Fichte declares that when a book is sold ownership of the physical object and its ideal content passes to the buyer.[51] The *form* of this ideational content, however, remains eternally the author's own:

> [T]hat which can simply never be appropriated by anyone, since it is phys-ically impossible, is the *form* of the thoughts, the connections between ideas, and the signs by means of which ideas are presented. Each person has his own manner of thinking, and his own unique way of forming con-cepts and connecting them.[52]

Whilst Fichte does briefly attempt to distinguish form from 'manner' [*Ma-nier*],[53] it is quite clear that his own understanding of 'form' is very similar to Buffon's notion of 'style': that which is proper to each individual. Fichte thus provided the rational grounds for literary ownership and authorship and, at the same time, for the illegality of piracy. In doing so, he helped fundament-ally to alter the understanding of what a writer was: no longer the patron-ised, neo-classical imitator of nature, but an *Urheber*, an originator and cre-ator.[54]

If we now return to Marx's article on censorship, we see it in a whole new light. This is not – or not *only* – Marx the Romantic, chafing at the bit of mundane restrictions on individual creation. On the contrary, when Marx states that a man's style is his property he means it quite literally. State censorship is a form of expropriation: the expropriation of form, of individual property. As Margaret Rose has observed,[55] in attempting to confer its identity upon its citizens, the state has succeeded only in expropriating them of their own identity – of what is *proper* to them. So we are left in somewhat of a quandary: the very Romantic theory of the author as unique, individual

---

article, with the German and English in parallel columns: cf. Mayeda 2008, pp. 171–98. This is the source of my quotations from Fichte.

51 Whereas in terms of the physical object, the author cedes all proprietary rights to the buyer on purchase, in terms of ideas the author remains a co-proprietor (Fichte in Mayeda 2008, pp. 175–6).

52 Fichte in Mayeda 2008, p. 176.

53 Fichte in Mayeda 2008, p. 177.

54 Woodmansee deals with this aspect in great detail.

55 Rose 1978, p. 29.

originator developed partly because of the very system of private property that Marx used it to criticise. Just as Marx attacked Proudhon for declaring that 'Property is theft!', since the concept of theft presupposes private property,[56] so Marx's attack on the censors for forcibly expropriating the formal property of man seems to presuppose an individual with property rights. Yet we must be careful not to confuse property as such with *private* property. For property is not an inert thing, any more than man's species-being is an inert genus. Property is a social relation, and private property for Marx is synonymous with the 'totality of the bourgeois relations of production'.[57] So what we have here, as throughout all of his various writings on censorship, is an attempt to stress the inner contradictions of the state. The censor's stylistic decrees are at one with the abstract universality of the system of rights: neither is capable of realising the concrete universality of man, the *Gattungswesen*, which would also contain within itself the particular and the singular, thereby fusing political and civil man in one.

If we now set the modern theories of style in the context of Aristotle's pronouncements we are surely forced to conclude that the shift from a collective and relational theory of style to one based on style as the non-relational, unique property of the individual is broadly in line with the transition from pre-capitalist modes of production to capitalism. Moreover, the nature of style as Marx understands it – as individual property potentially expropriable by the state – could only arise in a capitalist modernity premised upon private property and the abstraction of the state into a political sphere over and above the lives of the people of whom it nominally consists. The question we must now ask is this: if style as communal *lexis* or individual property were the pre-capitalist and capitalist manifestations of style respectively, and if their very existence is symptomatic of the social relations of their respective modes of production, then would the dissolution of capitalism spell the end of style? In other words, would Marx's implicit desire for what I have called a stylistic concrete universal not bring about the end of style as hitherto conceived? Or would we have to hypothesise some new, post-capitalist linguistic regime? These are questions directly related to Marx's overall philosophy of history, though as the next section shows: even at this level, style remains a constitutive aspect of his thought.

56   Marx and Engels 1956, p. 128.
57   Cited in Chitty 1998, p. 58.

5   Style and the Philosophy of History

A useful interlocutor at this stage is Nietzsche. His writing on style responds to the same set of problems as Marx's own later writings, but reaches very different conclusions. In the first of his *Untimely Meditations*, Nietzsche berates the German middle class for its lack of culture. Written in 1873, two years after the Franco-Prussian war, and against a wave of national triumphalism, Nietzsche castigates the German bourgeoisie for equating military might with cultural supremacy. 'Culture', he writes, 'is, above all, unity of artistic style in all the expressions of the life of a people [*Einheit des künstlerischen Stiles in allen Lebensäußerungen eines Volkes*]'; the opposite of culture is 'barbarism, which is lack of style or a chaotic jumble of all styles [*der Stillosigkeit oder dem chaotischen Durcheinander aller Stile*]. It is in such a chaotic jumble of styles that the German of our day dwells'.[58] For Nietzsche, the problem with the *Reich* is that it lacks a proper culture or stylistic unity. The self-conscious, virile, spiritual bond of the German *Volk* has been substituted by a motley array of semi-conscious 'tacit conventions',[59] whilst an awareness of historical relativism has purged them of the enthusiasm and fanaticism necessary for stylistic unification.[60]

Marx's philosophy of history also identifies the problem of modernity's lack of authentic unity of style. Yet his diagnosis of this problem differs from Nietzsche's in two respects: firstly, he extends the problem of the organic connection between social content and cultural style much further back than Nietzsche (to Luther) and, secondly, he explains it via a theory of history in which historical protagonists necessarily blind themselves to the social content of their own deeds by dramatically imitating long-dead events:

> [J]ust when they appear to be engaged in the revolutionary transformation of themselves and their material surroundings, in the creation of something which does not yet exist ... they timidly conjure up the spirits of the past to help them; they borrow their names, slogans and costumes so as to stage the new world-historical scene in this venerable disguise and borrowed language.[61]

---

58   Nietzsche 1997, pp. 5–6.
59   Nietzsche 1997, p. 8.
60   Nietzsche 1997, p. 11.
61   Marx 1973, p. 146.

The empirical, external Prussian censor of Marx's early writings thus transforms in his later writings into a nigh-on metaphysical, immanent censor of History itself. Just as in Freud's *Interpretation of Dreams*, censorship is the process by which unconscious wishes are distorted and disguised so as to enable their fulfilment without the sleeper's being awoken by the horror of recognising his secret desires, so in Marx's *Eighteenth Brumaire* the borrowed costumes and language of political revolutions are the result of a world-historical censorship in which men hide from themselves the true nature of their class's desire. Unlike Stephen Dedalus, they are not trying to awaken from the nightmare of history, but pretend to awaken so as to go on sleeping all the longer.

Traditionally, one of the most hackneyed of all definitions of style is that it is 'the dress of thought', an elegant turn of phrase draped fetchingly over a self-contained content. Yet in the *Eighteenth Brumaire*, this most trivial and dubious of definitions has been raised to a historiographical principle. If, in the article on Prussian censorship, it was better (though – precisely – not ideal) to hide one's head beneath the Roman toga than submit to the state's prescribed folds, we now read of Louis Bonaparte 'hiding his commonplace and repulsive countenance beneath the iron death-mask of Napoleon'.[62] What in the former article was a contradiction between the abstract modern state and the individual subjects through whom it was supposed to cohere has now become a contradiction internal to History as such. In the former, historical subjects hid from the state; now, they hide from themselves. Though for Marx not all such disguises are negative. On the one hand, there are those 'tragic' events of world history whose stylistic excesses are – *pace* Nietzsche – precisely the *source* of their protagonists' enthusiasm, but also of their self-blinding;[63] on the other, there are those farcical repetitions, in which the stylistic excesses are simply absurd.[64] It is in this precise context that Marx pens that most cryptic of paragraphs:

> The social revolution of the nineteenth century can only create its poetry from the future, not from the past ... Earlier revolutions have needed

---

62   Marx 1973, p. 148.

63   'And its [bourgeois society's] gladiators found in the stern classical traditions of the Roman republic the ideals, art forms and self-deceptions they needed in order to hide from themselves the limited bourgeois content of their struggles and to maintain their enthusiasm at the high level appropriate to great historical tragedy' (Marx 1973, p. 148).

64   'In these revolutions, then, the resurrection of the dead served to exalt the new struggles, rather than to parody the old, to exaggerate the given task in the imagination, rather than to flee from solving it in reality, and to recover the spirit of the revolution, rather than to set its ghost walking again' (Marx 1973, p. 148).

world-historical reminiscences to deaden their awareness to their own content ... Previously the phrase transcended the content, here the content will transcend the phrase [*Dort ging die Phrase über den Inhalt, hier geht der Inhalt über die Phrase hinaus*].[65]

The German *Phrase*, like the English word *phrase*, originates in the Greek *phrasis*, meaning speech, diction or style. In this light we can see a continuation of Marx's early concerns; just as the Prussian state was consciously forcing its writers to use a style which was not properly their own, so these revolutionary forerunners have always spoken *improperly*, in a borrowed language. The upshot of style is both anachronism and self-blindness: an inability to speak in one's proper name and to act on the basis of one's proper volition. Thus, it now becomes clear that the problematic of the Prussian censorship articles has been fused with the larger problematic of world history as such: it will only be possible to overcome the abstract state and the stylistic contortions it enforces on its citizens if we cease to inherit and parody past historical styles and create our poetry from the future.

At this point we should stress that the social revolution as Marx conceives it must, if our reading holds true, necessarily combine the two historical models of style we have thus far examined: the relational, collective style of the Greek *polis*, and the (apparently) non-relational individuality of modernity. Modern revolutionary innovation must recuperate the collective and fuse it with the singularity of modern political subjects. The social revolution is an act of collective self-constitution in which the abstract state is re-concretised in and through the daily life of the people – including their linguistic life together. But if this were to occur, would not the very conditions for 'style' as such be dissolved? Would not the content transcending the phrase spell the *end of style*?

6   The End of Style?

If the notion of the 'end of style' sounds familiar, it is because Fredric Jameson has argued that postmodernity – rather than socialist revolution – has already achieved it.[66] There is no space here to rebut this problematic argument in detail, but suffice it to say that it is based partly upon an insufficiently nuanced

---

65   Marx 1973, p. 149.

66   'The end of the bourgeois ego, or monad, no doubt brings with it the end of the psycho-
      pathologies of that ego – what I have been calling the waning of affect. But in the end it
      means the end of much more – the end, for example, of style – in the sense of the unique

reading of the theory of style contained in Roland Barthes's seminal work, *Le degré zéro de l'écriture* (1953). (Insufficiently nuanced because it overlooks ambiguities inherent to Barthes's argument between, on the one hand, style as something completely unconscious and beyond the realm of volition and, on the other, style as potentially rationally transformable).[67] Among other things, Barthes refers in this work to what he calls *écriture blanche* [white/blank writing]. This is a type of writing which would transcend all connotations of literariness or political stance. It is a type of neutral writing, a zero degree or amodal form shorn of all moral and political implication. It is, he says, an innocent writing – a 'style of absence which is almost an ideal absence of style'.[68] There are, however, two problems with this notion. Firstly, as Barthes himself recognised, what for one generation or class of people counts as a 'neutral' style has a habit of transforming over time and space into a *non*-neutral style, one which cannot help but emit the connotations of its social origins and accents. Secondly, having explained the *practical, historical* origins of the modern linguistic situation, in which to denote something has become simultaneously (and usually unwittingly) to connote tacit social affiliations, Barthes then proposes the purely *aesthetic* solution of *écriture blanche* – a type of writing which remains, for a short period of time, socially and politically indeterminate.[69] In other words, for Marx's full-blooded stylistic concrete universal – the stylistic practices immanent to an emancipated human collective – Barthes has substituted an aesthetic, reductive universalism premised upon a 'zero degree' of sociality. This is ironic given that the logic of his own argument, if followed to its conclusion, would suggest precisely that 'blank writing' is not something that can be aesthetically activated without having first been historically achieved.

---

and the personal, the end of the distinctive individual brush stroke' (Jameson 1991, p. 15). I return to this theme in Chapter 7.

67   Again, I return to this problem in Chapter 7.

68   Barthes 1953, p. 60.

69   On my reading, the historical logic of Barthes' argument can be summarised thus: a language must first undergo gradual national homogenisation into a *langue*; '*écriture* appears only at the moment when the *langue* [language], constituted nationally, becomes a sort of negativity, a horizon which separates what is forbidden and what is allowed, without people wondering about the origins or justifications of this taboo' (Barthes 1953, p. 45). This *écriture* remained homogeneous from the seventeenth century, through the French Revolution, to 1848, the year of the European revolutions. Only then did *écriture* become plural, a whole host of styles vying for the (abstract) universality that had once been that of the liberal bourgeoisie. This was still, according to Barthes, the linguistic situation in 1953.

It would be more accurate to argue that constructing a concrete universal – a society in which (according to Marx's logic) individual men and women will have become species-being in their empirical daily lives – would involve the partly conscious, partly organic construction of new styles (as opposed to Barthesian stylelessness).[70] This was precisely the case in post-revolutionary Russia. Trotsky's masterful *Literature and Revolution* (1924) is a unique record of the literary and stylistic upheavals brought about by social revolution. The book locates in the shape of a subclause or the use of a certain cadence the ambiguous political tendencies of its author.[71] In that sense, then, revolutionary crises are moments when the social origins of styles are brutally unmasked; the icy bourgeois conception of style as purely individual and non-relational begins to melt under the inner truth of the Aristotelian conception of style as an extension of the social logic of the *polis*.

But revolutions are also a time of genesis. Here is a passage from Trotsky which links the historical logic of *The Eighteenth Brumaire* with the notion of style found in Marx's writings on the press:

> The Constitutional Democrats who are living abroad today, divorced or otherwise, point almost maliciously to the literary weakness of the Soviet press. And truly, we write badly, stylelessly, imitatively ... Does that mean that we have regressed? No, it means a transition period between the skimming imitation of progress, between the hired lawyer's claptrap, and the great cultural movement forward of a whole people, which, given but a little time, will create for itself its own style, in journalism as well as in everything else.[72]

Trotsky refers to the Constitutional Democrats as 'culture-skimmers' because they lazily appropriate and idolise European bourgeois styles whose form-

---

70 Cf. Marx 1975c, p. 234.

71 E.g., Trotsky on 'the Aldanovs': 'The Aldanovs are not mystics in the full sense of the word. That is, they do not have their own positive mythology, but their political skepticism gives them an excuse to regard all political manifestation from the point of view of eternity. This is conducive to a special style, with a very aristocratic lisp' (Trotsky 2005, p. 40). Or again on Andrey Biely: 'You can see clearly that Biely himself is flesh of the flesh and bone of the bone of the old state, that he is thoroughly conservative, passive, moderate, and that his rhythm and his verbal twists are only a means of vainly struggling with his inner passivity and sobriety when torn from his life's pivot' (Trotsky 2005, p. 57).

72 Trotsky 2005, p. 46.

ation they played no active part in.[73] The 'perfected forms' of France, for example, were 'molded in the furnace of several revolutions' but the Democrats 'skim from history, free of charge', using these styles as standards abstracted from their historical origins superciliously to judge the literary quality of the fledgling Soviet press.[74] Against this, and also against the Russian futurists, who for Trotsky attempted to make stylistic innovation and formal breaks with past traditions a revolutionary end in itself abstracted from all social relations,[75] he offers the prospect of a new writing designed for and by a new human collective:[76] a writing no longer individual, but of a unified culture. Indeed, he sees the construction of a new style as a constitutive element of the construction of socialist culture as such. Yet he is ever aware that this was a period of simultaneous absorption of the old and apprenticeship in the new, a time of leave-taking and strange encounters: in short, a much more sober, grounded affair than Marx's idealised talk of creating poetry from the future.

There is, of course, a fine irony to Trotsky's acute sensitivity to matters of form and style. For it was precisely this sensitivity that was overridden with the official adoption under Stalin of the doctrine of 'socialist realism' in 1934. This instituted an infamous content-centred theory of literature totally at odds with the more dialectical conceptions of the relation between style and content that had hitherto existed within the Marxist tradition. As we saw in the previous chapter, it was partly against such theories of literature that much late twentieth-century Marxist literary criticism would be written, in an attempt to revive the intrinsic connections that had previously existed between social and formal analysis. If the problem of style as posed by Marx remains a contemporary one, however, it is because the social and political contradictions which gave rise to it have not yet been resolved.

---

73   Ibid.

74   Trotsky 2005, p. 45.

75   Trotsky 2005, pp. 115–16. Trotsky is a clear forerunner of Raymond Williams when it comes to circumspection with regards to the precise politics of modernist stylistic innovation. Cf. Williams 2007.

76   On the matter of what precisely this collective consists of, Trotsky is very precise: he distinguishes between, on the one hand, a transitional 'proletarian dictatorship' which will be primarily engaged in defending itself against attacks from class adversaries and, on the other, what he calls a 'socialist community' and 'human culture' – the society which will emerge, possibly after decades, once these struggles are over (Trostky 2005, p. 155).

CHAPTER 3

Mimesis from Plato to Ricoeur

In the introduction, I made a general case for the coherence and desirability of a Marxist poetics. Having supplemented that case with a detailed overview of the unusual historical and conceptual reasons why Williams, Eagleton and Jameson became interested in style, and with a survey of the role of style in the Marxist tradition, I shall now begin developing the theoretical apparatus which will link the broader project of a Marxist poetics to the specific analysis of literary styles (that is, to that single aspect of a Marxist poetics with which I am concerned in this book). Since in many ways this will be an attempt to modify Aristotle's *Poetics* so as to render it applicable to modern literary works (produced, quite obviously, under historical conditions entirely alien to the Greek *polis*), it is perhaps no coincidence that I shall draw here on the work of one of the great modern inheritors and adapters of Aristotle: Paul Ricoeur. His magisterial trilogy, *Time and Narrative*, constitutes nothing less than a *summa* of the major twentieth-century debates regarding the role of narrative in philosophy, literature and historiography (not to mention those surrounding structuralism and humanism). It is also one of the most sophisticated adaptations of Aristotle's *Poetics* of the last century. My use of his work here, however, is very much localised; I shall focus almost solely on his theory of the production process of narratives and their subsequent reception – what he calls the 'threefold *mimesis*'.[1] In terms of the philosophical economy of *Time and Narrative*, this is a subordinate but literally crucial aspect,[2] in that it is located at the precise point of mediation between the aporias of time generated by phenomenology and their poetic solution in narrative: 'the question of the relationship between time and narrative culminates in this dialectic between an aporetics and a poetics'.[3] In this chapter I shall set out the Aristotelian theory of mimesis it inherits and develops along with the basic features of the threefold mimesis before going on to assess the relative strengths and weaknesses of Ricoeur's conception.

---

1   Ricoeur 1984b, p. 52 ff.
2   'Allow me to recall once again that the interest brought to bear here on the unfolding of mimesis does not contain its end within itself. My explication of mimesis remains subordinated to my investigation of the mediation between time and narrative' (Ricoeur 1984b, p. 70).
3   Ricoeur 1984b, p. 71.

Before doing so, however, it is worth remembering that, beyond the quite specific overlaps and disjunctions between Ricoeur's theory of mimesis and the body of works by Williams, Eagleton and Jameson, there exist certain more general correspondences. The most obvious is Jameson's essay on *Time and Narrative* itself, 'The Valences of History'.[4] At 137 pages in length, it is longer than his book on Hegel (2010) and only just shy of his volume on Marx's *Capital* (2011). Significantly, the essay on Ricoeur reads far more like a *summa* of Jameson's oeuvre than these other two ostensibly more representative works. Beyond this, it is surely not insignificant that Williams and Eagleton have both written books on tragedy.[5] Despite Ricoeur's expansion of narrative far beyond Aristotle's theory of Greek tragedy, it is arguable that some of the resonances to be found between these two traditions have their origins in common sources. For all these reasons, then, the choice of implementing a modified version of the threefold mimesis in the development of a Marxist theory of style is a more obvious one than might at first appear.

1   Mimesis in Plato and Aristotle

The concept of mimesis first came to prominence in the works of Plato, whose conception was subsequently inherited and implicitly critiqued by Aristotle. Yet the term mimesis in fact pre-existed its use in these works; its meanings were multiple but centred on the basic notion of correspondence.[6] They divided into two general groups: formal mimesis, in which there is 'a directly perceived match between the medium of the mimetic object or act ... and the relevant aspect of the corresponding phenomenon',[7] and metaphysical mimesis, in which 'the relation between the sensible world of men and objects, and the hidden, ultimate, metaphysical world of numbers' is conceived as a mimetic one.[8] Formal mimesis included visual representations, behavioural imitations, impersonations and vocal imitations. Metaphysical mimesis, by contrast, was primarily the preserve of Pythagorean mathematicians.

This ambiguity between 'merely' formal and metaphysical mimesis is in certain key respects reproduced by Plato and has a determinate effect upon

---

4 Jameson 2009, pp. 475–612.
5 Williams 1979a and Eagleton 2002.
6 For the sake of brevity, I am relying here on Stephen Halliwell's now canonical account of the Platonic and Aristotelian conceptions of mimesis: Halliwell 1998, pp. 109–37.
7 Halliwell 1998, p. 115.
8 Ibid.

his theorisation. Halliwell is quick to point out, for example, that whilst most
people associate Plato with his attack in Book 10 of *The Republic* on (visual)
mimesis as a form of falsehood – an imitation of an imitation – which drags
the mind below the level of reality (let alone ideality), there are other passages
in which he inherits the more positive, metaphysical meaning of the term.[9]
Indeed, it comes to signify 'both the means by which the eternal produces and
fashions the world, and correspondingly the means by which the human mind
can ascend or aspire in its search for knowledge'.[10] Philosophy itself is perceived
as a mimetic activity which leads thought to the truth of eternal Ideas.

Aristotle subsequently inherited both the general multiplicity of meanings
of 'mimesis' and their two contradictory orientations in Plato's philosophical
system. But whereas in Plato, as M.H. Abrams has it, 'the poet is inescapably the
competitor of the artisan, the lawmaker and the moralist',[11] Aristotle narrows
the focus of mimesis specifically to poetic and artistic practices, thus endow-
ing them with a relative autonomy beyond the strictures of praxis and theory.
Where Plato's conception of mimesis is implicitly visual and literalistic (a direct
copy of sensible reality), Aristotle expands imitation beyond the visual to the
ideal:[12] 'since the poet ... is a mimetic artist ... it follows that he must produce
(at any one time) a mimesis of one of three things: reality past or present; things
as they are said or seem to be; or things as they ought to be'.[13] Nonetheless, there
exists a dual ambiguity in Aristotle's use of the term: it hovers simultaneously
between the senses of visual reproduction and enactment on the one hand,
and between mimesis as a general formula for the relation between art and the
world, and mimesis as a specific mode of poetic representation (in contradistinction to narrative) on the other.[14]

These ambiguities, which reflect the semantic range of 'mimesis' in Greek
antiquity, do not prevent us from distinguishing three crucial elements of Aristotle's development of the term. Firstly, out of his emphasis on mimesis as
enactment arises his unique sense of the poet's task, not as asserting or arguing,
but as displaying 'organised structures of action through direct verbal representation'.[15] Unlike the explicit philosophical and political stance required of
the poet by Plato, Aristotle seems to argue that 'any attitude the poet may be

---

9   Halliwell 1998, pp. 118–20.
10   Halliwell 1998, p. 118.
11   Abrams 1953, p. 9.
12   Halliwell 1998, p. 125.
13   Halliwell's translation of *Poetics* 60b 8–11, in Halliwell 1998, pp. 124–5.
14   Halliwell 1998, pp. 126–31.
15   Halliwell 1998, p. 132.

assumed to have towards his material must be wholly implicit, embodied in the shaping and the structuring of the events'.[16] By extension, we can infer that, in arguing for a view of art as free of an immediate subjection to the criteria of truth-telling and virtue, Aristotle is developing 'a concept of *fiction* which allows the poet's stance towards reality to be more oblique'.[17] Finally, in his famous proclamation that poetry is more philosophical than history because it deals in universals and not particulars, we can discern a continuation of the metaphysical grandeur accorded to *one* of the multiple meanings of mimesis – the very meaning which Plato associated with the ennobling task of philosophy. To summarise Aristotle's understanding of mimesis, then, we can state – following Halliwell – that its true mode is enactment and its true meaning the portrayal of universals.[18]

2   On the Threefold *Mimesis*

This is the complex history that Ricoeur will inherit and develop. His central addition to this inheritance will be the connection of narrative to time. At the beginning of the third chapter of *Time and Narrative*, having guided the reader through the aporias of temporality at work in Augustine (Chapter 1), followed by their potential resolution in Aristotle's *Poetics* (Chapter 2), Ricoeur makes his central claim: '*time becomes human to the extent that it is articulated through a narrative mode, and narrative attains its full meaning when it becomes a condition of temporal existence*'.[19] To make good on this claim, Ricoeur will attempt to establish 'the mediating role of emplotment between a stage of practical experience that precedes it and a stage that succeeds it'.[20] 'Emplotment' is Ricoeur's term, lifted from Hayden White,[21] for Aristotle's μίμησις (*mimesis*). Ricoeur understands the term as possessing three 'moments',[22] which he labels – rather uninspiringly – $mimesis_1$, $mimesis_2$ and $mimesis_3$. The first denotes the *prefiguration* of the practical field (the world of praxis which is the raw material of narrative), the second the *configuration* of emplotment (and thus the work itself), the third the *refiguration* of the practical field through the reception of

16   Ibid.
17   Halliwell 1998, p. 133; emphasis in the original.
18   Halliwell 1998, p. 137.
19   Ricoeur 1984b, p. 52; emphasis in the original.
20   Ricoeur 1984b, p. 53.
21   White 1975.
22   Ricoeur 1984b, p. 53.

the work. The second of these – textual configuration – is pivotal and mediates between the first and the third, a role that will become central for the very mediation between time and narrative on which his central claim depends.

Mimesis$_1$ is summarised thus: 'the composition of plot is grounded in a pre-understanding of the world of action, its meaningful structures, its symbolic resources, and its temporal character'.[23] In other words, literary compositions do not arise in a vacuum. They emerge from practical forms of life, and these forms of life are always already structured. Ricoeur highlights three ways in which this is so. Firstly, humans distinguish between a domain of action, organised around such concepts as 'why', 'who', 'how', 'against whom' etc., as against a domain of mere physical movement.[24] The phenomenological structure of our being-in-the-world is such that prior to all reflection upon the world, we are already engaged in tasks and projects within it. Narrative understanding presupposes this virtual practical understanding and actualises it by transforming its paradigmatic order into the syntagmatic order of narrative.[25] Secondly, human action is always already symbolically mediated, striated and informed by signs, rules and norms.[26] This refers to what might be called the culturally innate *Ur*-signs immanent to any possible meaningful action – that which provides the shared context that renders action *readable*. It also covers the normative and ethical values innate to a given culture. Thirdly, our pre-understanding of the world of action also has a temporal form: that which Heidegger calls 'within-time-ness' [*Innerzeitigkeit*]. It is a prereflexive sense of time characterised by Care [*Sorge*]. In all these ways, then, it should be obvious that no literary creation is a *creatio ex nihilo*: it emerges from a pre-understanding of the world of action that is always already meaningful, symbolically mediated and temporally constituted. Mimesis$_1$ insists: The world is *prefigured*.

Mimesis$_2$ is the *configuration* of this *prefiguration*. It is at this stage that the dynamic quality of Aristotelian *poiēsis* – in this context, the idea of mimesis as an operation rather than a structure – comes into its own. Emplotment mediates in three principal ways. It organises (serial) events into a (narrated) story; it transforms the paradigmatic elements of action into syntagmatic signifying chains; and it performs a synthesis of the heterogeneous.[27] What must be stressed here, however, is that Ricoeur is performing a Kantianisation of

---

23   Ricoeur 1984b, p. 54.
24   Ricoeur 1984b, p. 55.
25   Ricoeur 1984b, p. 56.
26   Ricoeur 1984b, p. 57.
27   Ricoeur 1984b, pp. 65–6.

Aristotle. He actively encourages a comparison between the 'synthesis of the heterogeneous' and Kant's notion of judgment, particularly the reflective and teleological modes. This must be distinguished from Aristotle's own concern with the components of poetic unity (wholeness, order, singleness and appropriate scale)[28] which shares certain formal similarities with Ricoeur's Kantian conceptualisation but is substantially different from it.[29] 'The configurational arrangement', Ricoeur argues, 'transforms the succession of events into one meaningful whole which is the correlate of the act of assembling the events together and which makes the story followable'.[30] This 'followability' conferred by the poetic act upon the twin poles of event and story is read by Ricoeur as a solution to the Augustinian aporia of distention and intention; it converts the paradox into a living dialectic with its own temporality. Integral to this followability is the way in which configuration produces closure – Frank Kermode's 'sense of an ending'. Thus, the primary operation of configuration is to form the elements of the prefigured world into a whole story with a beginning, middle and an end.

Beyond these crucial acts of mediating synthesis, however, there are two final features of mimesis$_2$ that must be stressed. The first is the schematism of the configurational act. Once more Ricoeur turns to Kant, comparing the production of this act to the work of the productive imagination. Where the productive imagination schematised the categories of the understanding in the first *Critique*, synthesising intellectual and intuitive elements, so emplotment synthesises 'the point, theme or thought of a story' with 'the intuitive presentation of circumstances, characters and episodes, and changes of fortune that make up the denouement'.[31] In that sense, says Ricoeur, 'we may speak of a schematism of the narrative function'.[32] Needless to say, we are a long way from the original Aristotelian problematic of necessity, probability and universals.

The second additional feature of mimesis$_2$, for us the most important, is *traditionality.* Just as mimetic production never takes place in an *experiential* void, nor does it ever take place in a *traditionless* void: prior to the act of writing, there exist certain literary paradigms – forms available for imitation, adaptation or rejection. Tradition is the interplay of what Ricoeur calls 'innovation

---

28   Cf. Halliwell 1998, p. 98.
29   Aristotle's concern with unity is situated within his (implicit) rebuttal of Plato's reduction
        of mimesis to anaemic literalism, and his endowment of poetic mimesis with a philosoph-
        ical value (because of its claims to universality).
30   Ricoeur 1984b, p. 67.
31   Ricoeur 1984b, p. 68.
32   Ibid.

and sedimentation'.[33] By sedimentation he means the still active remnants of past labours of the productive imagination. The sedimented paradigms fall into three categories: forms (e.g., the discordant concordance of plot), genres (e.g., tragedy or epic), and types (individual works).[34] Traditionality is related to schematism in that forms, genres and types are not only rule-bound, but rule-generating. Literary innovations are always already bound up with determinate paradigms that set certain limits on what is thinkable and doable: in Ricoeur's felicitous phrase, one which stresses both the possibility of innovation and its limits, 'the paradigms only constitute the grammar that governs the composition of new works'.[35] In this sense, tradition is both *produced* and *productive*.

Mimesis$_3$ is then the stage in which the world of the text (which is a configuration of a prefiguration) encounters the world of the reader (producing a *refiguration*). The hinge of the transition from mimesis$_2$ to mimesis$_3$ is the schematism and traditionality just outlined. Readers bring to the text a horizon of expectation governed by their familiarity with the very received paradigms that limited the configurational act of mimesis$_2$. Moreover, readers follow a story and, in doing so, actualise it.[36] At this point, Ricoeur insists on the continuing validity of Gadamer's notion of a 'fusion of horizons' – the potential for mutual understanding across time, space and different cultures. Opposing it to the 'antipoetics' of semiotics,[37] which argues for the 'strict immanence of literary language in relation to itself',[38] he calls for the necessity of seeing mimesis as a form of communication. Mimesis$_3$ consists in the process of being offered, not just a text, but a 'world that I might inhabit and into which I might project my own most powers'.[39] Reading unfurls an experience in language which is, in the final instance, a world with its own temporality; this world has the capacity to *refigure* the prefigured world of the reader. It refigures the semantics and the symbolic mediation of action and – most importantly for Ricoeur – the *time* of action (Heidegger's within-time-ness).[40] Moreover, contrary to Plato's claim that art produces only weakened images of reality, Ricoeur argues that it performs an 'iconic augmentation': it *adds* something to reality, rather than weakly

---

33   Ibid.
34   Ricoeur 1984b, pp. 68–9.
35   Ricoeur 1984b, p. 69.
36   Ricoeur 1984b, p. 76.
37   Ricoeur 1984b, p. 80.
38   Ricoeur 1984b, p. 79.
39   Ricoeur 1984b, p. 81.
40   Ricoeur 1984b, p. 83.

shadowing it.[41] Unlike Aristotle, then, for whom plot increases the audience's capacity to know universals and effects catharses, Ricoeur's understanding has more in common with Coleridge's notion of an 'imagination' which genuinely creates (as opposed to 'fancy' which merely copies and rearranges). Mimesis$_3$ thus completes the hermeneutical circle. The prefigured world of action has been configured by emplotment and refigured by the reception of this emplotment.

3   Historicising the Threefold *Mimesis*

What is the relevance of the threefold mimesis to a Marxist theory of style? Its principal advantage is that it roots poetic activity in everyday (signifying) practices. In doing so, it stresses Aristotle's insistence upon poetics *as* activity, as a configuration of a world which is *already* meaningful (even though it does so, problematically, through a Kantian lens). Two welcome consequences arise from this: firstly, content must be seen as pre-formed, as a raw material with a determinate shape and meaning already inscribed in it.[42] Secondly – and consequently – the author can no longer be seen as a romantic genius, as he who – at least in the reductive stereotype of Romanticism – creates from nothing in the pure void of his imagination. Rather, the author is now a *configurer* who works on and forms this raw material in various potentially innovative ways. This labour is determined and determinate, since it is limited both by the type of social content available and by the sedimented paradigms which the configurer inherits from the tradition. Finally, the process of poetic communication has as its endpoint a public. This cuts straight against the grain of those notions of *écriture* which emphasise its self-subsistent, purely immanent aspect. The poetic configuration invites readers to refigure their own everyday worlds, and to that extent they are a determinate aspect of literary production. Taken together, these strengths make for a formidable social theory of literature.

3.1   *Mimesis$_1$: Prefiguration*

There are, however, several weaknesses. Ricoeur's prefigured world is structured by many things, but force is not one of them. A Marxist rearticulation

---

41   Ricoeur 1984b, pp. 80–1.

42   The correspondence with Jameson's approach is then obvious: '*Content does not need to be treated or interpreted because it is itself already essentially and immediately meaningful* ... Content is already concrete, in that it is essentially social and historical experience' (Jameson 2008, p. 16; emphasis in the original).

of mimesis$_1$ would thus require a way of describing being-in-the-world which could account for prefigurative experiences of oppression and exploitation – and, more specifically, of their linguistic instantiations. What Ricoeur's irenic reflections conceal are the political struggles which occur at the level of language and symbolicity in general. We shall return to this in detail in Chapters 4 and 5, but there is no better place to start than Bakhtin's dialogical definition of language:

> As a living, socio-ideological concrete thing, as heteroglot opinion, language, for the individual consciousness, lies on the borderline between oneself and the other. The word in language is half someone else's. It becomes one's own only when the speaker populates it with his own intention, his own accent, when he appropriates the word, adapting it to his own expressive and semantic intention ... [M]any words stubbornly resist, others remain alien, sound foreign in the mouth of the one who appropriated them and who now speaks them ... Language is not a neutral medium that passes freely and easily into the private property of the speaker's intentions; it is populated – overpopulated – with the intentions of others.[43]

This vision of speech and writing as the attempt to tame and shape the residual intentions of others – many of which may be directly opposed to one's own existential and political presuppositions – is a much more appropriate starting point for a Marxist poetics. Moreover, it adds a new aspect to the process of 'configuration', expanding it from the operation of narrativisation and synthesis to the act of binding together potentially mutually contradictory expressive and semantic intentions.[44]

By extension, the second major weakness of Ricoeur's level of prefiguration can be located in the domain of symbols. 'Symbolism', as Ricoeur uses this word, refers to that which confers on action an initial readability or sense prior to overt, self-conscious linguistic description or narration.[45] What his account of symbolism lacks, however, is a theory of specifically *verbal* language. This is because Ricoeur inherits Aristotle's privileging of plot (*muthos*) over style (*lexis*) and is concerned only with narrative texts, his definition of 'narrative'

---

43 Bakhtin 1981, pp. 293–4.
44 In Chapter 4 we shall examine an exemplary case of this in Williams's reading of Thomas Hardy.
45 Ricoeur 1984b, p. 58.

presupposing the centrality of action (tragedy being, as we saw in the introduction, a *mimēsis praxeōs* – an 'imitation of action'). Given Ricoeur's express
desire to expand the scope of Aristotle's *Poetics*,[46] however, this is problematic
for two reasons: firstly, it either ignores or is forced to downplay the quite obvious rise of style as a dominant literary category in bourgeois modernity, i.e., the
demise of classical conventions of *elocutio*, socially and aesthetically regulated
by the *Stiltrennung*, and the concomitant autonomisation of individual writerly
styles.[47] Secondly, it broadens the scope of Aristotle's *Poetics* only to narrative
texts (the prominent modern form being the novel), yet fails to account for
such typically 'plotless' genres as lyric poetry. A Marxist poetics, then, whilst
recognising the importance of *muthos*, will wish to provide some basic theory
of language itself: the raw material on which the writer-configurer of any genre
necessarily goes to work.

Finally, a more general problem is that Ricoeur imagines the realm of prefiguration as ahistorical, as eternally possessing the same structure. Consequently,
the act of interpretation at the level of $mimesis_3$ apparently has no influence
on the fundamental structure of experience. But if $mimesis_1$ were to be seen as
historically variable, then this would change. The inheritance and interpretation performed at $mimesis_3$ could then be connected, in a circuit-like fashion,
with the form of experience in $mimesis_1$. Peter Osborne articulates the solution well: 'If the mediating role laid down in Ricoeur's account of historical
time is ontological, rather than merely poetic in significance ... level 1 will be
"always already" historical, and Ricoeur's threefold schema will actually be a
cycle in which $mimesis_1$ is the sedimented result of $mimesis_3$ from a previous
circuit'.[48] And with that we are thrust back into the realm of Marxism. For it
is one of the tenets of that tradition, not only that men make their own history yet not in circumstances of their own choosing,[49] but also that men make
those very circumstances that come to impose their limits upon them.[50] In
other words, the structures of experience of which $mimesis_1$ consists are, to

46   See especially Chapter 1 of Ricoeur 1985.

47   For a slightly more detailed overview of this process, see Chapter 1.

48   Osborne 1995, p. 156. He adds in a footnote: 'Ricoeur is blinkered by his use of Aristotle for
        his paradigm of action here, despite his impressive extension of the terms of Aristotle's
        poetics ... A similar problem occurs in Heidegger, despite his awareness of historicity,
        since his use of Husserl's phenomenological method relegates historicity to a secondary
        position, methodologically, which the subsequent course of the analysis fails to reverse,
        despite its intent' (Osborne 1995, p. 232, n. 167).

49   Marx 1973, p. 146.

50   Marx 1975, p. 422, thesis III.

a certain extent, *produced* by human praxis itself. For Marx, there is no eternally unchanging transcendental consciousness as there is for Kant; rather, the
structure of the 'world' is produced through labour. Human labour processes
(what Marx sometimes refers to as *Stoffwechselprozesse*) transform a pre-given
nature – or a pre-laboured residue of a previously transformed nature – into a
habitable world, and in so transforming the objective structure of such worlds
alter the possible modes of experience within them. In this light, the relation
between mimesis$_3$ and mimesis$_1$ is not a vicious circle swathed in mystery (i.e.,
Ricoeur's claim that at the heart of human experience there lies a 'secret' from
which stories arise and to which they return):[51] it is the rationally discoverable
relation between the inheritance of social and cultural forms and their constitution of the structure of historical experience.

3.2   *Mimesis$_2$: Configuration*

Ultimately, however, it is at the level of mimesis$_2$ that the affinities and differences between the hermeneutic and Marxist traditions become apparent. One
of the major insights of Marxist literary theory has been that the act of configuration is often simultaneously an act of compensation. There exist social
contradictions in the practical world which are symbolically resolved in the
'imaginary' realm. Jameson's central notion of a 'political unconscious' and
Eagleton's extensive work on the ideology of form offer two modes of thinking
through this claim. The upshot is that where, for Ricoeur, mimesis$_2$ constitutes
a relatively neutral act of mediation between time and narrative, for the Marxist tradition it can be seen to possess an ideological function: by symbolically
resolving certain practical contradictions, literary works prevent these latter
from being truly recognised in reality (that is, recognised in a non-distorted,
non-partial, non-refracted manner). In doing so, they enable – in no matter
how modest a manner – the reproduction of the social relations of production.

Beyond this difference, however, lies the somewhat more serious problem
of Ricoeur's theory of tradition. The crux of the matter is that traditionality in
Ricoeur's work is transcendental. Whilst he articulates the schematism of the
narrative function with the dialectic of innovation and sedimentation, hence
implying the intra-historical nature of the tradition, he nonetheless presupposes an underlying, transhistorical identity of the productive schematism. He
can account neither for the advent of formal or generic novelty nor for the
power relations which constitute canon formations; instead, he must treat the
coming-into-being of genres and forms as entirely contingent, simply proceed-

---

51   Ricoeur 1984b, pp. 75–6.

ing to order and classify them. His reliance on Northrop Frye for his account of narrative paradigms is telling in this regard, as is his crucial misquotation of him. Where Frye writes of poetry that it 'can *only* be made out of other poems' (before going on to omit history altogether: 'Literature shapes itself, and is not shaped externally'),[52] Ricoeur omits the 'only',[53] thereby eliding the total absence of the historicity of forms in Frye's account. Thus, literary forms in both Frye and Ricoeur have the status of irrational facticity, but this is masked by the ultimately transcendental self-structuring of traditions and of the transhistorical presence of the narrative schematism.

Precisely because he treats the existence of 'traditional' literary forms and genres as purely contingent, Ricoeur never stops to ask *whose* tradition it is. Phrases such as '[t]he order that can be extricated from this self-structuring tradition is neither historical nor ahistorical but rather "transhistorical"' are misleading because they conceal the active selections of past literature by culturally powerful social groups in the present.[54] The work of Raymond Williams is indispensable here. It provides a twofold theory of tradition which incorporates and surpasses that of Ricoeur: his notion of a 'selective tradition' demonstrates the power relations involved in any tradition-formation, whilst his lifelong obsession with inheritance and generationality suggests political and temporal repercussions for which Ricoeur's Gadamerian approach cannot account.[55] This is then connected to a more general problem with Ricoeur's transcendental traditionality: 'Ricoeur fails to grasp modernity ontologically, as a form of historical being ... Ricoeur's allegedly transcendental traditionality is a specifically modern form'.[56] That is, *traditionality only becomes transcendental in modernity*. By positing its transhistorical transcendence, Ricoeur fails to account for modernity as a qualitatively new historical temporality.

Finally, we must include a specifically verbal element to the act of configuration. As we saw at the level of mimesis$_1$, Ricoeur's major concern is with *muthos* over *lexis*, but for our purposes mimesis$_2$ must also include the configurational counterpart to the (verbal) linguistic situation in which a writer finds herself. The act of lexical configuration is the operation which unites the

---

52   Frye 1957, p. 97; emphasis added.

53   Ricoeur 1985, p. 164 n. 21. The ambiguity also occurs in the French original. Ricoeur quotes the original correctly, but omits the 'only' in his translation: 'Les poèmes se font à partir d'autres poèmes, les romans à partir d'autres romans' (1984a, p. 32, n. 3).

54   Ricoeur 1985, p. 15.

55   See chapter 5.

56   Osborne 1995, p. 132.

various levels of style (instance, idiom and interpellation),[57] as well as the various sociolects and jargons, parodies and clichés, into a unified stylistic totality.
As will become clear in Chapter 4, this act of lexical configuration is a socially
significant one, since it often involves the imposition of a new intentionality
on idioms and modes of phrasing which already possess socially connotative, residual intentions of their own. This act of stylistic totalisation is often
informed by a stylistic ideology, which may or may not be part of a larger aesthetic ideology.

3.3   Mimesis₃: Refiguration

In terms of what Ricoeur, after François Dagognet, refers to as the 'iconic augmentation' of reality that works of literature achieve, the Marxist tradition
offers a suggestive expansion. For Marxist thinkers like Williams, as for Ricoeur, literature possesses a real effectivity.[58] The difference between them is
their understanding of the precise modality and location of this effectivity. For
Ricoeur, for example, it is unclear whether iconic augmentation is a purely
phenomenal expansion of our 'horizon', or whether the expansion is in fact
ontological (in other words, there is some confusion as to the ontological status
of the horizon as such). For Marxist thought, however, literary effectivity can
have a range of modalities: it is either a symbolic resolution of real, historical contradictions, thereby enabling the reproduction of the social relations
of production (the counterpart in mimesis₃ to the symbolic resolutions performed in the act of configuration); the locus of a pre-emergent structure of
feeling which embodies novel social relations;[59] or an act of Utopian prefiguration – the joy we experience upon writing and reading fine styles offering
us a proleptic sense of the pleasures of non-alienated labour and communication.[60]

　　The more general expansion of Ricoeur's threefold mimesis will then take
the form of one of the major insights of a Marxist poetics: that *praxis* and
poiēsis are ultimately immanent to one another. For example, if it is true
to say, with Williams, that the development of the soliloquy form was not
simply a 'reflection' of a nascent capitalist individualism, but an immanent and
constitutive element in its expansion, it is also true that political and economic
praxis – via various degrees of mediation – inform and internally limit literary

---

57   See Chapter 4.
58   Though whether, strictly speaking, this applies to Jameson's perspective is debatable. See
　　　Chapter 7.
59   See Chapter 5.
60   These are just three of many possible modes of literary effectivity within a Marxist poetics.

production. Contrary to Ricoeur's primarily *phenomenal* description of 'iconic augmentation', then, Marxist poetics accords mimesis$_3$ an ultimately *political* effectivity.

Conclusion

We can now summarise the major components of the overall theoretical recalibration of Ricoeur's threefold mimesis which will be developed in the following chapters:

Mimesis$_1$

– An account of the political struggles which occur at the level of language and symbolicity in general.
– A theory of specifically *verbal* language in the realm of prefiguration.
– An active recognition that the structures of experience of which mimesis$_1$ consists are, to a certain extent, *produced* by human praxis itself.

Mimesis$_2$

– An account of the act of configuration as simultaneously an act of compensation with a concomitant ideological function.
– A theory of the active selections and inheritances involved in literary traditions.
– An account of the act of specifically *lexical* configuration.

Mimesis$_3$

– A theory of the political effectivity of literature.
– An elaboration of one of the major insights of a Marxist poetics: that *praxis* and *poiēsis* are immanent to one another.

It is now time to begin the development of these components via an examination of the work of Williams, Eagleton and Jameson. The conceptual armature with which Ricoeur has provided us will reappear throughout Part 2 as I attempt to think the work of all three critics within a single framework. Nonetheless, it is inevitable that in some places (such as Chapter 4, where I provide my working definition of style in prose fiction) I shall draw more heavily on Ricoeur's work, whereas in others, where his vocabulary is less immediately relevant (Chapter 5, for example), it will occasionally fade from view. Nevertheless, in the general theory of style offered in Part 3, the threefold mimesis will return to play a central role.

Part 2 of this book begins with an act of symbolic patricide: the now infamous 1976 article in which Eagleton attacked his one-time mentor, Raymond Williams, accusing him of idealism, reformism, and populism. Williams would respond to each of these charges, without specifically naming Eagleton, later that year. I begin with a summary of their arguments because I hope to suggest that the ideas about style contained in Part 2 cannot be reduced to purely academic exercises: they were integral to larger debates within the Marxist tradition on political strategy. How to achieve revolution in the capitalist West and what the role of culture and literature within it would be: this was the force field in which the following theories of style were elaborated.

PART 2

Theories of Style in Williams,
Eagleton and Jameson

∴

Overture: Patricide; or, Reformism Versus Revolution

Eagleton Contra Williams

'Harold Bloom', declared Eagleton, in typically provocative spirit, 'was once an interesting critic'.[1] Interesting enough, that is, to invent a theory of literary history as Oedipal combat: the great authors were those who freed themselves from the shadow of their forebears only by literarily murdering them. Something of the same might be said of Eagleton with regards to his own symbolic father, Raymond Williams. Having played the apprentice to the master from the early 1960s, in 1976 a new, structuralist Eagleton – armed with Althusser and Poulantzas – struck out at his one-time mentor in an article which gained immediate notoriety. He subsequently apologised for the occasionally shrill tone of the piece, but to this day stands by much of what he wrote.[2] In this section I shall outline the main attack and point to the ways in which Eagleton links Williams's perceived weaknesses to the very style in which the latter writes. The point of this overture (and of the forthcoming *intermezzo*) is to show that the theories of style each of these thinkers developed did not occur in a vacuum: they were caught up in far larger, personally and politically turbulent debates.

Eagleton made three major criticisms of Williams's work: it was reformist, idealist and populist. Williams had fused *Scrutiny*'s liberal humanist emphasis on the importance of individual experience with those 'radical' elements of the Romantic 'radical-conservative' lineage outlined in *Culture and Society* which could be 'ingrafted into a "socialist humanism"'.[3] This latter, however, was effectively a strand of labourist reformism. Indeed, Williams was only able to graft Romantic organicism to socialist humanism in the first place precisely because 'the working-class movement is as a matter of historical fact deeply infected with the Carlylean and Ruskinian ideology in question':[4]

> The manoeuvre was enabled ... by the fact that both Romantic and labourist ideologies are in partial conflict with bourgeois hegemony; but it is

---

1   Eagleton 2000.
2   Eagleton and Beaumont 2009, p. 141.
3   Eagleton 1976, pp. 24–5.
4   Eagleton 1976, p. 25.

precisely that partiality which allows them to embrace. Neither tradition
is purely antagonistic to bourgeois state-power: the first preserves it by
displacing political analysis to a moralist and idealist critique of its worst
'human' effects, the second seeks to accommodate itself within it. What
the book did, then, was to consecrate the reformism of the labour movement, raise it to new heights of moral and cultural legitimacy, by offering
to it values and symbols drawn in the main from the tradition of most
entrenched political reaction.[5]

Finally, to these charges of reformism and idealism (the latter the result of
'displaced political analysis') Eagleton added the charge of populism. What
he meant was the paradox by which Williams's 'belief in the *need* for a "common culture" was continually crossed and confounded with an assertion of its
present *reality*'.[6] This resulted in 'the contradictory position of opposing a crippling hegemony whose power he had simultaneously to deny'.[7] Interestingly
for our purposes, 'political polemic ... was effectively confiscated by the populist claim'.[8] In short, Eagleton's major criticism was that Williams's work was
not really *Marxist*; quite what Eagleton believed Marxism to be is a matter to
which we shall return.

    All of these factors – the *Scrutiny* emphasis on experience, the Romantic
radical-conservative lineage, the socialist humanism and labourism – came
together, so Eagleton claimed, in Williams's literary style:

> ... an elaborately formal, resoundingly public discourse in which an ab-
> stractive habit has become an instinctual reflex ... Concrete particulars
> are offered in such modified, mediated and magisterial a guise as to
> be only dimly intelligible through the mesh of generalities. Yet at the
> same time his ponderous pauses and stiffly rhetorical inflections, his
> ritualising of a cluster of key terms to the point where they seem less
> public concepts than private inventions, suggest the movement of an
> unmistakeably individual voice. What appears at first glance the inert
> language of academicism is in fact the stage of a personal drama ... It is a
> style in which the very act of assuming an unruffled, almost Olympian
> impersonality displays itself (not least in its spiralling modifications)

5   Ibid.
6   Eagleton 1976, p. 28.
7   Ibid.
8   Ibid.

as edgily defensive, private and self-absorbed ... the style of a thinker intellectually isolated to the point of eccentricity ...[9]

Ultimately, Eagleton implied, Williams's style was a product of its 'political moment', the overriding factor of which was his structural divorce from a working class which was, in any case, reformist in outlook.[10] His constantly self-modifying prose, with its academic cadence, was the stylistic index of this larger structural disjunction: without one's feet planted firmly in the soil of a revolutionary working class, one's prose loses its raw vitality and polemic edge. Polemic, Eagleton suggests, is the formal symptom of a fundamental social antagonism, but its coming-into-being requires that the writer recognise this antagonism in the first place; only an engagement in the ranks of a revolutionary working class could possibly generate and sustain such recognition and, by extension, such a style. Reformism, idealism and populism were as stultifying stylistically as they were politically.

Needless to say, Eagleton's attack was premised upon a set of unspoken assumptions as to what constitutes a supposedly 'authentic' Marxism. What were its attributes? Firstly, if labourism or Romanticism were only partially antagonistic to bourgeois state power, then true Marxism would be 'purely antagonistic'.[11] Secondly, Marxism is not to be contaminated with labourism or reformism: revolutionary politics is seen as almost categorically distinct from them. Thirdly, having criticised Williams for placing his own theory within the same horizon as the very writers he was analysing,[12] it is obvious that for this Althusserian Eagleton a clear distinction must be drawn within Marxist theory between ideology and science: 'For historical materialism stands or falls by the claim that it is not only an ideology, but that it contains a scientific theory of the genesis, structure and decline of ideologies. It situates itself, in short, outside the terrain of competing "long perspectives" in order to theorise the conditions of their very possibility'.[13] Finally, the literary style appropriate to any scientific Marxist discourse dealing with non-Marxist discourse was polemic. The fact that Eagleton himself demonstrated that Williams's lack of polemic was to a

---

9   Eagleton 1976, pp. 22–3.

10   Eagleton 1976, pp. 34–5.

11   Eagleton 1976, p. 25.

12   Cf. Eagleton 1976, p. 23: 'It is in some ways the voice of the social critics examined in *Culture and Society 1780–1950*; and indeed the key to that work is that Williams offers himself, not consciously or intrusively but implicitly ... as the latest figure in the lineage he traces, a character within his own drama'.

13   Eagleton 1976, pp. 16–17.

large extent explicable in terms of historical contingency is seen as no excuse for not engaging in it. The voluntaristic will-to-revolution inherent in Eagleton's conception of Marxism is in many ways at one with his will-to-polemic in the realm of style.[14]

What was at stake in this attack, which was reprinted in *Criticism and Ideology*, was far more than simply how to read a novel; it was about setting limits to the meaning of 'Marxism' and purging Marxist theory of reformist elements, the better to enable revolutionary practice in the present. That style cropped up in this debate at all was a sign of its origins in the unusual concatenation of circumstances surrounding English literary criticism.[15] It was an argument about contemporary political strategy mediated and overdetermined by literary critical discourse (which is not to say that the latter remained unaffected or was a mere apolitical screen). And it was as just such a statement of political strategy that Raymond Williams would respond to it.

Williams Strikes Back

It took Williams several months to publish his response, 'Notes on Marxism in Britain Since 1945'.[16] It appeared, tellingly, in an issue of *New Left Review* notable for its emphasis on the problematic translation of the Russian revolutionary 'model' to the advanced capitalist nations of Western Europe.[17] Williams does not mention Eagleton by name, but responds methodically to almost every accusation levelled against him. In a characteristic opening, he takes issue with the terminology that forms the basis of the whole exchange: 'Marxism', he says, has changed its meaning several times since the war, depending on the specific political conjuncture in which it was active;[18] likewise, the meaning of 'Labour Left' has also constantly shifted, as has its relations to 'Marx-

---

14   For an alternative reading of his perennial stylistic self-confidence, see Chapter 6.

15   See Chapter 1.

16   The earliest version of Eagleton's attack was published as 'Criticism and Politics: The Work of Raymond Williams' in *New Left Review* in the January–February 1976 edition. Williams's 'Notes on Marxism in Britain Since 1945' was published in the November–December 1976 edition.

17   Williams's essay featured alongside Perry Anderson's profoundly influential 'The Antinomies of Antonio Gramsci' as well as an interview with Ernest Mandel on 'Revolutionary Strategy in Europe'. See *New Left Review* I/100, November–December 1976. For a recent critique of Anderson's article, see Thomas (2009).

18   Williams 2010, pp. 233–4.

ism'.[19] In other words: 'What "Marxism" is at any time seems dependent, finally, less on the history of ideas, which is still amongst Marxists the usual way of defining it, than on the complex developments of actual social being and consciousness'.[20] By using the key terms from Marx's core formulation of historical materialism – namely, that social being determines consciousness and not the other way around – the cutting edge to this observation is clear: here, Eagleton is the idealist. The problem with Eagleton in this light is that he writes as if there existed some 'pure ... essence called Marxism'.[21] In that sense, he was an exemplar of the bad kind of what Williams named 'legitimating theory', one of the three theoretical strands he saw as constitutive of Marxist theory in Britain since 1945. Legitimating theory dealt with 'the legitimate inheritance of an authentic Marxism';[22] 'academic theory', the second of the three strands, was concerned with the insertion or reinsertion of Marxism into a range of strictly academic work ('the question of "communism" or one of its variants did not *necessarily* arise' in this context);[23] finally, 'operative theory' provided theoretical analyses of the specificities of late capitalist British society, with a view to intervening into it.[24] Eagleton, the text implies, offered the worst of academic Marxist theory – his was an 'academically congenial formalism' –[25] and the least helpful aspect of legitimating theory: 'it can lead, at its worst, to a series of self-alienating options, in which our real political presence is as bystanders, historians or critics of the immense conflicts of other generations and other places, with only marginal or rhetorical connections to the confused and frustrating politics of our own time and place'.[26] Eagleton was in danger of entering 'a form of internal exile'.[27] Thus, for Williams, politics is a matter of *immanence*: there is no 'outside' from which to look in; the outside is already a constitutive element of the inside.[28] In that sense, the emphasis on the 'lived' or 'experience' in his work is not simply a residuum of *Scrutiny* petit-bourgeois ideology;

19   Williams 2010, pp. 234–6.
20   Williams 2010, p. 246.
21   Williams 2010, p. 239.
22   Williams 2010, p. 237.
23   Ibid.
24   Ibid.
25   Williams 2010, p. 239.
26   Williams 2010, p. 238.
27   Williams 2010, p. 247. Williams first developed the notion of an 'exile' in *The Long Revolution* (1965, pp. 107–108).
28   I explore at length Williams's attachment to immanence as a political principle in Chapter 6.

it is a key component of his immanentist conception of politics and literature. For Williams 'experience' names at once one's mode of insertion into transindividual socio-material processes (one's affective attachments, belongings and alignments), and the constant imperative to remain one's own contemporary: to dwell within the true processual depths of the present.

Williams develops this attack on Eagleton's 'formalism', a phrase he repeats several times, when countering the accusation of populism. Like 'Marxism' and 'Labour Left', the meaning of 'populism' has shifted repeatedly depending on its political context. Marxism has been constantly imbricated with various forms of populism throughout its history, and was thus never as pure as Eagleton made out. Nonetheless, Williams stated overtly that he had never been a populist 'in the sense of that residual rhetoric': 'But because I saw the process as options under pressure, and knew where that pressure was coming from, I could not move either to the other most generally available position: that contempt of people ... which makes the whole people, including the whole working class, mere carriers of the structures of a corrupt ideology'.[29] Eagleton's blanket generalisation always smacked of Brecht's satirical remark that the government should dissolve the people and elect a new one; here, Williams hints at that angle, but adds to it a term taken from his reconfiguration of the Marxist concept of 'determination'. He understood determination as both the 'setting of limits' and the 'exertion of pressures'; such pressures 'are by no means only pressures against the limits ... They are at least as often pressures derived from the formation and momentum of a given social mode: in effect a compulsion to act in ways that maintain and renew it'.[30] By voiding theory of the lived pressures of daily existence, Eagleton's formalism was not only contemptible in its abstract denigration of an entire class, but also politically futile in that it lacked all felt connection to contemporary political reality. The better solution, claims Williams, is to 'stay with the existing resources; to learn and perhaps to teach new resources; to live the contradictions and the options under pressure so that ... there was a chance of understanding them and tipping them the other way'.[31] Formalism, in this light, was the insubstantiality of a thought that has failed to absorb the lived pressures of a political reality, to process them and, in doing so, to transform them into positive political potential.

Williams's response to the accusation of culturalism involved his earliest definition of 'cultural materialism': 'a theory of culture as a (social and material)

---

29   Williams 2010, p. 241.
30   Williams 1977, p. 87.
31   Williams 2010, pp. 241–2.

productive process and of specific practices, of "arts", as social uses of material
means of production (from language as "practical consciousness" to the specific technologies of writing and forms of writing, through to mechanical and
electronic communications systems)'.[32] Far from being a concern with 'merely'
superstructural affairs, cultural theory was 'a response to radical changes in
the social relations of cultural process within British and other comparable
societies'.[33] These changes included the rise of culture precisely as a realm
of marketable commodities, and therefore as an area of primary, rather than
secondary, production; in this context, it was 'impossible … to see cultural questions as practically separable from political and economic questions, or to posit
either second-order or dependent relations between them'.[34] To ignore these
fundamental changes would lead, not only to theoretical errors, but to a political practice divorced from reality. This is why 'cultural materialism' should not
be seen as opposed to or different from historical materialism; rather, cultural
materialism is a systematic application of historical materialist principles and
insights, not only to bourgeois theories of culture and society, but also to *those*
elements of historical materialism itself – often involving 'culture' and the 'arts' –
which are, or have become, residually idealist.[35]

It is in the section on reformism that Williams takes on Eagleton's self-
proclaimed 'pure antagonism' to bourgeois state power. He shows that at a
pragmatic level reformism has always been a constitutive element of Marxism,
not least because 'a working-class political formation which does not respond
to and represent the perceived, often short-term interests of the working class
becomes impotent'.[36] The problem with Eagleton's notion of revolutionary
strategy is that it relies far too heavily – and ahistorically – on the Russian
model of revolution (one which, as we have seen, this issue of *New Left Review*
was designed to interrogate). Williams argues that this model is premised
upon 'societies in which the *political and social* defences of the system were
very much weaker, and with its consequent reliance on simple breakdown
as the crisis of capitalism which makes possible the socialist transition'.[37] By

---

32   Williams 2010, p. 243.
33   Williams 2010, p. 245.
34   Ibid.
35   The best illustration of this argument is parts I and II of Williams's *Marxism and Literature*
     (1977).
36   Williams 2010, p. 247.
37   Williams 2010, pp. 248–9. Anderson's article cites Gramsci on this point: 'In the East, the
     State was everything, civil society was primordial and gelatinous; in the West, there was a
     proper relationship between State and civil society, and when the State trembled a sturdy

ignoring the complexly stratified layers of civil societies in advanced capitalist countries, ones which acted as a buttress to the bourgeois state, Eagleton's polemic was downright dangerous: 'There is now a real danger, in a kind of theoretical opportunism leading to political, economic and sub-military ("terrorist") opportunism, of using the rhetoric against "reformism" to the point where isolated militant sectors enter battles in which a totalizing alternative is precipitated against them'.[38] What had seemed, in Eagleton's attack, a version of pure Marxism has ended up running the risk of a descent into 'terrorism'.

Nowhere does Williams's essay touch on the issue of style, but what becomes clear from its use of 'formalist' as a derogatory appellation is that, whereas for Eagleton polemic is a style integral to any genuinely Marxist writing, for Williams Eagleton's polemic is merely a formal index of his obsolete and purist conception of Marxism. Eagleton's triumphalist tone is the anachronistic echo of a Russian victory whose precise strategic model, if repeated in the advanced capitalist nations of the West, would lead either to failure or political suicide. Would it thus be too much to see in Williams's infamous 'spiralling modific-ations',[39] those ever self-renewing sub-clauses, an attempt to render his style adequate to the complex mediations of Western civil society? This may well sound extravagant, but there is a key mitigating factor here: for Williams, lan-guage is a substantial and constitutive aspect of human reality, thereby endow-ing style and form with a productive, interventionary nature quite alien to the-ories of language derived from Saussurean linguistics in which language is not so much *of* the world as *above* it.[40] This, combined with his immanentist con-ception of Marxist theory and practice, produces not only a radically different conception of politics to Eagleton's, but also, arguably, a necessarily different understanding of style – of its meaning and function. It is to Williams's prin-cipal essay on prose style, and towards our preliminary definition of style in prose fiction, that we now turn.

---

structure of civil society was at once revealed. The State was only an outer ditch, behind which there was a powerful system of fortresses and earthworks: more or less numerous from one State to the next, it goes without saying – but this precisely necessitated an accurate reconnaissance of each individual country' (Anderson 1976, p. 10).

38   Williams 2010, p. 249.
39   Eagleton 1976, p. 23.
40   For an overview of Williams's theory of language see Chapter 5.

CHAPTER 4

Style in Prose Fiction: A Preliminary Definition

The major secondary literature on Raymond Williams is more or less silent when it comes to the introductory essay he wrote for his edited anthology, *The Pelican Book of English Prose (vol. 2): From 1780 to the Present Day* (1969).[1] This is unfortunate since it brings together some of the major innovations of his previous work and offers a sophisticated political theory of style which points towards some of the principal lines of argument of *The English Novel From Dickens to Lawrence* (1970).[2] This chapter aims to set out the basic arguments of that essay and to show how they relate to other important aspects of his work. In doing so, the basic political stakes of style will hopefully begin to emerge.

1   **Style as a Social Relationship**

The central argument of the essay is that 'good prose and style are not things but relationships; that questions of method, subject and quality cannot be separated from the changing relations of men [*sic*] which are evident elsewhere in changing institutions and in a changing language'.[3] At one point, Williams

---

1   Alan O'Connor (1989, pp. 69–70) refers to it twice in passing in his suggestive chapter on the concept of the 'knowable community'. John Higgins (1999, p. 195, n. 11) has a footnote describing it as a 'rich formulation and exemplification' of the topic of 'stance'. The volume of the Pelican anthology edited by Williams was the second of two; the first, covering the period from the Middle Ages to 1800, was edited by Roger Sharrock. Perhaps significantly, the organisational structures of the two volumes are identical except in one minor detail: whereas Sharrock organises his volume according to three chronological periods (Medieval, Renaissance, Augustan) and subdivides each period into the categories 'Life and Action', 'Imagination' and 'Argument', Williams shares the tripartite chronological structure (1780–1830, 1830–95, 1895–Present) and the tripartite categorical distinction, but replaces 'Life and Action' with the term 'Observation'.

2   Indeed, it is evident that the reading he carried out for the edited anthology formed the basis for his study of the English novel. The two were apparently written in tandem.

3   Williams 1969, p. 55. Throughout this chapter I shall refer to the original edition of Williams's essay. He later reprinted it in slightly modified form in Williams 1983b; the changes consist mainly in the addition of excerpts from the texts of the writers he is discussing, i.e., those texts which in the original edition were already contained in the anthology itself.

even refers to the conception of style he is opposing as a 'reification of style'.[4]
Such language suggests an underlying but never explicitly stated thesis: just
as Marx unmasked the structure and process of commodity fetishism as the
socially necessary illusion whereby 'the definite social relation between men
themselves ... assumes here, for them, the fantastic form of a relation between
things',[5] so for Williams style appears as a 'thing' abstracted from all social
relations, but is in fact one of their determinate linguistic modes. The task of the
critic would then seem to consist in demonstrating the specific social relations
embodied in and communicated through styles, not least since these relations
are concealed by a dogmatic criticism unaware of the social grounds of its own
supposedly absolute value judgments.

The essay is divided into five sections. The first section sets out some of
the basic statistical shifts that occurred between 1780 and 1950: these include
massive increases in population sizes and a concomitant explosion in the rate
of urban dwelling, rising literacy rates, large increases in the number of books
and newspapers being published, and a gradual increase in newspaper read-
erships. All of these factors are constitutive aspects of the changing relations
between writers and readers. Continuing his earlier concerns in *Reading and
Criticism* (1950), Williams also emphasises the power of the education system in
influencing conceptions of writing and style: 'In the twentieth century, as a result of some improved access from elementary to higher education, writers have
had more varied social origins than their immediate predecessors, but many of
their ideas about writing have been mediated through a minority area of higher
education, both directly and indirectly'.[6] This would suggest that, even where
the social origin of writers varies, a national education system can in some
sense homogenise – and hegemonise – ideas about writing. Williams ends the
opening section with a first definition of prose:

> In its most general sense, the writing of prose is a transaction between
> discoverable numbers of writers and readers, organized in certain chan-
> ging social relations which include education, class habits, distribution
> and publishing costs. At the same time, in its most important sense, the
> writing of prose is a sharing of experience which, in its human qualities,
> is both affected by and can transcend the received social relations.[7]

4 Williams 1969, p. 36.
5 Marx 1990, p. 165.
6 Williams 1969, p. 24.
7 Ibid.

The awkwardness of this definition, torn as it is between the self-evidently 'materialist' concerns of the empirical production process and the *Scrutiny*-like emphasis on experience, is indicative of the more general problem he faced in reconciling the nuanced texture of lived experience with the mechanical versions of historical materialism he had inherited. Nonetheless, what unites both impulses is the concept, not overtly stated here, to which Williams retained a lifelong attachment: communication. In *Keywords* he stressed the root meanings of 'communication' as 'to make common to many, to impart' and 'to share'.[8] And in *The Long Revolution* he had already insisted that all art is communication, 'the process of making unique experience into common experience'.[9] (Not that this communication was automatically accepted by its audience or readership: it was there to be 'accepted, rejected or ignored').[10] Thus, as an initial understanding of style as a social relationship we can say, firstly, that writing in general is a 'systematic skill that has to be taught and learned' and which therefore necessarily requires the mediation of an education system on which the political hegemon of the day exerts a gravitational influence.[11] Secondly, once basic literacy is achieved, there remains the network of material and economic factors which enter into literary production, consumption, distribution and exchange. Thirdly, there is the question of readership: whether readers are known to the writer or unknown, personally or in the abstract, of the same class or of an opposing class, and so on. Finally, there is the fact that for Williams styles are ways of incorporating unique experiences and of sharing them with others.

The second section of the essay provides the most detailed definition of style in Williams's entire oeuvre, and is for that reason worthy of close attention. The key passage begins by observing that '[o]ne of the marks of a conservative society is that it regards style as an absolute. A style of writing or speaking is judged as a question of manners, and appreciation of this style as a question of breeding and taste'.[12] The word 'absolute' is key. In general it signifies 'free from dependency',[13] but it also has crucial philosophical and political implications: 'not involving or implying relation; not dependent for meaning or significance

---

8   Williams 1983a, p. 72. He also notes the ambiguity in 'communication' between the sense of a one-way process (a transmission) and a mutual process.

9   Williams 1965, p. 55.

10   Williams 1965, p. 46.

11   Williams 1983b, p. 3.

12   Williams 1969, p. 26.

13   *OED*, sense A.I.

on a relationship with another term or concept'[14] and 'Of authority: free from all external restraint or interference; unrestricted, unlimited'.[15] An absolute style is one whose meaning is internal to itself and whose authority is beyond question. It is *authoritative unrelatedness*, the apparent polar opposite of a social relation. Yet, simultaneously, it nonetheless seems to imply a social relation of sorts: that of manners. Manners, however, are a form of social etiquette determined, in the final instance, by the mores of a particular social class, and 'good manners' by those of the dominant class. If anything, they imply social relations specifically *within* that class amongst members of its own kind.[16] Thus, the paradox of an absolute conception of style is that style really is in fact a mode of social relationship – both between members of a hegemonic class and between that class and the supposedly non-absolute, relative styles of other classes – but the ruling class denies this very relatedness. It reifies style in the precise sense that it strategically masks its inherent social relatedness.

The immediately proceeding passage challenges this conception of style:

> In important literary criticism since Coleridge, this conventional assumption has been set aside. Style is known, not as an abstract quality, but as inseparable from the substance of the ideas and feelings expressed. In modern communication theory, a new dimension has been added: style is inseparable also from the precise relationship of which it is a form: commonly the relationship, whether explicit or implicit, between a writer or speaker and his expected reader or audience. This relationship is never mechanical. The ordinary formula in communication theory – 'who says what to whom with what effect?' – characteristically neglects the real sources of communication. In practice, we have to ask 'why?' The precise relationship, which is only rarely static, is then inseparable from the substantial ideas and feelings, which might otherwise be abstracted as a 'content' without form. In almost all writing the language, which is at once form and content, includes, though often unconsciously, the real relationships and the tension between these and the precise relationships of the writer and other men.[17]

---

14   *OED*, sense A.2.b.

15   *OED*, sense 4.A.

16   When Arthur Quiller-Couch (1916) informed his students at Cambridge that style was 'good manners', this was exactly what he meant.

17   Williams 1969, p. 26.

For Williams, there are two defining features of style. Firstly, it is 'insep-arable from the substance of the ideas and feelings expressed'; that is, it is not indifferent or opposed to content, but rather a constitutive aspect of it. (The upshot of this is that the very notion of 'content' as something the-oretically extractable from the mere shell of form will have to be radically overhauled). Secondly, style is a form of the relationship between a writer or speaker and his or her expected reader or audience. Williams is careful to distinguish this latter feature from the theories of relationship at large in the then dominant communication models (such as Jakobson's, which has a technical communication system as its basis).[18] What these mechanical the-ories ignore is the *purpose* of communication, the 'why'. It is as if Williams is claiming that one will not have understood the substantial – as opposed to abstract – meaning of a text unless one has considered its social purpose. But this purpose is not always singular. Williams distinguishes between the 'precise relationships' and the 'real relationships' of the writer to the expected reader; these two types may even be in 'tension'. This – and the association of 'unconsciously' with 'real relationships' – would suggest that writing consists of two levels: the level of conscious authorial intention, in which the writer knows (or thinks she knows) for whom she is writing and why, and the level of unconscious actuality, in which the underlying 'pressures and limits' of pre-cise historical situations are played out through the writer without her aware-ness.[19]

1.1   *Abstract Universal Style versus Particular Style*

Williams gives examples drawn from the political writings of Edmund Burke, Thomas Paine and William Cobbett. He notes that in such writing – *pace* those for whom 'style is regarded ... as ... a merely tasteful or mannered addition to substance' – 'the kind of experience being drawn on and the version of other men indicated by a particular way of addressing them are not only substan-tial but are crucial to the precise nature of a political argument'.[20] Burke, for instance, writing against the revolutionary upheavals of 1789, adopted the form of a letter to 'a very young gentleman at Paris'. 'By writing as an Englishman to a Frenchman', says Williams,

---

18   Cf. Jakobson 1987, pp. 62–94.
19   I pursue some of the potential problems of Williams's position on this matter in the next chapter.
20   Williams 1969, p. 27.

he can assume what he could not prove: a representative quality, describing the English constitution *as if* to a foreigner, and thus enlisting behind him the feelings of a united patriotism ... Burke relied on a pretended unity of national feeling to which in fact he was trying to persuade his *English* readers. Thus the literary method becomes, if we are not careful, the political proof.[21]

Drawing on the above distinction, one might say that Burke's 'precise relationship' to his expected audience was at odds with his 'real relationship'. In comparison, Thomas Paine 'cut through to direct public address, against what he called Burke's theatrical performance'.[22] Yet even Paine's prose falters between 'open argument, in line with his appeal to government by reason, and what is really an anxious appeal to men of his own kind to understand the feelings of ... "the 'mob'"'.[23]

Ultimately, then, Williams distinguishes between two types of political prose that developed in this period: what I shall call (though he does not) 'abstract universal style' and 'particular style'. The former is the style of the eighteenth-century academic essay and is characterised by Williams as 'the climax of print': 'a uniformity of tone and address; an impersonality, assuming no immediate relation between writer and reader, but only possession, in a social way, of this language; a durability, as in the object itself, beyond any temporary impulse or occasion'.[24] The particular style, on the other hand, was a form of 'direct address to an ever-widening public, having the strengths of contact, of the sounds of actual voices and experience ... but in danger, always, of declining to opportunism – the devices of flattery ... – and to simplification'.[25] If this seems like a simple re-run of the age-old feud between philosophy and rhetoric, it is a mirage, since Williams sees the abstract universal style as having a quite particular social basis: the British ruling-class. Their calmness and coolness of tone was premised upon their social hegemony.[26] The particularistic tones of a radical like Cobbett, however, were coextensive with the drive for universal suffrage. What seems, rationally, to be the superior form of prose – the abstract universal style – 'assumes the political forms of open and rational discourse

---

21   Williams 1969, p. 28.
22   Williams 1969, p. 29.
23   Ibid.
24   Williams 1969, p. 31.
25   Williams 1969, p. 29.
26   Williams writes that 'what we can learn from looking at the institutions we can learn also from looking at the prose' (1969, p. 29).

which in fact it is trying to create'.[27] The conflict must then, in my view, be seen as that between two different conceptions of rationality: an abstract rationalism, whereby particular individuals mask their private interests behind the coolly composed prose of 'philosophy', or a performative drive for the historical actualisation of the political equivalent of abstractly universal prose. What appears on the surface to be 'mere rhetoric' could thus be said to embody a more concrete form of critical rationality than its abstractly 'philosophical' opponent. The struggle for 'good style' is synonymous with the struggle for adequate social forms. Style is both passive and active: it reflects the current social relations but it also strives to transform and to create them. An 'adequate' style for Williams will clearly be one in which the abstract universalism of open rational discourse is somehow fused with the directness of particular address.

1.2   *Prose Settled and Unsettled*

In the third section of the essay, Williams develops these insights and applies them to an analysis of novelistic discourse. As in section two, where he distinguished between what I have called the abstract universal and particular styles, so in this section he identifies two types of prose: sustained analysis and speech. Roughly speaking, the former is equivalent to the abstract universal style (its qualities of timelessness and assumed equality between writer and reader are alike) whilst the latter is equivalent to the particular. Using a passage from George Eliot's *The Mill on the Floss*, in which she argues that it is not only the material life of 'good society' which is of 'very expensive production', but also its associated tones of moderation and irony, based as they are on a nation-wide 'emphasis of want', Williams makes plain the social antagonisms which structure what might otherwise appear merely abstract stylistic differences. The abstract universal style, or sustained analysis, is based on a 'small educated class' whose livelihood and modes of writing and speech were premised upon the widespread exploitation and expropriation of the working class. But the increasing inclusion of direct speech in the novel was capable of counteracting this, of 'expressing the actual life of a hard-pressed, hard-driven, excluded majority' – that very majority on whose emphatic want the abstract universal style relied. Thus, it is no exaggeration to say that for Williams the formal struggles novelists faced when attempting to unify these two discourses within a single work were stylistic extensions of the experience of a class-divided society. What was ostensibly a battle between classes 'out there' in society became

---

27   Ibid.

internalised or reflected into the very writing process itself, generating stylistic discontinuities which a reified conception of style would simply brush off as either artistic or moral failures.[28]

The most dramatic example of a writer who lived out this struggle in the very fibres of his being is – on Williams's reading – Thomas Hardy.[29] Written off condescendingly by F.R. Leavis, and Henry James before him,[30] Williams consciously gives him pride of place in his alternative history of the English Novel. Hardy, he claims, has a fundamental 'problem of style':

> Hardy as a writer was mainly concerned with the interaction between the two conditions – the educated and the customary: not just as the characteristics of social groups, but as ways of seeing and feeling, within a single mind. And then neither established language would serve, to express this tension and disturbance ... An educated style, as it had developed in a particular and exclusive group, was dumb in intensity and limited in humanity. A customary style, while carrying the voice of feeling, was still thwarted by ignorance and complacent in repetition and habit. Hardy veered between them, and the idiosyncrasy of his writing is related to this ...[31]

The agony of Hardy's writing, its idiosyncratic shifts between customary and elevated diction are the scars left behind from his struggle to bind and unite them. The educated style was necessary for observational and analytical exactitude, but went hand in hand with a class with which Hardy shared no common sensibility and an education system overtly designed to set a superior class apart from other men.[32] The customary style was the one, put simply, with which Hardy could *feel* but not *think* – at least, not to the standards of sophistication which his novelistic art and the reigning aesthetic ideologies of the day required.[33] 'The writer moving through this history', writes Williams, 'had

28 Or, in Leavis's case, as both. John Higgins has rightly argued that for Leavis 'formal failure is always the symptom of moral failing' (1999, p. 76).
29 For an alternative reading of Hardy's stylistic project, see Taylor 1993 and Hartley forthcoming.
30 Cf. Henry James: 'The good little Thomas Hardy has scored a great success with *Tess of the d'Urbervilles*, which is chock-full of faults and falsity, and yet has a singular charm' (cited in Leavis 1962, p. 33).
31 Williams 1969, p. 44.
32 Cf. Williams 1969, p. 47.
33 For Williams, by the time of *The English Novel From Dickens to Lawrence*, this would

to explore, as if on his own, the resources of what seemed to be but was not in fact a common language'.[34] On paper, English was the universal language of the inhabitants of Great Britain, but in reality it was only an abstract universal, riven by the particular interests and viewpoints of class struggle: Hardy was forced to speak with a cleft tongue.

Yet the bulk of Victorian prose was 'remarkably settled and solid: an achieved, confident and still powerful manner'.[35] In the fourth section Williams considers such 'settled' writers as Trollope, Macaulay and Bagehot. The key difference between a Macaulay and a Hardy was that the former

> shared this essential [achieved, confident] outlook ... He shared so much with his readers, in ways of seeing and dealing with the world, that he becomes a kind of model: an admirable style. While the ways of seeing and dealing last, that is English, and the schoolboys can be set to learn it: the attitudes and the style in a single operation ...[36]

Because language for Williams is 'practical consciousness',[37] it is no surprise that actual historical practices generate 'ways of seeing and dealing' with the world which crystallise into literary styles. The point is that it will only be possible to inherit and utilise those styles if one of two (or both) preconditions are met: either one shares what Williams calls the 'structure of feeling' which a style embodies or one is simply unaware that by adopting a given style one is also adopting a particular worldview.[38] That is, the style itself possesses a minimal ideological effectivity. The dichotomy Williams is sketching here, between confident and disturbed styles, is thus the literary index of the wider social and political crises brought about by the dual Industrial and French Revolutions. The confident styles were written by those who either embodied or (unwittingly) sympathised with the structure of feeling of the reigning political – and, in this case, imperial – hegemon. The disturbed prose was written by those who could not see or feel in the same way, and yet who had been taught that such self-assured English simply *was* English in its entirety. Incongruities of style, far

---

also become the very important split between participant and observer: 'He sees as a participant who is also an observer; this is the source of the strain' (1970, p. 110).

34   Williams 1969, p. 47.
35   Ibid.
36   Williams 1969, p. 48.
37   See Chapter 5, section 1.2.
38   I explain Williams's concept of the 'structure of feeling' in the next chapter.

from being reprehensible, were symptoms that a new structure of feeling was struggling to emerge.

1.3   *Williams's Theory of Prose: A Balance-Sheet*

Overall, then, Williams's essay is a rich and deeply felt meditation on the literary consequences of a divided common language. Among its greatest strengths is that it offers a first real glimpse of what the phrase 'politics of style' might actually mean. It shows that style is a linguistic mode of social relation immanent to the political and economic factors affecting social relations more generally. It is a mode of offering an individual experience to the community and, whether consciously or not, it proffers a certain type of relationship to its readers. Because language for Williams is 'practical consciousness', the raw linguistic materials on which stylistic configuration goes to work are not simply neutral, but are haunted by the still-dormant intentions of the divided classes who once spoke them.[39] Thus, the undeniable virtues of the abstract universal style are bound up for Williams with a ruling class which actively enforced widespread illiteracy on most of the population. At the same time, particular styles were rich in feeling and a sense of occasion, but could not raise themselves to the intricate complexities of organised thought. In other work of this period, he develops this insight into what one might call a perspectival sociology: a theory of the effect of social position (which is also a point of view in the narratological sense) on ways of seeing and feeling.[40] Those who identified with the ruling ideologies of the day were able to craft self-assured styles because the linguistic hegemony of the dialect of the powerful never became an issue for them. But those like Thomas Hardy, who lived out the linguistic contradictions between the two, were forced to try and *configure*, to bring together, those discourses which pulled in opposite directions. For many – like Leavis and Henry James – Hardy was a bad writer, 'chock full of faults and falsity', but for Williams those faults were the fault lines of this inner struggle – the stylistic counterpart of the class struggle. Good style in Williams's understanding could only ever be 'good social relations'. But if language is 'practical consciousness' then 'good style' could presumably only ever be achieved once class society has been overcome.[41] It is only thus that the raw linguistic resources will be exorcised of their still-traumatising pasts.

---

39   The constant references to ghosts throughout Williams's oeuvre, an obsession born in his period of personal crisis and frantic research on Ibsen, are part of this sense of troubling inheritance. I pursue this point at length in the following chapter.

40   See, for example, Williams 1971 or Chapters 2 and 11 of Williams 1973. I develop this point in the next chapter.

41   We shall see in Chapter 6 that this is very different from Eagleton's approach, for which

These are the great strengths of the essay, but what are its weaknesses? For a start, Williams fails sufficiently to distinguish between literary and non-literary texts. His reasons for not doing so are, of course, sound. As he later wrote, '[t]he dichotomies fact/fiction and objective/subjective are ... the theoretical and historical keys to the basic bourgeois theory of literature, which has controlled and specialized the actual multiplicity of writing'.[42] One can, I think, agree with this sentiment, yet nonetheless feel that, when discussing a writer like Thomas Hardy, Williams makes no distinction between the narrator of the novels and the biographical author. What he lacks, in other words, is both a coherent theory of mimesis – of the process of literary production and configuration – and a nuanced narratological theory of 'voice'. I have already gone some way to providing the former in my justification for using Aristotle's *Poetics*,[43] but shall shortly reinforce those passages with some reflection on the relation between narration and fictionality; following that, I shall sketch out a theory of voice. Both of these will help towards my ongoing effort to formulate a first definition of style.

For the sake of such a definition, let us divide Williams's pronouncements into two overlapping but distinct emphases. On the one hand, style is a linguistic mode of social relation: a direct address from writer to reader which sets up a certain ground for communication. On the other, style is the configuration of several sub-styles or discourses. In the framework of the threefold mimesis, the former belongs to the transition between $mimesis_2$ and $mimesis_3$ (the position accorded to 'voice' in Ricoeur's scheme of things);[44] the latter belongs primarily to $mimesis_2$, the act of configuration itself. In order to flesh these out, I shall turn to the work of rhetorical narratologist Richard Walsh, both to rethink the notion of fictionality and to develop a theory of style premised upon the Platonic distinction between diegesis and mimesis, themselves subdivided into what Walsh calls instance, idiom and interpellation. In elucidating style as configuration, I shall draw on the writings of Bakhtin.

---

    aesthetic judgments of stylistic virtue are possible beyond the social judgments implicit in them.

42   Williams 1977, p. 149.

43   See Chapter 3.

44   See Ricoeur 1985, p. 99.

2   Narratology, Voice and Style

The two main weaknesses of Williams's theory of prose are, firstly, that it has an awkward tendency to conflate fictional and non-fictional texts, and, secondly, that it seems to assume – rather as Eagleton does – that the biographical author is always synonymous with the fictional narrator. The first problem is related to the larger one of distinguishing between literature and non-literature; the second comes under the narratological rubric of 'voice'. Both of these problems come together in a series of magisterial essays by the rhetorical narratologist, Richard Walsh.[45] In this section, in which I focus on simply one of those essays, I shall argue that Walsh's work provides us with some ingenious solutions to Williams's shortcomings, and that, vice versa, Williams's theory of conventions serves to buttress Walsh's theoretically fragile notion of 'fictionality'.

There is no need here to regurgitate the arcane debates that have raged for the last 30 years over the concept of 'voice'.[46] Suffice it to say that, whereas most of them are founded on one or another form of structuralism, in which narrative representation is seen predominantly as a *structure*, Walsh, from his rhetorical standpoint, sees it as an *act*: 'a real-world communicative gesture – which, in the case of fictional narrative, is offered as fictive rather than informative'.[47] To grasp the quiet brilliance of this manoeuvre, it must be understood in terms of the Genettian problematic to which it is a response. Genette famously distinguished between narrative 'persons' (heterodiegetic, homodiegetic) and narrative 'levels' (extradiegetic, intradiegetic). Walsh argues that the personal distinction is epistemological in nature, the level distinction ontological. The problem with the ontological distinction is that Genette 'assigns each narrating instance to the diegetic level that includes it, so that the first level of any narrative is necessarily extradiegetic. Well then, is the extradiegetic a diegetic level?'[48] As Walsh shows, Genette needs it to be both: in the case of fictional narrators, it must be diegetic (since the narrator is of the storyworld), but in the case of narrative's direct address to us, the readers in the real world, it clearly

---

45   The essays to which I am referring have been published as a single volume: *The Rhetoric of Fictionality* (Walsh 2007).

46   The foundational texts in this debate include: Genette 1980, pp. 212–62, Stanzel 1984, Bakhtin 1981, pp. 259–422, Bakhtin 1984, pp. 181–269 and Chatman 1978, pp. 146–260. Other important interventions include: Aczel 1998, Gibson 1996 and Nielsen 2011. For an overview of a whole range of contemporary positions on the concept of 'voice', see the summer 2001 edition of *New Literary History* (vol. 32.3) which is dedicated to the concept.

47   Walsh 2010, p. 35.

48   Walsh 2010, p. 39.

cannot be diegetic. The equivocal nature of the extradiegetic level arises, argues Walsh, 'from the assumption, fundamental to the communicative model, that every narrating instance is literal with respect to the events represented'.[49] In short: 'If narrative mediacy is always transmission, the communicative model of narrative levels allows for no point of ontological discontinuity', yet 'the distinction of narrative person depends upon ontological discontinuity'.[50] How is this paradox to be overcome?

Walsh's solution is to substitute a rhetorical theory of narrative for the structuralist-communicational one. For '[t]he problem of ontological discontinuity', argues Walsh, 'is simply the problem, in the communicative model's terms, of fictionality itself'.[51] The communicative model cannot cope with fictionality because it cannot deal with non-literal communication that does not conform to everyday norms of referentiality; likewise, structuralism's focus upon the products, rather than the acts, of representation leads it to self-contradictions whose resolution lies in a pragmatic (and hence situational) account of narrative representation. To articulate his solution to this very modern problem, Walsh turns to the ancients: Plato's age-old distinction between diegesis (the poet speaking in his own voice) and mimesis (the poet imitating the voice of a character).[52] This has the signal advantage of stressing the act of fictional representation whilst generating the 'recursive possibility that a narration may represent another narration', a split between the extradiegetic level (diegesis) and all the others (mimesis):

> A typology of narration based on Plato's distinction, then, recognizes two hierarchical modes of fictive representation, which may be a matter of information (diegesis) or imitation (mimesis). In fictive diegesis the information is offered and/ or interpreted under the real-world communicative regime of fictionality, in which an awareness of its fictive orient-

---

49 Ibid.

50 Walsh 2010, p. 40.

51 Walsh 2010, p. 41.

52 Ibid. Though, as Stephen Halliwell (2012) has shown, the initial distinction in Plato was more complex than this clean dichotomy would imply. In *The Republic* mimesis is often considered a *type* of diegesis, but one which is potentially psychologically menacing in that it induces the author to invite multiplicity into his soul by imitating and assimilating the voices of others. Socrates's comments on diegesis-mimesis are thus not merely *technical* but part of the larger ethical psychology developed in *The Republic*. Significantly, whilst Aristotle inherits and develops this distinction, he does not perpetuate the normative judgements found in Plato.

ation is integral to its rhetoric. In mimesis the imitation is specifically of an act of narration, so accordingly the informative function of diegesis is performed at one remove.[53]

When we read a work of fiction, we read it *as* a work of fiction, not as a literal communication. This real-world awareness of the work's fictionality permeates our reading consciousness like a barely perceptible vapour, capable at any moment of evaporating into the ether of the real. By regrounding the act of narrative representation in the real world, and by replacing a purely textual conception of fictionality with a conventional one, Walsh has gone a long way to resocialising literature.

The second half of Walsh's essay tackles head-on the labyrinthine debates and confusions that have arisen around the notion of 'voice'. He proposes an ingenious terminological solution, premised upon his revival of Plato's diegesis-mimesis distinction and Bakhtin's three types of discourse.[54] He delineates three subdivisions of voice: voice as instance, voice as idiom, and voice as interpellation. These subdivisions diagonally striate the informative (diegesis) and imitative (mimesis) modes of fictional representation. Voice as instance is a representational act, in which voice is not objectified, and carries out the task of narration.[55] Voice as idiom refers to an object (rather than an act) of representation, the voice being thus objectified; it invites ethical evaluation of the character whose discourse it represents.[56] In the case of a represented narrating instance – i.e., a narrative told by a character – both senses of voice apply: 'In *Moby-Dick*, Ishmael's narration considered as idiom tells us about Ishmael; as instance it tells us about Ahab and the white whale'.[57] The underlying assumption of voice as idiom is that voice is expression, that it offers an insight into the character of the enunciating subject.[58] In cases where the notional voice is not objectified, however – i.e., in narrative diegesis – 'the discursive features commonly embraced by voice are equally, and perhaps better understood as style: by *style* I mean discourse features understood in their relation to mean-

---

53   Walsh 2010, p. 41.
54   Walsh never overtly references Bakhtin in this section of the essay, but it is obvious that his first two definitions of voice are based on Bakhtin's first and second types of discourse respectively. Cf. Bakhtin 1984, p. 199.
55   Walsh 2010, pp. 48–9.
56   Ibid. The exception is when diegesis is viewed from the perspective of voice as idiom. See below.
57   Walsh 2010, p. 49.
58   Walsh 2010, p. 50.

ing ... rather than as the expression of subjectivity'.[59] Style, for Walsh, is the idiom of diegesis, the non-character narrator: it is as close as one can come to the author's own voice under the 'regime of fictionality'.[60] Finally, voice as interpellation – the third subdivision – has both a narrow and a general sense, though each refers to the production of a subject position: in its narrow sense it refers to perceptual and cognitive focalisation (the spatio-temporal, often character-aligned perspective through which the reader experiences the story, and which is an implicit premise of the rhetorical focus of the representational act); in its general sense it is the overall ideological subject position implied by any discourse and to which the reader (either consciously or unconsciously) imaginatively aligns herself.[61] Taken together, this tripartite definition of voice forms a powerful critical tool.

Walsh's essay enables us to pinpoint and transcend the central weaknesses in Williams's and Eagleton's respective positions: where Williams dubiously identifies the author's voice with that of the fictional narrator, and Eagleton (as we shall see in Chapter 6) reduces style to the idiom of the diegetic narrating instance, Walsh stresses, firstly, the multiple and internally stratified nature of style and, secondly, the fact that in prose fiction styles are read under the regime of fictionality.[62] To adopt an Aristotelian terminology, we might say that the dynamic operation of 'poietic' mimesis always produces a minimal gap – the gap of 'fiction' – internal to reality. Add to this the fact that intrafictional style is a conjuncture of multiple intra- and extra-literary factors and we begin to see that the 'politics of style' will not inhere directly in the words on the page, nor be reducible to their real-world effects, but is rather produced through their (intra-textual) idiomatic and (extra-textual) interpellative interrelations.

---

59   Ibid.

60   Though we must heed Walsh's warning: '... there is no inherent expression of authorial selfhood – no authentic self-presence – in such discursive features; nor indeed is there inherently a singular authorial subject ...' (ibid.).

61   Walsh 2010, p. 53. Here, Walsh makes use of Althusser's classic essay on ideology and interpellation.

62   For my insistence on using the concept of style over that of 'voice', see the conclusion to this section. It should be observed that the identification of the diegetic idiom with that of the author originates, not in the author alone, but in the reigning convention – i.e., in writers' and readers' habitual literary expectations which actively produce the text. Both Susan Lanser and Didier Coste stress the reader's activity in equating the narratorial idiom with the author's voice, unless otherwise advised in the text itself. Both are cited in Aczel 1998, pp. 473–6.

The other major gain is the 'communicative regime of fictionality' – the shift from a structural understanding of the literary artefact to a rhetorical emphasis on the literary act. Yet fictionality also happens to be Walsh's Achilles' heel. It presupposes certain writerly and readerly expectations without taking into account their historical mutability. This is where Williams's theory of conventions – those tacit agreements or agreed standards between writer, reader and text – comes into its own. Whilst one might, in the extreme, concede with Terry Eagleton that there has always existed something bearing at least a 'family resemblance' to what we now know as 'fiction' – a mimetic core running through the myriad literary permutations of human history – it is quite clear that this core alone is not enough to determine the totality of a literary convention. (If it were, then *The Iliad*, the plays of David Garrick, and *Harry Potter* would all be instantiations of the same convention). The 'regime of fictionality' is thus too vague a concept to be critically productive; its stress on what I have called 'poietic' mimesis is commendable, but it cannot account for those other elements of a convention which are equally constitutive in the writing and reading of literature.

How can Walsh's rhetorical reconsideration of voice be accommodated within the threefold mimesis? Ricoeur himself locates voice 'at the point of transition between configuration and refiguration' in that it 'addresses itself to the reader'.[63] This applies primarily to the third of Walsh's subdivisions: voice as interpellation, which produces subject positions. Voice as instance and voice as idiom, however, whilst also belonging to the point of intersection between text and reader, must surely be seen as pertaining primarily to mimesis$_2$: the former as the zero degree of style necessary for any narration whatsoever to occur, the latter as a mimesis of an other's discourse (or, in the case of Walsh's limited definition of style, as the author's own idiom). Thus, it is entirely possible to combine the dynamic operations of the threefold mimesis with the rhetorical, threefold theory of voice.

At this point, however, we have to perform a terminological shift. Anyone who has worked their way through the narratological debates about 'voice' will have noticed the way in which they gradually, almost imperceptibly, become debates about 'style'. This is not least because they deal with precisely the same textual phenomena. Consequently, much of the confusion generated by the concept of 'voice' when referring to written texts – precisely the confusion it was Walsh's task to dispel – could be limited, if not entirely avoided, by referring instead to 'style'. This is not least because it invites a primarily scriptural

---

63   Ricoeur 1985, p. 99.

problematic which the dubious vocal metaphor – with its Derridean spectres – does not.[64] In that spirit (to invoke another Derridean keyword), I propose to rewrite Walsh's tripartite distinction thus: style as instance, style as idiom and style as interpellation. All three of these will become important elements of my ultimate definition of style.

Finally, I wish briefly to draw attention to a footnote in which Walsh quotes, and dismisses, Richard Aczel's following claim: 'Narrative voice, like any other voice, is a fundamentally *composite* entity; a specific *configuration* of voices'.[65] To which Walsh retorts: 'If every voice is a configuration of voices, the term is being made to work too hard'.[66] Walsh's desire for definitional rigour is understandable but by rejecting Aczel's crucial emphasis on the *configurational* aspect of style, he can account neither for the dynamic element of *poiēsis* nor for that kernel of truth in people's speaking of an author's style in the singular. In other words, Walsh cannot account for the operation by which the various strands of style (instance, idiom, interpellation), along with the other elements of the text, become unified. Let us quote Aczel in full:

> Narrative voice, like any other voice, is a fundamentally *composite* entity; a specific *configuration* of voices. But it is, nonetheless, *actively* configured, and it is precisely in the traces of its (artistic) organization that its identity resides ... [Bakhtin treats] narrative discourse as an essentially quotational form where the quoting instance is not unitary and monological, but a configuration of different voices or expressive styles organized into an 'artistic' whole by means of a set of identifiable rhetorical principles. The ontological status of this configured quoting instance remains, however, unclear.[67]

This is in line with Bakhtin's claim that the myriad styles of novelistic heteroglossia 'are subordinated to the higher stylistic unity of the work as a whole, a unity that cannot be identified with any single one of the unities subordinated to it'.[68] There are two consequences to this plea for stylistic totality. The first is that the price we pay for unity is a tortured search for its source and

---

64   Whilst I concur with John Frow (2014, pp. 149–180) and Peter Boxall (2015, pp. 19–38) that 'voice' can never be *entirely* eradicated from the experience of reading novelistic prose, I hold that a focus on style would limit potential philosophical confusion.

65   Aczel 1998, p. 483.

66   Walsh 2010, p. 54.

67   Aczel 1998, p. 483.

68   Bakhtin 1981, p. 262.

principle: is it the author which unifies a literary work? *La langue* through the author? Convention? Technique? Or something else entirely? My own hypothesis is that the source of unity of a literary work is the dynamic operation of 'poietic' mimesis. This operation is informed by the techniques of literary composition – which are themselves crystallisations of forms of practical consciousness – and implemented by a writer who is their host and practitioner. Moreover, this operation occurs within the context of literary conventions coproduced by writers and readers alike. This is not, admittedly, the snappiest of explanations but it is, I hope, a comprehensive one. The second consequence of global stylistic unification is that we shall require an extra level to our definition of style: one for the subdivisions (instance, idiom and interpellation) and one for the overriding unity. It is to the first formulation of this definition that we shall now turn.

3 A First Definition of Style in Prose Fiction

Style, as it pertains to prose fiction, has three principal meanings:

1. It is a linguistic mode of social relation, which operates on and through, and is informed and internally limited by:
    a. the available linguistic resources (i.e., crystallisations of 'practical consciousness' past and present), which are often in themselves internally stratified and contradictory, in line with the broader social contradictions of the day (mimesis$_1$)
    b. the level of (formal or informal) education of the writer, which directly affects the quantity, quality and range of linguistic resources available to him or her (mimesis$_1$)
    c. the quasi-physical factors of writing: those lexical, syntactical and rhythmical compulsions beyond the realm of choice or consciousness (mimesis$_1$)
    d. the anticipated reader or audience, which ranges from a directly known or knowable individual to an anonymous mass public (mimesis$_2$)
    e. the genre and/ or literary form in and through which the social relation is proffered (mimesis$_2$)
    f. the reigning literary conventions of the day: that is, the specific aesthetic regime, or tacit horizon of expectation, in and through which a given author, text and reader come together (mimesis$_{2/3}$)
2. It is one of several subordinated, relatively autonomous, linguistic operations featured in a given fictional narrative. These can be roughly divided

into the three stylistic functions (which diagonally striate the two principal modes of fictive representation, diegesis and mimesis):

   a. style as instance (mimesis$_2$)
   b. style as idiom (mimesis$_2$)
   c. style as (narrow) interpellation (focalisation) (mimesis$_{2/3}$)

3. It is the total mode of configuration of these subordinate linguistic operations, unidentifiable with any one of them. Depending on whether analysis is text-oriented or reader-oriented, this can be seen as:

   a. style as lexical configuration (mimesis$_2$)
   b. style as (general) interpellation (mimesis$_{2/3}$)

Style, then, is first and foremost a linguistic mode of social relation. It is not, however, a social relation in the abstract. It requires the constitutive medium of language (1a), which can be defined as 'practical consciousness'. Language is not a neutral substance: it is a tissue of competing semantic intentions, words and phrases jostling against one another in the various directions that the multiple forms of human praxis have led it. It is a multitude of ways of being in the world, ways of seeing and feeling, each criss-crossing the others along complex verbal and semantic networks. This is the always-already preformed raw material on which a writer-configurer goes to work. But, of course, the available quantity, quality and range of these linguistic resources will be limited to various extents depending upon a given writer's level of education (1b). This is not to be confused with *formal* education, since both autodidacticism and the unofficial bequest of cultural capital are also types of education. Nonetheless, given that formal education has the most dramatic impact upon a society's overall literacy levels, it is ultimately the ruling class which has the greatest influence upon everyday reading and writing practices. These, then, are the two most profoundly 'social' elements of the linguistic basis of any style. Yet one must also take into account their contrary: the uniquely individual, quasi-physical factors of writing (1c). This includes those impulsive, unconscious verbal or syntactical tics that are beyond the realm of volition. Any precise idea of their ultimate scope is difficult to determine, but a materialist account of style must surely allow for them. These three elements form the raw materials on and through which the 'poietic' act operates.

    A conscious communication also involves, on the part of the addresser, some notion of the addressee (1d). At one extreme, a writer will know her reader personally (e.g., a literary coterie, or Bloomsbury); at the other extreme, her public will remain completely anonymous (e.g., authors of contemporary mass-market paperbacks). This can affect style in several ways: at the level of diction, it can affect linguistic formality (informal when addressing a friend, formal when writing for strangers); at the level of interpellation, it can subjectivate experts (by use of complex terminology or private codes unknowable to the uninitiated) or amateurs (by using simplified versions of complex terms). The tone of the writing will also be affected by the envisaged readership: George Eliot, for example, found it necessary constantly to interrupt her narrations with half-pleading, half-castigating moral appeals to her readers – so many attempts to convince them that working people were worth taking seriously. Richard Wright, on the other hand, wrote for a split public (poor blacks and rich whites), and the respective modes of address geared to each public mutually complemented one another.[69]

An even greater determinant of literary style, however, is the overriding genre or literary form in which a writer writes (1e). The modern-day detective novel, for instance, invites the configuration of a whole gamut of social idioms, ranging from Scots obscenities to Italian-American slang, all the way to the high-falutin prose of the city's well-to-do. Moreover, certain literary forms come, over time, to be associated with certain styles: hard-boiled detective fiction has a stylistic norm which gravitates towards the macho *bon mot*, whilst much contemporary mainstream British poetry (e.g., Don Paterson, Carol Ann Duffy) tends towards a falling cadence with a final silence that accompanies the poem's (pseudo-)profundity. Needless to say, each of these styles harbours within it a quite specific structure of feeling. All of these factors, however, are mediated by the ultimate literary conventions through which they occur (1f.). A large group of people seated in the dark, paying almost no attention to one another, and watching a small number of other people under spot-lights on wooden planks below them, these latter pretending to be people they patently are not: this can only be 'normal' under the strict literary convention of theatrical performance. Without such conventions styles would have no abode.

These, then, are the general constituents of style as a linguistic mode of social relation. We now have to differentiate between these and the individual linguistic operations of which a work consists (2). Adapting Walsh, I have argued for the various operations to be divided into three broad narratological categories, depending on their vocalic (or, in my terms, stylistic) function; each of them applies equally to diegesis (the author 'speaking in her own voice' under the regime of fictionality) and mimesis (the imitation of an act of narration). Style as instance (2a) refers to the representational act and is

---

69   Cf. Sartre 2001, p. 61: 'Had he [Wright] spoken to the whites alone, he might have turned out to be more prolix, more didactic, and more abusive; to the negroes alone, still more elliptical, more of a confederate, and more elegiac. In the first case, his work might have come close to satire; in the second to prophetic lamentation'.

primarily *informative* in nature; style in this sense is thus object- or story world-oriented, a lexical zero-degree necessary for any act of verbal narration whatsoever. Style as idiom (2b), except when applied to diegesis (that is, except when the language of the authorial narrator is examined for its ethical or artistic connotations), refers to all those moments of represented discourse. This ranges from the inclusion of direct speech into an overarching narratorial idiom all the way to a represented narrating instance as such (e.g., Ishmael in *Moby-Dick*). Here, the verbal tone and texture of the idiom is an index of the ethical or political traits of the represented discursive instance (whether this be a character or simply a generic sociolect). Finally, style as (narrow) interpellation (2c) refers to the subject position offered to the reader by the text via its perspective (spatio-temporal and cognitive-affective).

The relation between these relatively autonomous linguistic operations is not one of simple contiguity; they are bound together in a unified totality by the act of configuration. Whereas 'style' at level 2 of the definition indicated one of a text's sub-styles, style at level 3 refers to the totality of relations between them. In the strict sense, this means that the overall act of poietic configuration includes a lexical configuration by which a writer forces the multiple voices of a text to cohere (usually by making one of them – the authorial idiom – dominant). Even those texts which aspire to pure heteroglossia are limited by the dominant literary conventions which presuppose them to constitute hermetic unities. To that extent, heteroglossia is always limited by the (current) hegemony of monologic readerly expectations.[70] The totality of sub-styles also generates a total subject position: a general ideological perspective which the reader is invited to inhabit (and which he or she must inhabit, either consciously or unconsciously, for any reading to occur) (2b). This overall 'stance' of the work is – crucially – *not* necessarily coterminous with the author's self-conscious ideological position.

4   Possible Elaborations

The preceding section offers a working definition of style in prose fiction, developed through a critique of Raymond Williams's major 1969 essay on English prose. In the following chapters it will become clear that there are many other aspects of style which must be taken into consideration in performing a

---

70   Monika Fludernik (1996, p. 33) recognises as much in her conception of 'narrativisation' – level IV of her '"natural" narratology' model.

fundamental recalibration of style as a critical concept. What is distinctly lacking in this definition, for example, above and beyond the activity inherent to lexical configuration more generally, is any real sense of a self-conscious project of stylisation on the part of the author. Given that, as we shall see, the restless search for *le mot juste* and the perfectly sculpted sentence is one of the defining features of the modern conception of style, this element of self-conscious elaboration will be a necessary addition. As we shall see in the next chapter, its absence here is not coincidental: it connects with a curious feature of Raymond Williams's conception of historical temporality. Put simply, Williams has a tendency to emphasise the unconscious attachments of tradition over the modernist temporality of a conscious break with the past; by extension, he tends to overemphasise the pre- or un-conscious aspects of literary production at the expense of an author's self-conscious aesthetic or conceptual project. It is to this and many other related issues that we now turn.

CHAPTER 5

Raymond Williams: Style between Immanence and Naturalism

'Now, for us there is no exteriority, no absolute outside of politics with regard to institutions, of the event with regard to history, of truth with regard to opinion. The outside is always within. Contradictions explode from the inside. And politics does not consist in eluding them but in installing oneself in them so as to bring them to the point of rupture and explosion'.

    – DANIEL BENSAÏD[1]

∴

The main argument of the previous chapter was that style is a linguistic mode of social relation. This relation involves, not only the offered relationship from writer to (potential) reader, but also the internal relationship of narratorial to characterological stylistic idioms within the prose work itself. Yet Williams's theory of style actually went much further. 'Style' in his work constitutes the point of intersection between five themes and problems, the first three of which relate to different aspects of one of his major conceptual innovations, the 'structure of feeling'. These include: a theory of the collective formation of subjectivity (the structure of feeling in its articulation of individual styles and period styles); a theory of the advent of historical novelty, which is also a theory of historical temporality understood in terms of 'inheritance' (the structure of feeling as a pre-emergent phenomenon); an attempt to map the range of what is ultimately sayable (the structure of feeling as an expression of that which is not yet utterable in terms of currently existing modes of articulation); the dramatic and prose ideal of the stylistic integration of multiple idioms; and, finally, as in Chapter 4, style as a linguistic mode of social relation – here rearticulated from the perspective of Williams's fully developed 'cultural materialism'. The great difficulty is that these five approaches to style do not neatly cohere. Con-

---

1   Cited in Bosteels 2011, p. 17.

sequently, the task of this chapter will be to reconstruct in some detail each of
the sub-conceptions of style, whilst indicating the ways in which they overlap
yet ultimately come to emphasise different approaches to the same problem.

One of the major claims of this chapter is that Williams was a thinker
for whom immanence was a central theoretical and political principle. This
involves a reconception of Williams's oeuvre which tries consciously to connect it to more recent work on immanence in Marxist philosophy and cultural
theory. The chapter begins with a systematic presentation of Williams's understanding of immanence – a concept he never overtly employs – as it relates
to language and form. Consequently, the reader will notice a certain shift in
valence between the first and second halves of the chapter: whereas the first
employs a relatively synchronic and systematic mode of presentation, moving between Williams's works with little consideration for their chronological
development, the second half is structured according to a more traditional
mode of philological reconstruction. Nonetheless, the reader will require the
systematic overview of Williams's immanence in order to perceive the stakes
of the philological reconstructions. I will also attempt periodically to suggest
the intrinsic connection between immanence and a second principle informing Williams's work: complexity. Though less important than immanence, the
principle of complexity – by which I mean Williams's sustained emphasis on
the potentially infinite multiplicity of social relationships, practices, and values – is important in grasping the unique intellectual tenor and methodology
of his work.

1   On Williams and Immanence

Thanks to recent Marxist scholarship, we are now in a position to reconceptualise our understanding of Williams's intellectual and political project. One
of the key concepts of this recent work has been that of immanence. Prominent among the advocates of immanence have been those Marxists affiliated
with the Italian *operaismo* (workerism) tradition,[2] though it is work on the production of subjectivity in Marx and especially on Antonio Gramsci's detailed
elaboration of the notion of 'absolute immanence' that informs my rereading
of Williams.[3] I claim that we will not fully have understood the work of Willi-

---

2   Such thinkers include Antonio Negri, Paolo Virno, Franco 'Bifo' Berardi, and Christian Maraz-
    zi. For a critical overview of the *operaismo* tradition, see Turchetto 2007.
3   Read 2003 and Thomas 2009.

ams until we realise that it is everywhere informed by a principle of immanence which strongly resembles Gramsci's concept of 'absolute immanence'.

The term 'absolute immanence' first entered the Marxist lexicon via Gramsci's critical reconfiguration of its use by Croce (who used the term in his 1908 work, *Logica come scienza del concetto puro*). Gramsci's aim was to elaborate Marx's second thesis on Feuerbach, in which Marx stresses the secular 'this-sidedness' [*Diesseitigkeit*] of thinking, an absolute 'being-within-history'.[4] Gramsci believed that Marx's inheritance of David Ricardo's notions of 'tendential laws' and 'determinate markets' had enabled him to break definitively with the speculative philosophical tradition by positing 'laws which have a validity within determinate and historically limited social formations'.[5] Gramsci held that by extending Ricardo's insights to the whole of human history, Marx had produced a new concept of immanence understood as a ' "unitary synthetic moment" which allows the transformation of the three pre-Marxian movements of classical German philosophy, French politics and classical [British] economy into theoretical moments, in relations of continual translation, of the philosophy of praxis'.[6] Thus, for Gramsci, immanence means the mutual imbrication, constitution and translatability of politics, economics and thought via the philosophy of praxis. It is my claim that the principle of immanence informing Williams's work shares crucial similarities to this Gramscian sense of 'absolute immanence'. I take Williams's assertion that 'the theory of culture [is] a theory of relations between elements in a whole way of life' as exemplary of the notion of mutual translatability just outlined.[7]

Williams himself, however, never refers to his own theories in terms of immanence, so my initial task will be to reconstruct the central immanentist strands of his work in order to justify my larger claim. For the purposes of developing a Marxist theory of style, there are four relevant elements of Williams's work which presuppose this principle of immanence:

1. His theory of words and concepts.
2. His theory of language in general.
3. His theory of forms.
4. His development of a sociological perspectivism.

The following sections deal with each in turn.

---

4   For a detailed overview of this elaboration, see Thomas 2009, pp. 307–83.
5   Thomas 2008, p. 241.
6   Ibid.
7   Williams 1963, pp. 11–12.

1.1   *Keywords*

The basic building-block of Williams's theory of language is the word. The type of word he takes as fundamental is not the concrete noun describing what J.L. Austin once called 'medium-sized dry goods' (tables, chairs, doors – the basic stock of the analytic philosopher's lexicon), but rather abstract nouns delineating complex, non-sensuous concepts (culture, society, literature).[8] This is deeply significant because such words do not lend themselves easily either to philosophies of language premised upon questions of referentiality (the relation between language and the reality it refers to or denotes) or to traditional communication models premised upon a 'sender', 'receiver' and 'object' or 'state of affairs'.[9] The former model implies a relation of externality between a realm called 'language' and a realm called 'reality'; the latter implies this same separation into realms, plus a covert methodological individualism. Both models imply (potentially, at least) a theory of language as instrument: a tool which is malleable to our individual whims. The difference between words like 'table' and 'chair' and those like 'culture' and 'society', however, is that where the former denote clearly delimitable things *within* reality, the latter are in some sense *constitutive* of the very conception of reality to which they supposedly 'refer'.

We can build on these basic observations by studying Williams's introduction to his 1976 work, *Keywords*, plus various puzzling comments in *Marxism and Literature*. He describes *Keywords* as 'the record of an inquiry' into 'the [general] vocabulary we share with others, often imperfectly, when we wish to discuss our common life'.[10] It began as an intended appendix to his earlier work, *Culture and Society* (1958), but the publisher suggested he omit it for reasons of space. From 1958 until 1976, he continued to collect examples of all those 'keywords' which arise in 'general discussions, in English, of the practices and institutions which we group as *culture* and *society*'.[11] He goes on: 'Every word which I have included has at some time, in the course of some argument, virtually forced itself on my attention because the problems of its meanings seemed to me inextricably bound up with the problems it was being used to

---

8   This is not to suggest that a noun now deemed abstract was not once concrete – as Williams consistently points out in *Keywords*.

9   An extension of the 'referential' problematic would be the Marxist one of 'reflection', which Williams duly criticises in *Marxism and Language* (1977a, pp. 95–100). Examples of traditional communication models include Karl Bühler's (2011) 'organon model' and Roman Jakobson's (1987, pp. 62–94) six-part model.

10   Williams 1983a, p. 14 and p. 15.

11   Williams 1983a, p. 15.

discuss'.[12] Here, again, we are confronted with a conception of words totally at odds with prevailing linguistic ideologies.[13] There is a clear mutual imbrication between historical antagonisms as they exist in 'reality' and the concepts which are deployed to think those antagonisms; thought – the domain of concepts – is not transcendent of social being, but *immanent* to it, and this immanence must result in a theory of logical coherence at odds with traditional conceptions of analytic rigour.[14] To fully grasp Williams's attachment to the principles of immanence and coherence, we must first examine a crucial passage of *Marxism and Literature*.

Williams opens the first chapter thus:

> At the very centre of a major area of modern thought and practice, which it is habitually used to describe, is a concept, 'culture', which in itself, through variation and complication, embodies not only the issues but the contradictions through which it has developed. The concept at once fuses and confuses the radically different experiences and tendencies of its formation. It is then impossible to carry through any serious cultural analysis without reaching towards a consciousness of the concept itself: a consciousness that must be ... historical. This hesitation, before what seems the richness of developed theory and the fullness of achieved practice, has the awkwardness, even the gaucherie, of any radical doubt. It is literally a moment of crisis: a jolt in experience, a break in the sense of history; forcing us back from so much that seemed positive and available – all the ready insertions into a crucial argument, all the accessible entries into immediate practice. Yet the insight cannot be sealed over. When the most basic conceptions – the concepts, as it is said, from which we begin – are suddenly seen to be not concepts but problems, not analytic problems either but historical movements that are still unresolved, there is no sense in listening to their sonorous summons or their resounding clash. We have only, if we can, to recover the substance from which their forms were cast.[15]

---

12   Ibid.

13   Its relation to Saussurian and post-Saussurian theories of language will be discussed below.

14   I choose the word 'coherence' here quite consciously to highlight the affiliations between Gramsci's theory of conceptuality and that of Williams. Cf. Thomas 2009, pp. 364–79.

15   Williams 1977a, p. 11.

The philosophical presuppositions of this passage are central to everything Raymond Williams ever wrote.

The first thing to note is that concepts such as 'culture' play a constitutive part in the practices they were thought merely to describe. It is not just that they delimit a certain area of 'society' (itself a deeply problematic word) or a certain set of practices within it, but that they internally inform the nature and self-understanding of the practices and those who practise them.[16] Moreover, because concepts embody – 'through variation and complication' (i.e., complexity) – the contradictions through which they have developed, their internal incoherence is not analytical or theoretical, but a residue of past and ongoing practical struggles. Cultural analysis which ignores the complex and contradictory histories of these words – i.e., which fails to raise itself to historical consciousness – is thus inadequate. What is required is 'radical doubt' (a term whose Cartesian pedigree can be glimpsed in such passages). It is a force immanent to the situation which can overcome all that seems 'positive and available'. What Williams calls 'the ready insertions into a crucial argument, all the accessible entries into immediate practice' are what I.A. Richards termed 'stock responses', now extended beyond the field of literature.[17] Central words like 'culture' and 'society', because they are used so often and so confidently, tend to become automated, such that we use them without having submitted them to critical scrutiny. In doing so, it is the words themselves, via the hegemonic powers' accentuation of only the most congenial of their meanings, which do our thinking for us and – consequently – perpetuate our current practices.

In such a context, radical doubt is a moment of determinate or absolute scepticism (and it is no mistake that Williams was drawn to Hume, whom he described as 'the skeptic who wished to affirm')[18] which opposes to all that is 'positive and available' a critical negativity that is 'literally a moment of crisis'. A constitutive aspect of the automated positivity which such negativity took as its target are those keywords which Williams refers to as 'the concepts, as it is

---

16   Later in the book, in a chapter entitled 'The Multiplicity of Writing', Williams notes that 'the crippling categories and dichotomies of "fact" and "fiction", or of "discursive" and "imaginative" or "referential" and "emotive", stand regularly not only between works and readers ... but between writers and works, at a still active and shaping stage' (1977a, 146). Such categories inform not only the reception of literary works, but the very act of writing itself.

17   Richards describes them thus: 'The button is pressed, and then the author's work is done, for immediately the record starts playing in quasi- (or total) independence of the poem which is supposed to be its origin or instrument' (2004, p. 14).

18   Williams 1983b, p. 141.

said, from which we begin'. The 'it is said' is crucial: what appear to be timeless, natural concepts like 'culture' and 'society', precisely because of this apparent naturalness and timelessness, come to assume the role of conceptual *a prioris*. When using these words as they seem to wish us to use them, we unconsciously engage in pre-critical philosophy since we have not rationally deduced their a prioricity. Yet, any serious analysis of these terms will soon find that they are 'not concepts but problems, not analytic problems either but historical movements that are still unresolved'. Thus, what had initially appeared as unproblematic concepts which transcended the reality they were presupposed to describe, once submitted to radical doubt and critical negativity, become 'problems' in their own right. They are not 'analytic problems' because that would imply that they can be resolved in terms of internal logical coherence according to systematic theoretical rigour and the laws of logical consistency. Instead, they are 'historical movements that are still unresolved'. That is, they are *immanent and constitutive factors of ongoing historical struggles*. The resolution of the problems of which they are a constitutive factor must be practical. Yet, this must not be taken to mean that conceptual thought is null and void. On the contrary, precisely because these concepts are constitutive factors in the historical process, a conceptualisation of the contradictions they contain – i.e., a theoretical and philological elaboration – will be a necessary part of any *practical* intervention into those struggles. Theory and practice are not opposed here but become two modes of the same historical substance.

When Williams returned in a late essay to Marx's theory of culture, he stressed the affinities with those passages of Marx which emphasised just such a mutual imbrication of consciousness and practice. He cites the following well-known passage in Marx:[19]

> We presuppose labour in a form in which it is an exclusively human characteristic. A spider conducts operations which resemble those of the weaver, and a bee would put many a human architect to shame by the construction of its honeycomb cells. But what distinguishes the worst architect from the best of bees is that the architect builds the cell in his mind before he constructs it in wax. At the end of every labour process, a result emerges which had already been conceived by the worker at the beginning, hence already existed ideally.[20]

---

19   It was the work of Paul Jones (2004, p. 48) that drew my attention to this passage from Marx and the proceeding one from Williams.

20   Marx 1990, pp. 283–4.

Williams then comments:

> This convincing account of the specifically human character of work
> includes ... not only the foreseeing concept of what is being made but
> ideally integrated concepts of how and why it is being made ... Thus
> 'real active men', in all their activities, are full of consciousness, foresight,
> concepts of how and why, or to the degree that they are not have been
> reduced from this fully human status.[21]

Human labour is thus the ultimate exemplar of what Williams subsequently
calls 'integrated consciousness':[22] the concepts and ideas of what, how and why
we do what we do are immanent to, and constitutive aspects of, all human practices, informing both them and us from the inside. It is on these precise grounds
that Williams criticises the inaccuracy of Marx and Engels's polemic against
German philosophy in *The German Ideology*. Whereas German metaphysics,
wrote Marx and Engels, 'descends from heaven to earth, we here ascend from
earth to heaven. That is to say, we do not set out from what men say, imagine, or
conceive ... in order to arrive at men in the flesh. [We set out from real, active
men ... etc.]'.[23] Whilst Williams endorses the general thrust of the argument –
that 'we must begin any inquiry into human development and activities from
actual human beings in their actual conditions'[24] – he observes, quite rightly,
that the logic of Marx and Engels's metaphor is dubious: if 'real, active men' are
on earth, then what they say, imagine and conceive must be in heaven. It is this
celestialisation of thought and imagination which Williams, using alternative
passages from Marx, seeks to overcome. For what this does is merely reproduce
the very transcendent dualism of bourgeois thought against which it was written. In this light, then, Williams – as so often in his later writings – is doing
nothing less than attempting to save historical materialism from its incipient
tendencies towards the idealism it in principle opposes. He does so by constantly stressing the *immanence* of theory to practice.

Here, however, we must enter a caveat. Williams's claim that words, language
and concepts – what he would later come to call 'signifying systems' – are *constitutive* aspects of the social process must not be misread as the superficially
similar, but actually very different claims, that they are either 1) the *fundamentally* constitutive aspect of the social process (as in Herder, or in any number

21 Williams 1989b, p. 204.
22 Ibid.
23 Cited in Williams 1989b, p. 203. The square brackets are Williams's.
24 Williams 1989b, p. 203.

of bourgeois intellectuals thereafter) or 2) *equally* constitutive aspects of the social process (i.e., equally as constitutive as productive human activities, their possible separation therefrom being thus implied). By positing the immanence of language to practice, the two are always united. When it comes to religious and metaphysical speculation or 'ideologies' more generally, it is not because they are predominantly 'linguistic' or 'theoretical' as opposed to 'practical' that makes them potential forms of 'false consciousness': it is because, as a result of the historically locatable division of labour between intellectual and manual work, *two distinct types of practice emerged. Both* intellectual labour and manual labour are practices and *both* of them involve theory and practice. It is simply that the former practice is a predominantly contemplative one, whilst the latter is predominantly active. Consequently, the real split is not one between signifying systems on the one hand, and production and praxis on the other; the division of labour between manual and intellectual work forms a diagonal which cuts through the totality of social practices. Signification is a constitutive aspect of the social process in both manual practices and intellectual practices, but the nature of these practices and their mutual relations determines the understanding and the extent of elaboration of signification inherent to each. In his late work, *Culture*, this distinction becomes one between activities in which 'signifying practice is deeply present' but 'more or less completely dissolved into other needs and actions' and, on the other hand, activities in which 'those other needs and actions are deeply present in all manifest signifying activities' but here 'those other needs and actions are, in their turn, more or less completely dissolved'.[25] Signifying systems and productive practices are both terrestrial; they are immanent at once to the social totality and to each other.

1.2   Language as 'Practical Consciousness'

The second relevant 'immanentist' element of Williams's project is his theory of language.[26] The main error of almost all previous theories of language, Williams argues, was that they presupposed a primordial split between 'language' and 'reality', their driving force (including much of philosophy) thus being to understand the relation between the two.[27] Williams, on the contrary, will insist

---

25   Williams 1981a, p. 209. He continues: 'The metaphor of solution is crucial to this way of looking at culture, and the qualification "more or less" is not a casual phrase but a way of indicating a true range, in which relatively complete and relatively incomplete degrees of solution, either way, can be practically defined' (ibid.).

26   I shall reconstruct this theory from a different angle in the second half of the chapter.

27   Williams 1977a, p. 22.

time and again that this split is a reification of a social process in which the two are always inseparable. What these theories ignore, but what eighteenth-century theories of language (e.g., Vico and Herder) first began to realise, is that language is 'a distinctively human opening of and opening to the world: not a distinguishable or instrumental but a constitutive faculty'.[28] Language is essential to what humans are as social beings; they do not pre-exist language and subsequently wield it as a tool: it is constitutive of humanity as such. The problem was that the old ways of viewing language based on the split between 'language' and 'reality' were compounded by the new forms of language-study developed in the nineteenth century. European exploration and colonisation had dramatically increased the available linguistic material, but the subsequent theories were marked by this political history:

> On the one hand there was the highly productive application of modes of systematic observation, classification, and analysis. On the other hand there was the largely unnoticed consequence of the privileged situation of the observer: that he was observing (of course scientifically) within a differential mode of contact with alien material: in texts, the records of a *past* history; in speech, the activity of an alien people in subordinate (colonialist) relations to the whole activity of the dominant people within which the observer gained his privilege. This defining situation inevitably reduced any sense of language as actively and presently constitutive.[29]

Language under such conditions could only ever be grasped as an '(alien) objective system', and speech as a mere epiphenomenal instantiation of (dead) written languages. This was the reified understanding of language which reached its apotheosis in Saussure's linguistics, and on which a new structuralist Marxism – the very kind from within which Eagleton had attacked Williams in 1976 – was based. The irony could not be clearer: contemporary Marxism had turned to a structuralism premised on a view of language which was a rerun of the classic 'individual versus society' logic integral to the very bourgeois ideology it aimed to overcome.

The seeds of a way out of this impasse, claimed Williams, were sown in Marx and Engels's *The German Ideology*.[30] There, we find the definition of language that Williams will make his own: 'Language is as old as consciousness, language

---

28   Williams 1977a, p. 24.
29   Williams 1977a, p. 26.
30   Marx and Engels 1978.

is practical consciousness, as it exists for other men, and for that reason is really beginning to exist for me personally as well; for language, like consciousness, only arises from the need, the necessity, of intercourse with other men'.[31] What draws Williams to this definition is its emphasis on language as an '*indissoluble* element of human self-creation'.[32] In other words, the chicken-and-the-egg question – which comes first, language or labour? – is false: language is necessarily an indissoluble element of labour. Williams thus demonstrates, *pace* thinkers like Habermas, that intersubjective communication cannot be separated from the labour process: the 'life-world' – to risk a phenomenological vocabulary – is a constitutive aspect of the purposive rationality of production, and vice versa.[33] The problem as Williams sees it, however, was that after this

---

31   Cited in Williams 1977a, p. 29. The English translation on which Williams relies is poor. The original German reads: 'Die Sprache ist so alt wie das Bewußtsein – die Sprache *ist* das praktische, auch für andre Menschen existierende, also auch für mich selbst erst existierende wirkliche Bewußtsein, und die Sprache entsteht, wie das Bewußtsein, erst aus dem Bedürfnis, der Notdurft des Verkehrs mit andern Menschen' (Marx and Engels 1978, 30). A more accurate translation would be: 'Language is as old as consciousness – language *is* that practical, real consciousness that exists also for other men, and for that reason alone it really exists for me as well; language, like consciousness, arises primarily from the need, the necessity of intercourse with other people'.

32   Ibid.

33   Jacques Bidet (2008, p. 681) is even more precise on this point: 'In ... identifying "labour" with "rational-purposive action", Habermas operates a surreptitious conceptual revolution from the outset. For Marx's concept of labour does not apply to the one-sided adequacy of means to an end [*Zweckrationalität*], but to the bilateral relationship between end and means. Labour in general is not only abstract labour characterised by an "economy of time" for a given end. It is also, and correlatively, concrete labour, with a view to a determinate use-value, where use assumes a *social norm*. Labour is a means gauged by an end, but which is "stripped of meaning" only with respect to the meaning that it imparts to the end it pursues. It is a *rational* activity only with respect to an end that is posited as *reasonable*. And Marx's whole endeavour consists in showing how, in the conditions of capitalism, these two terms are dissociated, because its concrete purpose – its end as use-value – is threatened by the profit motive, which is the particular goal of capitalism, an "abstract" purpose pursued for its own sake, whatever the consequences for humanity and nature – in other words, the effects in terms of use-value. Marx thus deconstructs the notion of "purposive rationality", dismantling the ideological unity of the categories of "production", productivity, or "productive force". Capitalist production is not "production" *tout court: it is defined by a specific, contradictory tension between these two ends*. The concept of "sub-systems of rational-purposive action" restores the ideological unity of the category of "productive force", the artificial unity that was shattered by Marx's analysis. Habermas can thus attribute to "labour", in as much as its quintessence is embodied in

brief illumination in the writings of Marx, the Marxist tradition itself failed to develop the insight. Consequently, theories of language remained divided into two camps: the positivists, for whom language was a matter of mere physicality and not of activity (hence falling prey to Marx's first thesis on Feuerbach)[34] and the idealists – beginning with Herder and Humboldt – for whom language was an activity, but only of a spiritual kind. If the former camp tended to stress the instrumental nature of language, the latter reacted against this by emphasising its expressive power: '[The theory of language as expression] could include the experience of speaking *with* others, of *participating* in language, of making and responding to rhythm or intonation which had no simple "information" or "message" or "object" content'.[35] It was this split which gave rise, in Williams's eyes, to those fatal divisions that haunt literary theory to this day: referential versus emotive, denotative versus connotative, 'ordinary' language versus 'literary' language. Thus, Williams's theory of language must be seen as a counter-movement against this schism internal to linguistic theories, but one which sees itself as in keeping with one of Marx's fundamental insights: that language is practical consciousness – a constitutive element of all activity and an indissoluble element of all human self-formation.[36]

Williams had been working towards such a theory of language throughout his whole career, but it was his discovery of Voloshinov's *Marxism and the Philosophy of Language* which provided him with the final impetus for his overt theorisation of language. This was, after all, a book in which Voloshinov laid out the rival expressivist and objectivist theories of language and attempted to sublate them into a historical materialist understanding. There are three main points of interest in Williams's exposition of Voloshinov. Firstly, he emphas-

---

the commodity-form of the "sub-systems of rational-purposive action", the burden that Marx makes capital as such bear, at the same time as he legitimates the market as the consummate form of productive rationality'.

34   'The chief defect of all hitherto materialism ... is that the thing, reality, sensuousness, is conceived only in the form of the *object or of contemplation*, but not as *sensuous human activity, practice*, not subjectively' (Marx 1975, p. 421; emphasis in the original).

35   Williams 1977a, p. 32.

36   It is important to note, however, that 'practical consciousness' is not as unproblematic a concept as Williams would have us believe. As Paul Jones observes, Marx is in fact providing the reader with an inventory of forms of consciousness, from myth to critique. Thus, for Marx, 'sheep-like or tribal consciousness' could also be included under the rubric 'practical consciousness' (Jones 2004, p. 103). Nonetheless, unlike Jones, I do not see this as a major problem: Williams makes it quite clear that in *his* use of the term (irrespective of his ignorance of its larger context in Marx's text) 'practical consciousness' is simply meant to stress that language is an indissoluble element of all social practices.

ises the latter's argument that language is an ongoing social process. To speak or to write in such a present is not merely instrumentally and neutrally to convey information between a sender and receiver, but to *participate* in – to be determined by and to determine – the ongoing and formative process of human self-realisation. It is in this context that the second point of emphasis becomes clear: 'Signification, the social creation of meanings through the use of formal signs, is then a practical material activity; it is indeed, literally, a means of production. It is a specific form of that practical consciousness which is inseparable from all social material activity'.[37] Thus, a sign 'must have an effective nucleus of meaning but in practice it has a variable range, corresponding to the endless variety of situations in which it is actively used'.[38] Contrary to those linguistic and social theories which have their roots in Saussurian linguistics – i.e., those which distinguish between a pre-given linguistic system (*langue*) and a momentary instantiation of that system in an act of speech (*parole*) – Williams is here propounding a theory of language analogous to Marx's famous dictum on historical change more generally: 'Men make their own history, but not of their own free will; not under circumstances they themselves have chosen but under the given and inherited circumstances with which they are directly confronted'.[39] Human language is, indeed, ruled by certain structured conventions beyond the subjective whims of individuals, but these conventions themselves are nothing but the accumulated sedimentation of past *and ongoing* language-in-praxis. Consequently, whereas for structuralism the synchronic is a fixed, immovable system, for Williams and Voloshinov – as for Marx's historiography – the synchronic is an optical illusion, an alienated timeless snapshot (taken by a non-participant, non-immanent observer) of what was and is a process of ongoing practical struggle.

Finally, in fundamentally altering our conception of synchronic objectivity via the dialectical sublation of structure and instantiation, the very notion of individuality is itself transformed. For an individual is simultaneously constituted by and constitutive of language. Thus, 'individuality, by the fully social fact of language ... is the active constitution, within distinct physical beings, of the social capacity which is the means of realization of any individual life. Consciousness, in this precise sense, is social being'.[40] Individuals come to self-consciousness in the medium of a language striated by the divisions

---

37   Williams 1977a, p. 38. Williams develops this argument in 'Means of Communication as Means of Production' (2010, pp. 50–66).

38   Williams 1977a, p. 39.

39   Marx 1973, p. 146.

40   Williams 1977a, p. 41.

and 'multiaccentuality' of practical social life at large.[41] Because individuality is the internal activation of social language, what appear to be *external* divisions inherent to language itself can quickly become *internal* divisions within subjectivity, creating inner emotional and cognitive crises in the individual.

1.3   *Forms, Techniques and Technology*

We have now seen that, for Williams, neither words, concepts nor language in general are mere conduits, indifferent to a hypothetically pristine content which they convey. Rather, they are the 'productive means' of human social relations:[42] humans do not wield language as a tool, but live together in and through it. Language is immanent to humans and their social activities; they themselves constitute and are constituted by it. This has direct consequences for Williams's theory of form and style. His mature theory sublates two contrary positions: on the one hand, what he calls 'expressivism' – the view that language is 'a pure medium through which the reality of a life or … an event or an experience or the reality of a society can "flow"',[43] and on the other hand 'formalism' – which focuses on the 'specific and definitive uses of literary forms of many kinds' but which 'deflects our attention from the more than formal meanings and values, and in this sense the defining experiences, of almost all actual works'.[44] The former presupposes the indifference of content to form whilst the latter ignores that which is expressed by overemphasising the constitutive importance of form.

It is worth noting that Williams's own earlier work was often haunted by this very dualism. As we shall see shortly, there was always a certain ambivalence regarding the relation between social experience and style: on the one hand, writing was understood as a productive and constitutive act in its own right. It did not simply convey a prepackaged experience, but rather *realised* and constituted that experience in the act of articulation.[45] On the other hand,

---

41   This proved a crucial insight to much of Williams's literary analysis of the novel – not least of those writers like Thomas Hardy whose life-path led him to inhabit two socially distinct linguistic worlds: that of customary, working-class diction and that of Oxbridge educated prose. As we saw in the previous chapter, Williams reads the formal disjunctions of Hardy's novels as a symptom of his unsuccessful lexical unification of a language internally divided by the external class divisions inherent to an *apparently* unified English language.

42   Williams 1977a, p. 171.

43   Williams 1977a, p. 166.

44   Williams 1977a, p. 165.

45   Cf. Williams 1965, p. 40: 'This vital descriptive effort – which is not merely a subsequent

however, there was always a looming sense that an author does indeed have a preformed experience which he or she seeks to communicate.[46] Williams was torn between the expressivist theory of T.S. Eliot's 'objective correlative' (in which the artist uses 'a set of objects, a situation, a chain of events' to express a previously understood experience) and an alternative theory which emphasises that forms themselves are constitutive of experience as such.[47] By the time of *Marxism and Literature* (1977) Williams had developed a much more dialectical conception of the relation between the two: of the extent to which the (re)production of literary forms informs, enables and limits experience as such whilst changes in experience (specifically, of 'structures of feeling') generate shifts in old forms and the production of new ones.[48] Paul Jones has called Williams's mature position that of 'social formalism';[49] Williams himself suggests the appellation 'sociology of forms'.[50]

Williams is quite clear of the stakes of an investigation of form: 'For a social theory of literature, the problem of form is a problem of the relations between social (collective) modes and individual projects'.[51] Forms, for Williams, are 'the common property, to be sure with differences of degree, of writers and

---

effort to describe something known, but literally a way of seeing new things and new relationships'.

46   This is prevalent throughout *Drama from Ibsen to Brecht* in such passages as this on Ibsen: 'Already, in these early plays, elements of the curiously consistent pattern of experience which Ibsen wished to communicate may be discerned, struggling for expression in an uncongenial form' (Williams 1973b, p. 25). I return to this point below.

47   The influence of Eliot on Williams's theory of conventions and expression in his early work on drama is obvious. Only John Higgins (1999, pp. 30–31) has noticed the importance of Eliot's theory of the 'objective correlative' – and of Williams's ambiguous relation to it – for his later theory of language and form. Higgins sees Williams as hovering between an endorsement of Eliot's emphasis of total authorial control and a reluctant acceptance that certain elements of literary composition – the constitutive efficacy of form being one of them – are beyond authorial volition.

48   He writes of the false opposition between the neo-classical emphasis on the existence and availability of definite forms and the romantic stress on the active making of them: 'Thinking which begins from such categories ... fails to give adequate recognition to the constantly interactive and in this sense dialectical process, which is real practice' (Williams 1977a, p. 187).

49   Jones 2004, pp. 92–126. The term 'social formalism' is actually Williams's own; where he applied it to Mukarovsky and Voloshinov (Williams 1983a, p. 139), Jones extends it to Williams himself.

50   Williams 1981a, p. 143.

51   Williams 1977a, p. 187.

audiences or readers, before any communicative composition can occur'.[52] That is, form – like style more narrowly – is a relationship, which is activated during the processes of composition, performance and response:[53]

> What is at issue in form is the activation of specific relations, between men and men [*sic*] and between men and things ... [Forms are] physical and material relational processes. This is as true of the most 'subjective' generative moments – the poem first 'heard' as a rhythm without words ... – as of the most 'objective' moments – the interaction of possible words with an already shared and established rhythm ... the selection and reworking of sequence to reproduce an expected narrative order.
>
>   This whole range of conscious, half-conscious, and often apparently instinctive shaping – in an intricate complex of already materialized and materializing forms – is the activation of a social semiotic and communicative process, more deliberate, more complex, and more subtle in literary creation than in everyday expression, but in continuity with it through a major area of direct (specifically addressed) speech and writing. Over this whole range, from the most indifferent adoption of an established relational linguistic form to the most worked and reworked newly possible form, the ultimately formative moment is the material articulation, the activation and generation of shared sounds and words.[54]

The breakthrough term here is 'activation': by posing the problem of form as the activation, as part of an individual project, of a collective mode, which is itself a social relation, Williams definitively transcends the Romantic, individualist conception of literary production. It is no longer a question of the individual writer pitting his or her creativity against the collective; rather, the collectively shared modes provide the very material on and through which the writer's individual agency operates, informing it even as the writer herself pushes those modes in new directions. To paraphrase Marx, writers make their own forms, but they do so within collective semiotic modes which are not of their choosing. For Williams, moreover, literature is not qualitatively different from literacy as such: it is simply a more elaborate version of it, thus refuting the formalist dogma that literary language is unique. This is a truly social conception of literary forms.

---

52   Williams 1977a, pp. 187–8.
53   Williams 1977a, p. 187.
54   Williams 1977a, pp. 190–91.

For those who equate form with mere techniques from which an author can choose, Williams's understanding must sound odd indeed. Yet it was just such a technicist conception of form, in the guise of the Russian formalists' notion of the 'device', on which Williams set his sights. The problem of the relation between the two conceptions can be posed thus: how do forms, which are in fact relationships, come to seem like inert techniques, to be manipulated at will or inhabited by new social experiences? Williams answers this question (among others) by introducing a relative scale of formal stability and innovation. In *Marxism and Literature* there are only three grades: shared communal forms (relatively transhistorical), intermediate forms (individual variations on relatively unchanging forms, such as myth, heroic tales, romance) and innovative forms. By the time of *Culture*, this has become a fourfold typology: modes, genres, types and forms:[55]

a. *Modes* are forms which persist in and through quite different social orders, and are thus relatively independent of changes within and even between specific social orders. They are best referred to an anthropological dimension rather than to the sociological in its ordinary sense.[56]
   i. Examples include drama,[57] lyric, narrative and the new mode of cinema.
b. *Genres* are forms which persist through radically variable social orders but which are more dependent than modes on changes between social orders in their epochal sense.[58]
   i. Examples include tragedy, comedy, epic and romance – the latter two having died out with the emergence of the bourgeois epoch.
c. *Types* are radical distributions, redistributions and innovations of interest, corresponding to the specific and changed social character of an epoch. They are effective general forms 'typical of a particular social order, which in its characteristic relations and distributions of interests continually reproduces them, and of course reproduces them as normal, as 'self-evident' definitions of what various arts should be'.[59]
   i. Examples include bourgeois drama, the realist novel, and landscape painting.

---

55 For a useful table, containing all four and their attributes, see Jones 2004, p. 122.
56 Williams 1981a, p. 194.
57 For the social and historical origins of the dramatic mode, see especially Williams 1981a, pp. 148–54.
58 Williams 1981a, p. 195.
59 Williams 1981a, p. 196.

d. *Forms* – the term usually used as a general label for all of the above –
   are smaller-scale distributions, redistributions and innovations of interest,
   reaching down to the level of formal dispositions: 'a particular stance, an
   appropriate selection of subject matter, a specific mode of composition'.[60]
   Significantly, at the level of form, the classic Williams tripartite temporality
   (of residual, dominant and emergent)[61] reoccurs at the level of relative
   formal innovation. Innovation ranges from *replication*, in which variation
   on a shared form is so limited that the formal qualities outweigh it; to the *reproduction* of a form, in the sense of a fuller or newly directed realisation of
   its possibilities; to *innovation*, which means that 'within a certain persistence
   of typical factors, there [are] radical alterations of both internal formal
   elements and of socio-formal relations with audiences and institutions'.[62]
   i. Examples include the development of the soliloquy and the breaks to
       naturalist drama and subjective expressionism.

This is a nuanced theory of the 'collective modes' in, on, through and beyond which individual literary projects go to work; it is designed the better to
adequate the concepts of literary theory with the true range and complexity,
the true multiplicity, of writing.[63] It also offers an implicit suggestion as to
the relation between forms and techniques. Forms become 'techniques' when
they have become widely accepted as conventional and when their historical
and social conditions of innovative emergence have faded. Significantly, not all
formal innovations will become conventional: some will continue to be rejected by audiences accustomed to previous dominant collective modes, while
others will simply wither away without having generated significant opposition.

   Why does this conception of form lend itself to the claim that Williams
is a thinker for whom immanence is an informing principle? Firstly, because
even those forms which are relatively independent of epochal historical shifts –
mode and genre – began as social innovations immanent to a specific configuration of social and political forces. Secondly, because the emergence of
new forms plays an immanent, constitutive role in historical transformation;
it does not 'reflect' changes in the 'base', but plays an active – even if modest – part in social shifts. Thus, Williams demonstrates that the emergence of

---

60   Williams 1981a, p. 197.
61   I return to these concepts below.
62   Williams 1981a, p. 199.
63   For a detailed overview of the 'multiplicity of writing', see the eponymous chapter of
     Williams 1977a, pp. 145–50.

the soliloquy was 'the discovery, *in dramatic form*, of new and altered social relationships'.[64] Certainly, the rise of Protestantism and a nascent capitalism were producing new conceptions of the autonomous individual, but it was the dramatic mode which lent itself to their initial articulation in the form of the soliloquy in a way in which other modes could not: 'the formal innovation is a true and integral element of the changes themselves: an articulation, by technical discovery, of changes in consciousness which are themselves forms of consciousness of change'.[65] This consciousness was 'beyond immediately available and confirmed social relations but within newly available dramatic relations'.[66] The counterpoints between the multivocal and univocal which only the dramatic mode afforded were supplemented by the precise conditions of dramatic practice in the English theatre at that time.[67] Together, the formal innovations internal to the dramatic mode, along with the conditions of dramatic practice in Elizabethan and Jacobean England, were immanent and active elements of social change. There is no way of constructing a relation between 'literature' and 'society' because without the literature the society is not actual. Literature is immanent to society, a constitutive force within it.

1.4   *Sociological Perspectivism*
At the same time, the social relations of which literature is a mode are immanent to that literature and active within it. It is possible to extract from Williams's writings what I call a theory of sociological perspectivism: the intrinsic relation between the social position of a writer – in the sense of class belonging and a quite literal geographical location, plus the shifts in these wrought by a biographical trajectory – and the interpretations and selections of reality which are embodied in their literary works. Williams analyses actual historical individuals (as opposed to literary narrators) in a manner strongly reminiscent of the narratological concept introduced in the previous chapter as 'style as interpellation' – perceptual and cognitive focalisation or the overall ideological subject position implied by any discourse. He uses perspective as a conceptual

---

64   Williams 1981a, p. 142; emphasis in the original.
65   Ibid.
66   Williams 1981a, p. 146.
67   These included 'a new kind of audience, within new kinds of theatre, no longer formally defined by terms, places and occasions of an extra-dramatic authority, but socially mixed and socially mobile within an expanding urban society, served by its own characteristic forms of commercial-enterprise theatres and specializing professional dramatists' (Williams 1981a, pp. 146–7).

tool for analysing the precise vectors of social relationships.[68] Indeed, more significantly for our purposes, Williams's work suggests that there is a strong sociological connection between style as interpellation and diegesis (an author's idiom under the regime of fictionality), and between style as interpellation and style as the total mode of configuration of a text's subordinate linguistic unities.[69] In other words, the social position of a writer strongly informs both their narratorial idiom and their total stylistic configuration.

We saw in the previous chapter that Hardy's biographical trajectory enabled him to experience multiple social positions, each of which possessed a predominantly educated or colloquial idiom. His burden was then to unite them. But a more extreme example of sociological perspectivism can be found in the chapter entitled 'Three Around Farnham' in *The Country and the City*. Superficially, this chapter is an analysis of the respective ways of seeing and writing of three writers – William Cobbett, Jane Austen and Gilbert White – who lived in or near Farnham at roughly the same time. But the chapter is also partly composed as a narrative – 'Imagine a journey ...' begins the second paragraph –[70] with three characters (the writers) and an animated setting (Farnham). The mode of analysis is thus just as much a 'poietic' configuration as it is a purely conceptual discourse.

The central antagonism is between the ways of seeing of Cobbett and Austen respectively: 'Jane Austen was writing from a very different point of view, from inside the houses that Cobbett was passing on the road'.[71] Austen's 'unity of tone', her 'settled and remarkably confident way of seeing and judging' – that is, her style as both idiom and total configuration of sub-styles – was a precise result of her incapacity to see, from her social perspective, the existence of classes: 'All her discrimination is, understandably, internal and exclusive. She is concerned with the conduct of people who, in the complications of improvement, are repeatedly trying to make themselves into a class. But where only one class is seen, no classes are seen'.[72] Cobbett's tone, on the other hand, was of 'the voice of men who have seen their children starving, and now within sight of the stately homes and the improved parks and the self-absorbed social patterns at the end of the drives'.[73] Thus, precisely because Cobbett could see

---

68   That is, from our retrospective perspective. He was not self-consciously translating narratological concepts into a sociological idiom.

69   See part three of the definition of style I gave in the previous chapter.

70   Williams 1973a, p. 108.

71   Williams 1973a, p. 112.

72   Williams 1973a, p. 117.

73   Williams 1973a, p. 118.

the unity of Austen's social world as one based on economic class, and had experienced the brutality on which its cultural refinements rested, his *style* is one of anger, rage, exclamation and satirical bitterness. His precise social position (the meeting point of class status and geography) produced a way of seeing and experiencing the world which was quite simply unavailable to Austen and which became a constitutive shaping force within his style. Thus, the sociological perspective of a writer – the social coordinates of her ways of seeing and feeling – is in variable and complex ways immanent to her style.

2   Williams's Multiple Approaches to the Problem of Style

Having explored Williams's thought in relation to the concept of immanence, I shall now turn to a more philological reconstruction of his multiple approaches to style. My trajectory here will draw heavily on Williams's oft-neglected writings on drama, which offer a different set of emphases from his equivalent writings on prose – not least because they deal with writing for speech rather than for reading. The reader will, I hope, find that the preceding systematic and thematic account of the principle of immanence in Williams's theory of style provides the theoretical foundation for what follows.

2.1   *Language in Naturalist Drama; or, the Relation of 'Structure of Feeling' and Style*

When Williams described the chapter on language in *Marxism and Literature* (1977) as 'pivotal' for a comprehension of the book as a whole, adding that he could easily have written a volume on it in its own right,[74] he was emphasising an aspect of his work that had concerned him since his postwar return to Cambridge. In that 1977 work he states that '[a] definition of language is always, implicitly or explicitly, a definition of human beings in the world',[75] thus making quite clear what was at stake. As we have seen, in that chapter he was to attack the then dominant linguistic ideology of structuralism, though structuralism was not his only opponent. For much of his career, but especially in his writings on drama from the 1940s to the 1960s, he had been concerned with naturalism and the problems of speech which it posed to the dramatist. Since his initial approach to the problem of dramatic speech also drew on the work

---

74   Williams 1979, p. 324.
75   Williams 1977a, p. 21.

of T.S. Eliot and *Scrutiny*, this was more than a purely literary critical endeavour: it was an attempt to develop the basic insights, yet firmly to rebut the wider political implications, of the linguistic ideologies of this locally dominant intellectual formation. It was also, significantly, the production of a linguistic genealogy of modernism.

According to *Scrutiny*, modern economic development had resulted in a fourfold linguistic degradation.[76] Firstly, journalistic standards had become degraded in the service of commercial interests. Secondly, and perhaps most significantly, the economic and social process of industrial society had actually sapped the signifying capacities of language: behind the inadequacy of the use of words lay an inadequacy in experience itself. This included the view, prevalent among modernists of varying persuasions, that contemporary linguistic usage was 'a hazy medium which smothers [man's] essential human nature, which interposes between him and things as they are'.[77] Thirdly, contemporary language use was rootless. The major literary achievements of the pre-industrial era had drawn on the resources of a vital popular speech rooted in a stable and homogeneous social life. Shakespeare's language, for example, was that of a 'community which forged it as a vital medium'.[78] In contrast, the modern writer was rootless: the styles of Faulkner, Mallarmé and Joyce were clear examples of this disembedding from the socially homogeneous lifeworld. Finally, and as an extension of the third feature of linguistic degradation (here I extend Mulhern's account), what no longer existed in industrial modernity was the spontaneous linguistic integration innate to the pre-industrial *Gemeinschaft*. Where Shakespeare's plays 'were at once popular drama and poetry that could be appreciated only by an educated minority',[79] drawing at once on learned and demotic idioms, concrete and abstract registers, modern writers (Leavis cites Eliot, Pound and Joyce) wrote in a style which was inaccessible to the populace.

What should be clear is that this linguistic ideology contained an implicit critique and rejection of capitalist modernity as such, a point Williams would only emphasise towards the end of his life.[80] But it was with this theory of language in mind, strongly influenced by T.S. Eliot's emphasis on the import-

---

76   The first three types follow Mulhern 1979, pp. 54–7.

77   Knights 1936, pp. 57–8.

78   Knights 1936, p. 57.

79   F.R. Leavis cited in Hilliard 2012, p. 51.

80   See the next section. He did, of course, make the connection between the concept of 'culture' (as opposed to language) and a critique of the 'long revolution' of modernity in his postwar years at Cambridge.

ance of conventions and, crucially, by his insistence that good drama must also be good literature,[81] that Williams went on to tackle naturalist drama – from its inception in Ibsen to its critical climax in Brecht and Beckett. Thus, Williams's *Drama From Ibsen to Eliot* (1952) (which in 1968 became *Drama From Ibsen to Brecht*) abounds with *Scrutiny* commonplaces such as: 'contemporary spoken English is rarely capable of exact expression of anything in any degree complex'.[82] Yet, as Higgins has shown,[83] it also includes a certain self-distancing from these views, pointing towards what will become his notion of the structure of feeling: the decline of dramatic speech is 'related, in fact, not only to the impoverishment of language but to changes in feeling'.[84] Nonetheless, if Higgins rightly stresses the importance of *Scrutiny* and especially of T.S. Eliot for Williams's early theory of drama (as well as his budding attempts at intellectual independence), he fails to articulate the strange amalgamation that is at work in it. For Williams's theory of drama, precisely because it grew out of the context of *Scrutiny*'s organicist linguistic ideology, is also a theory of language, and of language as a way of being together in a community.

Where Eliot had claimed that a fully serious drama was impossible in a society where there is no common system of belief, Williams shifted the emphasis: 'the condition of a fully serious drama is less the existence of a common faith than the existence of a common language'.[85] This common language would be the 'expression' of the 'common sensibility' uniting the dramatist and her audience.[86] Higgins has criticised this talk of common sensibility as 'one of the weakest points of Williams's thought',[87] but this is a misunderstanding. As we saw in Chapter 5, Williams's desire was for a style – a linguistic mode of social relation – capable of uniting the abstract universalism of formal prose with the colloquial and experiential immediacy of popular speech. Where Higgins seems to presume – implicitly following E.P. Thompson's earlier criticisms –[88] that 'common language' and 'common sensibility' are idealist notions, ignoring the fundamental matter of class struggle, the logic of Williams's overall project would imply the contrary: a 'common language', precisely because language

---

81   See, e.g., Eliot's 'Four Elizabethan Dramatists', in Eliot 1972.
82   Williams 1952, p. 26.
83   Higgins 1999, p. 28.
84   Williams 1952, pp. 22–3.
85   Williams 1952, p. 26.
86   Ibid.
87   Higgins 1999, p. 29.
88   Thompson 1961a and 1961b.

is an indissoluble element of all social practices, can only be achieved once communality itself has been politically, economically, socially and culturally realised.

More significantly for our purposes, there is a clear connection between Williams's writings on drama and his development of the concept of a 'structure of feeling', both of which originate in this immanent critique of *Scrutiny*'s pessimistic evaluation of the contemporary condition of language. Higgins has already reconstructed the link between the two and offers a convincing account of it.[89] What I offer here is in many ways an alternative reconstruction, but one which accepts both of Higgins's basic claims: that the concept of 'structure of feeling' does indeed originate in Williams's work on drama and film, and that it is 'a concept deployed as a conscious alternative and direct challenge to the available Marxist formula'.[90]

What Higgins overlooks, however, is that the concept of 'structure of feeling' arose from Williams's consideration of two problems commonly associated with *style*: firstly, in the sense of individual style, there is the problem of the relation of an individual work or writer to collective literary conventions such as forms and genres; secondly, in the sense of period style, there is the more general issue of periodising and of generationality as such – that ineffable quality common to a distinct number of disparate phenomena at a certain point in time. This is most clear in the introduction to *Drama From Ibsen to Brecht*:

> All serious thinking about art must begin from two apparently contra-
> dictory facts: that an important work is always, in an irreducible sense,
> individual; and yet that there are authentic communities of works of
> art, in kinds, periods and styles ... The individual dramatist has done

---

89   The other well-known account, which Higgins himself draws on, is David Simpson's (1992). It must be said that whilst Simpson's overview of the development of the concept of 'structure of feeling' is insightful, he uses it to produce a radically wrongheaded reading of Williams's work. His essay claims that Williams's supposed preference for voice over writing is proof of both his preference for the individual as against the system and a rejection of modernity. The first claim (voice over writing) could be proved only with grossly selective quotation; the second (individual versus society) ignores the entire impetus of his work (and, ironically, *especially* of the 'structure of feeling'), which was precisely to overcome the bourgeois individual-society distinction; the third (his rejection of modernity) is simply absurd when one considers works ranging from *Culture and Society* and *The Long Revolution* to *Towards 2000* and *The Politics of Modernism*.

90   Higgins 1999, p. 41.

this, yet what he has done is part of what we then know about a general period or style.

It is to explore this essential relationship that I use the term 'structure of feeling'. What I am seeking to describe is the continuity of experience from a particular work, through its particular form, to its recognition as a general form, and then the relation of this general form to a period.[91]

This is an early formulation of what will become, in *Culture*, the much more sophisticated differentiation between mode, genre, type and form (outlined above). But the close relation between style and 'structure of feeling' remains even as late as *Marxism and Literature*, where 'structure of feeling' is reformulated as a predominantly emergent or pre-emergent phenomenon: 'What really changes is something quite general, over a wide range, and the description that often fits the change best is the literary term "style"'.[92] Thus, the concepts of style and structure of feeling intersect at the crossroads of the collective formation of transindividual subjectivity and a theory of historical temporality. To understand both of these, and hence to grasp the profound unity of style and structure of feeling in Williams's work, it will be necessary to reconstruct his theory of inheritance, which is itself a theory of historical temporality. At the end of each of the following sections, I provide a brief summary of the 'lesson' which can be learned from that particular sub-conception of style.

2.2   *Historical Temporality and Stylistic Inheritance: Against the Ideology of Modernism*

When Williams returned to Cambridge after the war to complete his studies, he felt it had become an alien world: the people here seemed to speak a different language from the Cambridge he had known before.[93] In the context of this feeling of alienation – one in which the seemingly unproblematic political optimism of the 1930s had given way to a wave of political apostasy – Williams experienced a powerful connection to the drama of Ibsen, whom he studied for many months while producing a 15,000 word thesis for the Tripos. The intensity of this connection is significant: Williams says overtly that the central structure of feeling of Ibsen's plays – that everybody is defeated, but that this does not cancel the validity of the impulse that moved them – was precisely his own

---

91   Williams 1973b, pp. 8–9.
92   Williams 1977a, p. 131.
93   This was the basic feeling and insight which sparked his idea for what would become *Keywords* (Williams 1983a, p. 10).

structure of feeling from 1945 to 1951.[94] He even goes so far as to state that it was Ibsen's plays which 'protected him from the rapid retreat from the thirties' which his former Party comrades were now performing, and that it was at this time that 'a quite different personality emerged, very unlike [his] earlier self'.[95] The importance of Ibsen's plays in the formation of Williams's intellectual and political project is thus central: they touched the roots of his deepest personal and political commitments.

Their thematic material also provided him with the basis for some of his theoretical concepts. That is, Williams translated certain dramatic themes from Ibsen's plays into a theoretical register. The most important of these for our purposes was the theme of filial inheritance: from financial bequeathement and indebtedness to genetic diseases.[96] I believe there are three reasons why this theme appealed to Williams so intensely: firstly, Leavis's mode of literary criticism – the mode which affected Williams most deeply – was one based on the construction of lines of literary inheritance, which Leavis called either 'traditions' or 'bearings';[97] secondly, as we have already seen, the situation of postwar Cambridge confronted Williams with the starkest possible embodiment of the discrepancy between two generations – that is, his obsession with generationality was born from the unique historical circumstances of his return to Cambridge; finally, as his autobiographical novel *Border Country* (1960) testifies, Williams himself felt his relation to his own father to be torn between biological inheritance and social inheritance, this latter being disrupted by the changing patterns of economic development (whereby fathers no longer pass on knowledge of a specific trade to a child who will follow in their footsteps). Consequently, Williams was attuned to Ibsen's broadening of 'inheritance' from the primarily familial sphere to the social sphere more generally. After quoting a key passage from Ibsen's *Ghosts* – 'I almost believe we are all ghosts ... It is not only what we have inherited from our fathers and mothers that walks in us. It is every kind of dead idea, lifeless old beliefs and so on. They are not alive but they cling to us for all that' –[98] Williams concludes: 'We are, Ibsen insists, the creatures of our past. From the moment of our birth we are inevitably haunted, by every inherited debt'.[99]

---

94   Williams 1979, pp. 62–3.
95   Williams 1979, p. 63.
96   The whole of the chapter on Ibsen in *Drama From Ibsen to Brecht* focuses primarily on this theme.
97   E.g., Leavis 1962 and 1932.
98   Cited in Williams 1973b, p. 49.
99   Ibid.

It is then no wonder that Williams would later modify Gramsci's theory of hegemony, which sees 'relations of domination and subordination ... as in effect a saturation of the whole process of living',[100] by fusing it with his own tripart-ite schema of inheritance: dominant, residual and emergent. This schema is nothing less than an immanentist theory of historical temporality. It involves a suturing of past, present and future via what one might call a conception of three 'modes of presence' – three modes in which the present presents itself. There are residual social inheritances which 'have been effectively formed in the past', but are 'still active in the cultural process ... as an effective element of the present', as is the case with the monarchy or with organised religion;[101] the dominant which is a totalising but non-total incorporation of the social as such – indeed, the dominant order *defines* what counts as the social; and the emergent which is the making-becoming of an alternative future – that which the present will bequeath to future generations, provided it escapes incorporation into the dominant. The concept of the 'structure of feeling' is applicable primarily to this third mode of presence: 'The idea of structure of feeling can be specifically related to the evidence of forms and conventions – semantic figures – which, in art and literature, are often among the very first indications that such a new structure of feeling is forming'.[102] The very pro-cess of communication will then be seen as the refunctioning, the activation or the entirely novel production of various shared, inherited – residual, dom-inant and emergent – forms. Indeed, the story of *Drama From Ibsen to Brecht* is very much structured around two of these modes of presence:[103] in the Ibsen chapter, for example, Williams traces both the inheritance of domin-ant forms (French melodrama), which are becoming objectively residual in that they no longer embody the contemporary 'structure of feeling', and the subsequent production of emergent forms of naturalism, which have since become dominant and decayed into mere external conventions in their own right.

There is, however, a major problem with this early work, and one that will haunt much of Williams's later work. It is at once too intentionalist and too formalist: too intentionalist, because it presupposes the existence of some

---

100 Williams 1977a, p. 110.
101 Williams 1977a: p. 122.
102 Williams 1977a, p. 133.
103 At this point in Williams's work, there remained some confusion between residual and dominant. His comments on melodrama throughout the chapter on Ibsen in *Drama From Ibsen to Brecht*, for example, cannot ultimately decide between its residuality and its continuing effective dominance.

pristine 'experience' or personal 'structure of feeling' which the dramatist wishes to 'communicate',[104] thus instrumentalising styles and forms into passive means of expression. Yet it is too formalist because whenever it locates the presence of so-called 'residual' forms, such as melodrama in Ibsen, it is too quick to reject the work as 'regressive' – not, it must be added, because its mere presence renders it obsolete but because its conspicuousness is a sign that it has not been reabsorbed into a new, full dramatic substance.[105] By reducing Ibsen's intentions to a single desire to communicate a single 'experience' (this intention itself being effectively a post-factum interpretation),[106] Williams ignores the potential multiplicity of authorial intentions, thereby overlooking other possible interpretations of Ibsen's use of residual forms.

Nowhere does this become clearer than when comparing Williams's reading of *A Doll's House* to Toril Moi's. Albeit perhaps overstating his case out of determination to release Ibsen criticism from the stranglehold of George Bernard Shaw, Williams uses the presence of melodramatic intrigue and stock characters to justify his verdict on *A Doll's House* as 'theatrical' and regressive, describing it as 'simply *anti*-romantic', a 'rejection of the conclusions [of the earlier morality]' but 'not a rejection of the limited kinds of experience'.[107] Yet Toril Moi demonstrates conclusively that Ibsen was *intentionally* exploring theatricality and melodrama as modes of existential authenticity.[108] In the scene in which Nora performs the tarantella, the mode is purely melodramatic, and yet, as Moi shows, this is Nora's most *authentic* moment. The authenticity (in this case, naturalism) or inauthenticity (here, melodrama) of the scene is strictly undecidable, thus throwing into doubt the very opposition of authentic and inauthentic in the first place – it being precisely this feature of Ibsen's work that makes him, in Moi's eyes, the father of modernism. To throw this opposition into doubt is simultaneously to question the expressivist bias in Williams's writings on drama, premised as they are on the conception that writers proactively seek out forms of expression which are adequate to their unique 'structure of feeling' or 'experience' – the relation of adequation between the form and the experience *constituting* authenticity itself.

For Williams's oeuvre, then, Ibsen has a symptomatic importance, precisely because Williams translated some of its dramatic themes into theoretical con-

---

104   Williams 1973b, p. 25.
105   Williams 1973b, p. 47.
106   He once stated that structure of feeling 'was developed as an analytic procedure for actual written works' (Williams 1979, p. 159).
107   Williams 1973b, pp. 46–7.
108   Moi 2006, pp. 225–47.

cepts; any reinterpretation of Ibsen's work has repercussions internal to Williams's theoretical project. Toril Moi's magisterial rereading of Ibsen as father of modernism produces just such a repercussion. It pinpoints, principally, Williams's occasional incapacity to deal with a multiplicity of authorial intentions over a range from unconscious, pre-conscious, semi-conscious to self-conscious. As we saw in Chapter 4, Williams's usual method of interpretation of literary styles is the critical revelation of the social relations to which they are immanent; that is, he takes styles which *appear* absolute and reimmerses them in the conflictual and contradictory social relations from which they emerged (thereby, in his mind, dereifying them). In doing so, he hovers between a hermeneutics of suspicion, for which intentionality is largely unconscious (and thus the critical act is one of *exposure* of a real, *historical* intention), and a more concerted authorial intentionality (whereby the author is credited with self-conscious literary and social effectivity). Ultimately, however, this difficulty in harmonising reflexivity with relatively unconscious automation is the symptom of a larger structural peculiarity of Williams's work: his unique theory of historical temporality.

The place where inheritance and reflexivity converge in Williams is precisely the site of what has been interpreted as an *absence*: his supposed lack of a theory of modernity.[109] On one reading, of course, this is absurd; his entire oeuvre, structured as it is around the central notion of the 'long revolution', is nothing but an epic mapping out of modernity. Yet at the same time, it is true that Williams's work does not overtly recognize a sense of modernity as a qualitatively new experience of time (an experience premised upon the primacy of novelty as such). The reasons for this are complex. Modernity has been defined as 'the product, in the instance of each utterance, of an act of historical self-definition through *differentiation, identification* and *projection*, which transcends the order of chronology in the construction of a meaningful present';[110] it is a logic of temporal negation, valorising the present over the past, a registration of contemporaneity in terms of the (valorisation of the) new, with an openness towards an indeterminate future, and a tendency to reduce the present to a vanishing point in the permanent transition from past to future.[111] It is quite clear that Williams's theory of inheritance, especially as it is spelled out in his theory of drama, is implicitly premised upon just such a logic of temporal negation in its championing of the search for new dramatic

---

109   This absence has been noted by Jones (2004, pp. 181–94) and Grossberg 2010.
110   Osborne 1995, p. 14.
111   Cf. Osborne 1995, p. 14.

forms freshly adequate to the new structure of feeling. Yet there is also a second, competing temporality at work in his writings.

This is the time of tradition. As a form of temporalisation, 'tradition is distinguished by its apparent prioritization of the past over both present and future' and is thus the antithesis of modernity; it 'shadows the biological continuity of generations at the level of social form' and 'its primary medium is not self-consciousness, but what Adorno describes as "the pregiven, unreflected and binding existence of social forms"'.[112] The sheer strangeness of Williams's conception of historical temporality, I claim, is that it combines a valorisation of novelty typical of modernity with an emphasis on the force of biological, generational and (relatively) unconscious attachments typical of tradition. Williams's is precisely an *immanent, self-conscious traditionality*. Its immanence becomes clear when contrasted with Ricoeur's conception of historical temporality, which holds that 'the transcendental narrativity of the schema of the productive imagination underlies (and underwrites) the basic structure of historical consciousness'.[113] For Williams – as for Walter Benjamin, about whom Osborne is speaking here – 'there is only the *historically specific variety* of social [and cultural] forms of memorative communication',[114] plus – crucially (and differently from Benjamin) – *their modes of inheritance*. That is, the social and cultural forms themselves offer specific mediations of historical time, but these are limited further by the active process of selective tradition in the present, through which, via ideological filtering, only those works are selected which legitimate the political status quo.

Williams's immanent historical temporality is thus a traditionalism against (selective) tradition. It rejects the futurism of modernism, the desire abstractly to negate all traces of the past – 'a freedom with which no memory interferes, a freedom upon which no past weighs', as Levinas has it –[115] but at the same time connects the constitution of the present by the past with a potentially different future. This is then the source of many of the ambiguities – though especially those between conscious and unconscious inheritance – at work in Williams. It explains why, at one moment, he will stress intentionality and proactive selection (as in the selective tradition), whilst the next he will demonstrate unintended repetitions of previous lines of inheritance.[116] It is his greatest

---

112   Osborne 1995, p. 127.
113   Osborne 1995, p. 133.
114   Ibid.
115   Levinas 1987, p. 124.
116   Cf. Williams 1989a, p. 86: 'When I hear people talk about literature, describing what so-and-so did with that form – how did he handle the short novel? – I often think we should

strength but also a partial weakness. The strength is that it opens up the present to a consciousness of its attachments and selections, its determining lines of inheritance, the very *traditional immanence* of which means that they cannot be simply wished away (in that modernist abstract negation of the past) but must be *worked through*. His *traditional* traditionality thus retains from 'tradition' its sense of binding attachments through time. At the same time, however, it often leads him to underestimate the processes of self-conscious conceptualisation and intentionality that enter into the production of literary works. This explains those moments in which the unveiling operation of the hermeneutics of suspicion, whereby the critic exposes the social relations which secretly structure apparently absolute styles and forms from the inside, tends to fall short. Perhaps it is this fundamental ambiguity in Williams's work – between self-conscious modernist futurity and traditionalist boundness to the past – that Steven Connor senses when he describes Williams's reflections on modernity as 'at once refreshingly robust and alarmingly rustic'.[117] Whereas Connor concludes from this that 'Raymond Williams's time is not our time',[118] I claim, on the contrary, that Williams's time is *self-consciously untimely* in the context of the ideology of modernism – that mode of thought which believes it can break with the past by sheer voluntarism.[119] That is why it is not entirely true to say, as certain critics have done, that he *lacks* a theory of modernity: it would be more accurate to say that his conception of modernity is a strictly oppositional one, in that it is a historically specific, political and theoretical *rejection* of the ideology of modernism.

What does this have to do with style? It will be recalled from Chapter 1 that style as a literary category achieved its autonomy and centrality along with modernity. Indeed, 'style' in the two senses of 'a unique manner of verbal phrasing' and of 'fashion' were coeval products of capitalist modernity. For Walter Benjamin, fashion was the most advanced embodiment of modern temporality per se; it was generated by both the constant innovation and the eternal recurrence of the new produced by the commodity form. Style as a literary category, which as we saw in Chapters 1 and 2 was linked to both bourgeois property

---

✳ reverse the question and ask, how did the short novel handle him? Because anyone who has carefully observed his own practice of writing eventually finds that there is a point where, although he is holding the pen or tapping the typewriter, what is being written, while not separate from him, is not only him either, and of course this other force is literary form'.

117 Connor 1997, p. 173.

118 Connor 1997, p. 175.

119 For a far more detailed account of the 'ideology of modernism', see Jameson 2002.

rights and Romantic individualism, was then the literary verbal equivalent of this temporal logic of negation immanent to modernity. Thus, constant stylistic innovation was very much bound up with the qualitatively new experience of temporality with which I claim Williams refused to come to terms, precisely because he associated it with an ideological concealment of the true lines of inheritance which internally limit any given present. His refusal to abandon the alternative temporality of tradition was a self-conscious choice to acknowledge these unspoken and often invisible inheritances.

Nowhere do these matters become clearer than in his writings on language and modernism, which are in many ways developments of his earlier writings on naturalist drama. His basic charge against the purely ideological notion of a unified 'modernism' was its undeclared selectivity, its abstraction from all social conditions, and its overreliance on modernists' own accounts of their activities.[120] To counteract this, he makes three moves: he reinstates lines of intergenerational inheritance between 'modernists' and their supposedly non-modernist predecessors; he stresses the profound political and artistic differentiations internal to 'modernism' (a further example of what I called the 'principle of complexity' informing his work); and he recontextualises the social conditions of the principal modernists – namely, that they were exiles or émigrés whose abstract experimentations arose partly out of their profound disconnection with the metropolises and native cultures in which they found themselves.[121] He thereby counterposes a logic of inheritance (with its imminent historical temporality of tradition) to the modernists' own accounts, which are narratives of clean breaks with the past (and thus *modern* in form):

> If we are to break out of the non-historical fixity of *post*-modernism, then we must search out and counterpose an alternative tradition taken from the neglected works left in the wide margin of the century, a tradition which may address itself not to this by now exploitable because quite inhuman rewriting of the past but, for all our sakes, to a modern future in which community may be imagined again.[122]

This is the clearest example of Williams's untraditional mode of traditionality: the self-conscious construction of an alternative line of inheritance – one whose internal complexity defies the homogenising bent of the hegemonic

---

120   Williams 2007, pp. 31–5.
121   Cf. Williams 2007, pp. 31–80.
122   Williams 2007, p. 35.

term 'modernism' – intervenes into our present in order to capacitate an alternative future. It is here that we see most clearly the way in which his supposed
lack of a theory of modernity is in fact never that: it is a self-conscious *counter-
narrative* to the ideology of modernism, informed by his historically specific
appropriation of the Ibsenite theme of inheritance.

It was the same logic he applied to language. Despite the great variety of
experimentation, which he explores at length,[123] the modernist avant-garde
could essentially be divided into two camps: the modernists in practice but
not in theory and the modernists in both practice and theory.[124] The former
(the reactionaries) essentially saw the 'modern' as an 'eternal contemporaneity'
rather than as a 'historical time'; for them, modernity was an ontological condition which prevented man from achieving authentic consciousness. Their
analyses of modernity were typically selective: they picked out one aspect of
modernity and blamed it for all social ills (just as *Scrutiny* had done with the
catch-all word 'industrialism'). The true modernists (effectively, the revolutionaries), however, were those who saw modernity as a historically produced situation that arose from specific historical and social formations. Because of this,
they could attempt to intervene into it and change it. Whereas the modernists against modernity saw language as blocking authentic consciousness, the
revolutionary avant-garde '[engaged] with received form and the possibilities
of new practice, [treating] language as material in a social process'.[125] For Williams, then, a truly radical politics of style is not one which aims at formal
and stylistic innovation for its own sake, but one which accepts the immanent, constitutive efficacy of inherited styles and, by tarrying with them, extends,
develops or transcends them. Innovation is necessary, but it is progressive only
if it struggles with the (self-consciously) traditional, inherited resources.

*Lesson 1: A politics of style includes a politics of time. Attitudes towards stylistic
innovation necessarily involve, at the level of language, attitudes towards the past,
the present and the future.*

2.3   Stylistic Integration

It is now clear, then, that Williams's theory of inheritance, born initially from
his work on Ibsen, developed into a powerful and (un)timely theory of historical temporality. In his later work, he extended this theory into a critique of

---

123   Williams 2007, pp. 65–77.
124   Williams 2007, p. 77.
125   Ibid.

modernism whose self-comprehension he attacked as abstractly modern and formalist. He also used it to develop an implicit politics of style. We shall now trace another strand of Williams's overall theory of style which, likewise, begins in his writings on naturalism but extends into his later critique of modernism.

It must be said immediately that the overriding impetus of all his work on drama is to denaturalise naturalism, to demonstrate that the convention of verisimilitude in the reproduction of everyday human speech is precisely that: a convention, a tacit agreement or accepted standard, not an eternal given. The second major aim is to show that naturalism itself is not synonymous with verisimilitude or probability. Naturalism proper – which is variously described as a 'creative purpose',[126] as naturalism '*as a form*',[127] or as 'high naturalism' – [128] is constantly opposed to an inauthentic or degraded variant, ultimately referred to as 'naturalist habit'.[129] The basic opposition is between an authentic desire to represent human actions in exclusively human and secular terms (as opposed to supernatural ones), these actions themselves being contemporary, secular and socially inclusive (i.e., opposed to premodern codes of dramatic propriety) and, alternatively, a 'naturalist habit' which is 'the naturalized assumption of an immediately negotiable everyday world, presented through conventions which are not seen as conventions'.[130] Many of the attacks on naturalism, which have been ideologically recast as simply 'modernist', can thus be seen as *extensions* of the original naturalist project (or 'high naturalism') at the expense of 'naturalist habit': what began as a revolutionary dramatic innovation in, amongst other things, the representation of human speech (Ibsen: 'My desire was to depict human beings and therefore I would not make them speak the language of the gods'),[131] became in its turn a merely 'external' convention, thus necessitating new formal innovations to carry on the naturalist project.[132]

The basic problem faced by dramatists (and which is traced throughout *Drama From Ibsen to Brecht*) is that 'once a certain level of conversational speech is set, you can never move beyond it: people are confined to its limits

---

126   Williams 1973b, p. 385.
127   Williams 1973b, p. 389.
128   Williams 1977b, p. 2.
129   Ibid.
130   Ibid.
131   Cited in Williams 1973b, p. 40.
132   '[T]o realize the full possibility of the naturalist project, as a new secular view of personal character and social relationships, drama had to move on to other forms' (Williams 1979, p. 205).

at moments when a greater intensity of expression is needed'.[133] At the other
extreme, however, '[w]hat becomes intolerable is either the adoption of an
overall verse form which pitches everything at the level of myth, or the descent
from the metaphysical to the trivial within a uniform verse medium, such as
you find in Eliot's later plays'.[134] Thus, if a dramatist faithfully reproduces probable human speech, she risks an inadequacy of expression at crucial moments
of intensity, but if she pitches her diction at too uniformly formal a level, she
risks either negating the naturalist ideals of verisimilitude or of inviting com-
ically bathetic switches from the sublime to the everyday.[135] It is no wonder,
then, that Williams's implicit ideal of dramatic speech, from first to last, is an
integration of multiple stylistic levels. Yet – and this is crucial – this is no mere
abstract formalist ideal of dramatic excellence: it is strictly in line with the original naturalist project of a drama attached to history, society and secularity. It
aims, firstly, to register and incorporate the actually existing gamut of spoken
idioms into an artistically controlled polyphony, and, secondly, to produce a
dramatic speech adequate to the expression of the entire range of human feeling, from the seemingly most personal and pre-conscious affective fluctuation
to the most officially, formally and publicly recognised emotions.

If, however, Williams's guiding ideal for dramatic speech is an integration
of multiple stylistic levels, then the word 'integration' has three meanings: the
integration of multiple idioms, the integration of speech with other formal
elements, especially that of action, and the integration of the writer in the
total process of production. Again, it is important to stress that these ideals
of integration are not aesthetic ends in themselves. If the early Williams did,
admittedly, occasionally sail close to a certain formalism in his dramatic analyses, a shift occurs throughout his work on drama from a *formalist* conception of integration and expression to a *formational* one – one that takes into
account those sociological groups, ranging from guilds, through schools and
movements, to class fractions, to which writers belong.[136] The greatest indication of this shift was his changing attitude towards the drama of T.S. Eliot.
The early Williams was torn between a profound political opposition to Eliot's

---

133   Williams 1979, p. 208.
134   Ibid.
135   'The biggest single mistake that Eliot made was his attempt to find an all-purpose dramatic
       verse which could function as a substitute for conversation. For the whole case for verse
       as capable of greater precision and intensity of meaning collapsed when characters had to
       ask whether someone had bought an evening paper, a perfectly ordinary conversational
       exchange, in a uniform poetic mode' (Williams 1979, p. 207).
136   Cf. Williams 1981a, pp. 57–86.

writings on culture (best captured in *Culture and Society*) and a championing of Eliot's attempts to move beyond the impasses of naturalist drama, especially its problems of speech. Consequently, where the young Williams praised Eliot's 'remaking of a fully expressive dramatic speech',[137] the late Williams would come to describe his work as a form of 'modernism ... against modernity' and a 'dramatic counter-revolution'.[138] This shift in evaluation is central to understanding a further aspect of Williams's politics of style.

It will be recalled that the third and fourth elements of *Scrutiny*'s linguistic ideology bemoaned the loss of linguistic integration which they saw as arising with 'industrialism'. The early Williams saw the drama of T.S. Eliot as the pinnacle of attempts to move beyond the speech conventions of naturalist habit, and one of the reasons for this was precisely because it achieved an integration of stylistic idioms. The finest example of this new drama was *Murder in the Cathedral*.[139] The key to its success lay in its ingenious resolution of two aspects of the problem of naturalist speech. Firstly, it partially solved the problem of naturalist conventions: it overcame the audience's conventional expectations of spoken verisimilitude by being set, and actually performed, in a cathedral. Moreover, it drew on a story – the martyrdom of Becket – which was already well known. Taken together, the setting and the legend opened the audience's receptivity to a linguistic range and formality which exceeded that of the average naturalist play. Secondly, the setting of the cathedral provided certain *formal* possibilities to surpass the limited conversational prose of the typical naturalist play. The chorus function, long alien to the bourgeois theatre, could be reintroduced and conventionally accepted by the audience, under the guise of the choir;[140] the sermon provided an excuse for introducing soliloquies;[141] and the liturgy naturalised the use of a very formal stylistic register.[142] It thus achieved a nuanced stylistic intensity quite alien to the naturalist habit.

Yet, despite the fact that Williams's analyses of stylistic integration were not yet truly 'formational', even at this stage they were not purely formalistic. It is worth comparing his praise of Eliot to the comments he made on the styles of Jane Austen and D.H. Lawrence respectively. Superficially, all three of them achieve stylistic integration: Eliot between formal, rhetorical speech and everyday conversation; Austen and Lawrence between the narratorial and

---

137   Williams 1973b, p. 219.
138   Williams 2007, p. 76; Williams 1979, p. 206.
139   Williams's analysis of the play can be found in Williams 1973b, pp. 199–204.
140   Williams 1973b, p. 200.
141   Williams 1973b, p. 201.
142   Williams 1973b, p. 200.

characterological idioms (that is, broadly speaking, what in Chapter 5 I called 'style as instance' and 'style as idiom'). But Williams also shows that Austen's unity of tone was only possible because she took as her purview the superficial field of decorative, reified, *neutral* signs of social improvement without having to embody in her writing the brutality of the colonial plantations and the basic, backbreaking labour that produced them.[143] At a formal level, Lawrence achieved the same unity of tone as Austen, but in his case Williams refers to it as 'a miracle of language'.[144] How are the two so formally similar and yet, in terms of Williams's evaluations, so absolutely different? Jeff Wallace is the only commentator to have grasped the full significance of this discrepancy:

> What is 'really new' is not the unity of idiom itself ... the real change lies in the use of a narrative voice which feels *with* working-class experience rather than about it; as there is no disconnection between the narrative language and the language of the characters, Lawrence denotes the authority of that experience from within rather than imposing it upon the external authority of 'observation'.[145]

If, on the level of a purely formal analysis, the stylistic integration (which is not to say the diction) of Austen and Lawrence is 'the same', at a sociological level it is completely opposed: Lawrence wrote from within and about the working class, with full knowledge and first-hand experience of the labour processes behind the making of polite society, whereas Austen's more or less total excision of those processes was built into the very fibres of her prose. When it comes to Eliot, a similar unveiling of the real social relations immanent to his stylistic integration is employed: the cathedral may well allow him to broaden his stylistic range, but it also embodies his central structure of feeling – 'the many unconscious, the few conscious', that is, precisely the elitist and authoritarian conception of society which Williams exposed in *Culture and Society*.[146]

Thus, it is now clear that Williams's call for the integration of a multiplicity of stylistic idioms was not a purely formalist one, but was not yet 'formational'. By the time of his late work, however, this desire for integration has matured into a critique of what he takes to be the formalist, non-sociological championing of Bakhtin's notion of polyphony (stylistic integration par excellence). In a crucial essay on language and the avant-garde, he writes that

---

143   Williams 1970, pp. 21–2.
144   Williams 1970, p. 172.
145   Wallace 1993, p. 111.
146   Williams 1963, pp. 224–38.

... the 'multivocal' or 'polyphonic', even the 'dialogic', as features of texts, have to be referred to the social practice if they are to be rigorously construed. For they can range from the innovatory inclusion of a diversity of voices and socio-linguistic relationships ... to what is no more in effect, but also in intention, than the self-absorbed miming of others: a proliferation and false interaction of class and gender linguistic stereotypes from an indifferent and enclosing technical consciousness. The innovatory inclusion can be traced to its formation, but the isolated technique is more usually traceable to its agency, in direct or displaced domination. Similarly, the important inclusion, within a highly literate and culturally allusive context, of the active range and body of everyday vernacular has to be distinguished not only formally but formationally from that rehearsal and miming of what is known in the relevant agencies as *Vox Pop*: that linguistic contrivance for political and commercial control.[147]

Contrary to the view of an increasingly obsolete American poststructuralism, a work which composes a multiplicity of voices and styles is not *in and of itself* politically progressive. In order to discern the *politics* of the multivocity of the work, it is necessary to perform a formational analysis. This entails, firstly, the recognition that 'every act of composition in writing' is precisely that – an act, and one necessarily structured by intention and content, and that this act of composition itself enters into social processes and practices whose purposes and intentions may inform, suppress or override those of the writer.[148] For example, the late Williams constantly observed that techniques developed by consciously marginalised and oppositional avant-garde formations, whose politics were internally extremely diverse, were, one generation later, adapted and incorporated by a burgeoning paranational capitalist system of advertising and publicity. The second move, which proceeds naturally from the first, is to supplement this translation of an (apparently intentionless) form into an (intentional, practical) act by the location of the act within the social formation from which it proceeds. A formation is a non-institutional, group self-organisation, with specialising, alternative or openly oppositional external relations to more general organisations and institutions within society at large.[149] Often, formations belong to particular class fractions (as in the case

---

147   Williams 2007, pp. 79–80.
148   This is my strongly adapted paraphrase of Williams 2007, p. 76.
149   Williams 1981a, pp. 57–86.

of the Bloomsbury group, which belonged to the professional and liberal fraction of an imperial ruling class) or to specific social groups, such as the exiles and émigrés who made up a significant part of the modernist avant-garde. The crucial lesson to take from this shift in Williams's work, then, is that it is only by combining formal with formational analysis that one can be said to be carrying out *political* analysis proper: *without formational analysis, there is no 'politics of style'.*

Lesson 11: The politics of a style, whether it be monological or integrated heteroglossia, does not inhere in the mode(s) of verbal phrasing alone, nor solely – in the case of heteroglossia – in their mutual internal relations. It resides in the articulation of the style with the intentions, purposes and social formations through which the style achieves its efficacy.

2.4   *Transindividual Subjectivity: Style and 'Total Expression'*
At this point, the problem of stylistic integration encounters the problem of transindividual subjectivity. As we have seen, reflection upon this problem was integral to Williams's development of the concept of the structure of feeling. Beyond its more immediate relation to style, however, the concept of structure of feeling was a direct foray into the territory, not only of *Scrutiny*, nor of the Marxist base-superstructure metaphor,[150] but also of the very naturalist and modernist writers themselves: it was an attempt to win back for the common all social experience which, in an alienated society, people take to be purely individual or 'merely' subjective. Williams wanted to show that even our innermost thoughts and deepest desires are *social* and potentially *articulable*; only in doing so could forms be developed which would be adequate to their expression and ultimate satisfaction. This is why the early Williams, to the unease of his mature counterpart (who preferred the term 'total form'),[151] advocated what he called 'total expression'. This was first and foremost (as we shall see below) an ideal of the total integration of all elements of a drama,[152] but it was also quite clearly a desire for the possible verbal articulation of *all* human feelings.

Williams had long noticed the significance in naturalist drama of the domestic setting:

---

150   Higgins 1999, p. 41.
151   When the interviewers quote his early definition of 'total expression', he responds: 'The idea is inadequately put there: I should have spoken of total form' (Williams 1979, p. 230).
152   Cf. Williams and Orrom 1954, p. 31.

It is perhaps a particular stage of bourgeois society, in which the decisive action is elsewhere, and what is lived out, in these traps of rooms, are the human consequences: in particular, the consequences of a relatively leisured society. To stare from a window at where one's life is being decided: that consciousness is specific ... The rooms are not there to define the people, but to define what they seem to be, what they cannot accept they are.[153]

In contradistinction to the innate total integration and expression of ancient Greek drama,[154] the linguistic embodiment of this bourgeois structure of feeling is a style condemned to superficiality, one that is forced to hint at hidden depths of experience beneath what is actually articulated, and in constant danger of mere 'wished significance'.[155] This means, as Vladimir Nemirovich-Danchenko once observed in relation to Chekov, that '[t]he dialogue the author has written is merely a pale reflection of those emotions, their outward manifestation, which still leaves a great deal over'.[156] These observations became crucial to his insight into the inadequacy of contemporary Marxist approaches to culture, as he understood them (essentially, variations on the base-superstructure model). These approaches all depended on 'a *known* history, a known *structure*, known *products*'[157] – on internally complete systems of thought with an assumed fully achieved articulation without remainder. What such approaches to culture ignored was precisely that realm of pre-articulated transindividual experience which naturalist drama was constantly forced to hint at, and to explain which Williams developed his theory of the 'structure of feeling': 'social experiences *in solution*, as distinct from other social semantic formations which have been *precipitated* and are evidently and more immediately available'.[158] Thus, Williams's recognition of the constitutive inadequacy of lin-

---

153   Williams 1973b, p. 387.
154   Cf. Williams on *Antigone*: 'The more one looks at the text of the play, the more one realizes that a simple, yet radical, pattern, a controlling structure of feeling, has been clearly isolated and designed in the writing. And then, if one looks at the performance, one sees that this design is being continually enacted, in the parts as in the whole. For it is a design made for performance; the purpose of the play is not report, not description, not analysis, but enactment of a design. The structure of feeling is the formal written structure, and also the structure of performance' (1991, p. 39).
155   Williams and Orrom 1954, p. 45.
156   Cited in Williams and Orrom 1954, p. 46.
157   Williams 1977a, pp. 106–7.
158   Williams 1977a, pp. 133–4.

guistic expression in the early naturalist drama simultaneously provided his key line of attack and, ultimately, the basic trajectory of his attempted reconstruction of Marxist theories of literature and culture.

In terms of solutions to the problem of stylistic inadequacy, Williams called for two developments: the reintegration of speech with other dramatic elements (especially with action and movement), and the reincorporation of the dramatist into the whole process of production and direction. Since language is an indissoluble element of practice, it is no surprise that conventions of movement and action on stage can severely limit or enable certain types of stylistic expressivity. Williams was concerned to show that those modes of verisimilar acting and gesture which had been developed within naturalism were just as much a problem for total expressivity as the linguistic styles themselves. Only once new relations could be established between a wider repertoire of gestures and a broader array of idioms would the drama have any hope of integration. But, of course, such innovations cannot be wished into being by sheer fiat alone; they have to connect with and negotiate the hegemony of current dominant theatrical conventions, which are themselves usually held in check by their relation to the dominant ideologies of a society at large. What is stylistically achievable on the page and what can be actualised on the stage are two very different things.

The second proposal – the reincorporation of the dramatist into the whole process of production and direction – took as its model Brecht's Berliner Ensemble. Whereas most contemporary dramatists were the victims of a capitalist division of dramatic labour,[159] Brecht had achieved at least an intra-dramatic solution by effecting a total integration of dramatic vision at all levels of the small theatrical institution. Yet again, then, Brecht's written style itself cannot be evaluated in purely formalist terms. It has as its condition of possibility Brecht's own integration into the total process of production – not to mention the radically enlarged receptivity of his audiences to dramatic experimentation which was a concomitant of the general extremity of the historical situation at large.

Lesson III: Literary styles can, on occasion, embody aspects of newly emergent transindividual subjectivity, ones which may well be in opposition to the ruling, formally articulated modes of subjectivity which are officially or commonly recognised.

---

159 'The idea of total form was designed to indicate that all the elements of a dramatic work should be under coherent control, rather than vagaries of the dissociated process typical of capitalist relations of production' (Williams 1979, p. 230).

A politically radical conception of style is thus characterised, firstly, by its recognition of subjectivity and experience as always already social, secondly, by its recognition of style's power immanently to constitute and embody newly emergent transindividual subjectivity and, thirdly, by a resolute linguistic optimism for which nothing is verbally inexpressible. At the same time, it must be seen that style is an essentially relational phenomenon, dialectically constituted both by its relation to other formal elements of a medium (in the drama: action and movement), and by the writer's power to activate the totality of a convention congenial to her stylistic intentions, itself limited by the cultural hegemony of pre-existing conventions.

2.5   *Style and Cultural Materialism*

The final element of Williams's theory of style relates more directly to what he came to call 'cultural materialism': 'a theory of culture as a (social and material) productive process and of specific practices, of "arts", as social uses of material means of production (from language as material "practical consciousness" to the specific technologies of writing and forms of writing, through to mechanical and electronic communications systems)'.[160] A theory of style constructed from this angle would emphasise, firstly, that language is a social activity which assumes two principal forms, in line with the two principal types of communicative resources: inherent bodily resources (speech) and a use of non-human means of communication (writing and print). Style could then be defined either as the elaboration of verbal phrasing (the art of which was best exemplified in rhetoric) or as the elaboration of written phrasing. The difference between the two is that '[w]riting as a cultural technique is wholly dependent on forms of specialized training, not only ... for producers but also, crucially, for receivers'.[161] Consequently, 'writing has from the beginning been a special form of privilege and social discrimination ... It has to be carefully taught and learned, and until comparatively recently, and still in some respects today even in the most literate societies, access to this skill has been carefully and at times malignly controlled'.[162] Thus, it is clear that the production of *literary* styles always presupposes a certain social distribution of the technology of writing; as we saw in Chapter 4, the social relations of writing are necessarily connected to the system of education and reproduction of any given social formation. Writing is not a neutral technique that can be learned in the abstract; it has,

---

160   Williams 2010, p. 243.
161   Williams 1981a, p. 93.
162   Williams 1989b, p. 53.

historically, been a form of power learnt in combination with a set of ideologies and ways of seeing, often themselves built into the dominant modes of writing – 'the attitudes and the style in a single operation'.[163] O'Connor sums it up well: 'Writing is a material production of human sociality and it is also marks on a surface. These two come together in ways that are both complex and social'.[164]

Literature must then be seen, at the most basic level, as 'the process and the result of formal composition within the social and formal properties of language'[165] – a process which is not separate from the ordinary processes of linguistic (re)generation.[166] At the same time, however, it is also 'a specializing social and historical category',[167] which has an observable effect on what is produced in its name. Whilst there is no *absolute* distinction between that which comes to be categorized as 'literature' and 'the practical history of writing and of forms of writing' in general,[168] the terms in which writers understand their practice internally affects the styles and forms they produce. Taken together, we can say that literary style is located at the intersection of three forces: the general ideological charge generated by the fact that writing is a cultural technology requiring specialised training, and hence mediation via a ruling class (or mediation in opposition to a ruling class, as in the case of, say, the Irish hedge schools); the historically variable and politically directed definitions of literature, which attempt to defy the basic fact of the multiplicity of writing by enforcing writers to think of their work in limiting categories (fiction/ non-fiction, objective/ subjective, etc.); and, finally, the force of a Marxist theory which attempts to *reconnect* the ideologically selected representations of literature and writing to, firstly, the formal composition of language in general and, secondly, the fact of writing as a significant social act and practice in its own right.

---

163   Williams 1969, p. 48.

164   O'Connor 1989, p. 117.

165   Williams 1977a, p. 46.

166   I use the word 'ordinary' here quite consciously, since there is an analogy between the early Williams's famous claim that 'culture is ordinary' (that is, that the creation of values and meanings is not limited to an elite 'cultural' clerisy) and the later Williams's refusal to 'restrict linguistic generation and regeneration to works of literature': 'The process of language itself is a continual possibility of shift and change and initiation of meanings and this range of possibility is embedded in the 'rules' of both the linguistic and the social system' (1981b, p. 60).

167   Williams 1977a, p. 53.

168   Williams 1983b, p. 2.

Lesson IV: Style is both a linguistic mode of social relation and a social use of the material means of production. It has as its presupposition a learned technology of writing mediated predominantly by the ruling class via the education system. Specifically literary styles are then the coming together of both the ruling ideologies learned through literacy (themselves historically varying in intensity) and the likewise historically various and ideologically selective definition of 'literature'.

Conclusion

We must now attempt to unify the theory of style developed in the previous chapter with the multiple developments traced here. It will be recalled that in Chapter 4 the struggle for 'good style' was seen to be synonymous with the struggle for adequate social forms. An 'adequate' style for Williams was one in which the abstract universalism of open rational discourse could somehow be fused with the directness of particular address. For Williams, the formal struggles novelists faced when attempting to unify these two discourses within a single work were quite literally stylistic extensions of the class struggle. What was ostensibly a battle between classes 'out there' in society became immanent to the very writing process itself, generating stylistic discontinuities which a reified conception of style would simply brush off as either artistic or moral failures. Actual historical practices were seen to generate ways of seeing and dealing with the world which crystallise into literary styles. The raw linguistic materials on which writers' stylistic configurations go to work are not simply neutral, but are haunted by the still-dormant intentions of the divided classes who once spoke them.

We can now add several elements to this account. Firstly, at the smallest scale, styles are micro-registrations of shifts in socially mediated, transindividual subjectivity (a *constitutive* and *expressive* theory of style). From the perspective of Williams's late theory of the structure of feeling, styles are the prime locus of the emergence of historical novelty. Literary styles are often attempts tentatively to articulate, via some new form of verbal phrasing or elaboration, emerging forms of practical consciousness – especially those that have been thus far denied or suppressed by the dominant styles of articulation. Seen from this angle, style is 'political' in the sense that it is the most microscopic articulation of transindividual subjectivity with the collective forms of society.

Secondly, styles are informed and internally limited by the modes, genres, types and forms of the works in which they are actualised, and by the internal constellations of formal elements within them (e.g., in drama, the constellation of speech, movement, gesture and action). Stylistic innovations that are purely verbal, affecting in no way the other elements of a particular form, are, if not impossible, then at least condemned to linguistic superficiality. Any lasting stylistic innovation will generally require a simultaneous innovation in the other constitutive elements of a mode, genre, type or form (especially of the latter two). To that extent, any politics of style is intimately bound up with the broader conception of the politics of form: the way in which cultural forms embody, criticise and perform ideologies.

Thirdly, as further proof of the claim examined in the previous chapter that good style is a matter of good social relations, we can now see that even those styles which achieve an integration of multiple idioms (potentially an index of the actual *social* integration of the groups they represent) are not in and of themselves politically 'progressive'. It is not just that there is no one-to-one correlation between the overt political stances of an author and the styles and forms in which they write, but that stylistic polyphony, void of all formational and hence *intentional* context, cannot be political in any meaningful sense. There is no purely immanent politics of style in the sense of 'immanent to the words on the page'; there is only a politics of style as immanent to a linguistic project structured both by 'poietic' intentions and by the (potentially unconscious or misrecognised) political intentions of the formation itself (or, as with the modernists, by both at the same time).

Fourthly, style is both a linguistic mode of social relation and a social use of a material means of production which has as its presupposition a learned technology of writing. Here, the politics of style resides, initially, in the learning of literacy via an education system which is deeply influenced by the hegemony of the ruling class. In modern liberal democracies, the function of literacy, which involves the transmission not only of (neutral) techniques of writing and reading but also of the linguistic ideologies that accompany them, is fundamental to the reproduction of the social relations of production.

Fifthly, any politics of style includes a politics of time which is simultaneously a politicisation of our stylistic inheritances. Whereas the theory of style in the previous chapter remained predominantly synchronic, we can now see that Williams's theory of style includes what I have called an immanent self-conscious traditionality. This renders political not only the act of configuration itself (as an act of mediation between the mutually contradictory idioms of the internally divided *polis*) but also the processes by which specific styles, conceptions of style and stylistic models are handed on from one generation to the next: all those processes of canon formation and education (formal and informal) whose purpose is to reproduce in the present and future the social relations of production that existed in the (immediate) past (or in a *perceived* past which is politically active in the present). From this perspective – the *rela-*

tional perspective – style is political both because it is an immanent aspect of the reproduction of the social relations necessary for the maintenance of the political and economic status quo, and because new styles might potentially embody new social relations.

Finally, and here I am developing an insight based on the blind spot I located in Williams's theory of historical temporality, style does not always reside solely in the words on the page: it can also be the name of the relation between a literary or artistic *concept* and a verbal inscription. This understanding of style is crucial in accounting for experimental literature ranging from, say, Kenneth Goldsmith's project of 'uncreative writing', which involves the simple copying of preexisting texts from one medium or context to another, through to literary collages of citations.[169] 'Uncreative writing' is the true zero degree of style as phrasing. The intrinsic relation between language and social relations is here sublated into an abstract conceptuality. The politics of this type of style – style as conceptuality – resides in the structure and effect of the concept behind the various inscriptions; it is not *immanent* to them. The literary collage, on the other hand, still exhibits a certain lexical configuration, though the operation draws, not on the verbal element of $mimesis_1$ but on pre-existing literary and non-literary texts, citations from which are orchestrated into new stylistic constellations.

Ultimately, then, Williams offers us a genuine range of conceptualisations of style, each of which implies a different sense of 'politics'. He expands our sense of the theoretical and practical issues buried deep within the production and evaluation of literary styles, whilst augmenting our sense of what 'politics' can mean both in general and within the context of literature more specifically. It is his work, arguably the most nuanced of the three thinkers featured in this book, which sets the benchmark for all political theories of style.

---

169   Goldsmith 2011.

Intermezzo: Style and the Meaning of 'Politics' and 'Culture'

Eagleton Contra Jameson

Williams was not alone in linking the problem of style to the meaning and scope of politics itself. In 1982, six years after his devastating attack on his former mentor,[1] Eagleton renewed his reputation as a combative figure with an essay entitled 'Fredric Jameson: the Politics of Style'. Aligning himself with Jameson's comment in *Marxism and Form* that 'any description of a literary or philosophical phenomenon – if it is to be really complete – has an ultimate obligation to come to terms with the shape of the individual sentences themselves, to give an account of their origin and formation',[2] Eagleton states his aim: '[to enquire] into the political determinants of Jameson's style'.[3] The essay consists of three stages. Firstly, Eagleton claims that Jameson's style hovers ambiguously between the pared-down lucidity of traditional Anglo-American prose and the *jouissance*-fuelled marauding of the signifier writ large in certain French poststructuralist texts (Barthes's chief among them). He attributes this to Jameson's 'historical responsibilities as one of the few American critics for whom "radicalism" extends beyond the terrors of tropology ... to embrace the fate of the political struggles in Poland or El Salvador'.[4] In this sense, Jameson's style can be read as a form of political maturity, indulging in a certain utopian excess – a small slice of historically proleptic pleasure this side of world revolution – but constantly reining it back in so as to maintain the coherence of his thesis. It is a 'dialectical figure' which 'both compensates for and adumbrates pleasures historically postponed, goals as yet politically unrealisable, and is to this extent both a bleak and politically instructive displacement'.[5] The second stage of the essay then reinterprets the ambiguity of Jameson's style from another angle, this time seeing it as 'a curious doubling of commentary and critique'. When reading a work like *The Prison-House of Language*, one is never entirely sure whether Jameson is offering a survey of a given theory (in this case, structuralism and formalism), or whether he is

---

1 See the overture to Part II.
2 Jameson 1971, p. xii.
3 Eagleton 1982, p. 14.
4 Eagleton 1982, p. 15.
5 Eagleton 1982, p. 16.

critiquing it. Eagleton sees this problem as 'the stylistic index of a more fundamental dilemma, that of his relationship as a revolutionary to bourgeois theory'.[6] Jameson appropriates such texts both too much and too little: he 'transcodes' a vast panoply of works ranging from Hjelmslev to Hegel, from Freud to Foucault, into a Marxist 'master code', but at the same time leaves them 'relatively untransformed, intact in their "relative autonomy"'.[7] Jameson's tendency 'to invest in description all those dramatic intensities which one would usually associate with argument' is then yet another stylistic index of this theoretical dilemma.[8]

The third stage of the essay broadens the scope and significance of this stylistic trait. Eagleton argues that Jameson has misunderstood the point of Marxist criticism: his residual Hegelianism necessitates the demonstration that a suitably vague 'History', the progressive version of *Geist*, is the hidden truth of all phenomena. Thus for Jameson the point of Marxist criticism is to provide a 'political hermeneutics', such that all contextual dots can be joined and the mind can catch an occasional, liberating glimpse of that rarest of beasts: totality. Such a theory of the function of Marxist criticism is seen to result from the special esteem in which Jameson holds Lukács's theory of reification and, conversely, from his failure fully to have digested Althusser's attack on historicism. Finally, this *theoretical* inclination is exposed as a *political* choice. A focus on commodification (and here Eagleton quotes his own earlier essay, 'The Idealism of American Literary Criticism')[9] 'links the economical to the experiential only at the cost of displacing the political'.[10] In contrast, urges Eagleton, Jameson should '*start* with class-struggle; ... begin, theoretically, from the political; ... take off from institutions rather than from discourse or "consciousness": ... it cannot be *incorporated* in quite the [same] way'.[11] Eagleton recognises that Jameson's proclivity for theoretical *Aufhebung* is no doubt a reflection of the 'current relative quiescence of the class-struggle in the United States', but nonetheless claims that, as it stands, Jameson's critical project is in violation of Marx's eleventh thesis on Feuerbach: 'The philosophers have only *interpreted* the world, in various ways; the point is to *change* it'.[12] Just as in his attack on Williams in 1976, then, Eagleton reads Jameson's style as an indication of his (false)

---

6   Eagleton 1982, p. 17.
7   Ibid.
8   Eagleton 1982, p. 18.
9   Eagleton 1981.
10   Eagleton 1982, p. 21.
11   Ibid.
12   Marx 1975, p. 423.

conception of Marxism. His essay must thus be seen as an intervention into contemporary debates about the changing nature of Marxism and the revolutionary task of literary theory.

Jameson's Reply

Jameson responded to some of Eagleton's central charges in an interview which featured alongside the attack in the same volume of *Diacritics*. He followed two lines of argument. The first was associated specifically with the relation between Marxism and literature departments. Where Eagleton had asked sardonically of *The Political Unconscious* 'how is a Marxist-structuralist analysis of a minor novel by Balzac to help shake the foundations of capitalism?', Jameson replied that, as a Marxist, he could not have chosen a worse example. For Balzac was precisely one of the few authors on whom Marx and Engels wrote at any length, so 'to propose a new reading of Balzac is to modify *those* debates' in Marxist aesthetics.[13] Thus, the first, modest function of a Marxist attention to literature is to modify debates internal to that tradition itself. The second function was a matter of Marxist pedagogy and consisted in a critical intervention into the university teaching of the 'canon'. For 'the ideologies in which people are trained when they read and interpret novels are not specialized at all, but rather the working attitudes and forms of the conceptual legitimation of this society'.[14] By intervening into these debates, Marxist teachers could, at the least, put a chink in the armour of the hegemonic discourse of liberal humanism. Finally, Jameson frames these comments in the context of the desolate political landscape of America at that time: 'I happen to think that no real systemic change in this country will be possible without the minimal first step of the achievement of a social democratic movement'.[15] The two preconditions for this were the creation of a Marxist intelligentsia and of a Marxist culture. In this light, Jameson's critical readings of canonical texts were cast as a first step in a propaganda exercise designed to demonstrate the subtleties and strengths of a Marxist discourse which many presupposed inferior to the most advanced currents of bourgeois thought. Ultimately, Eagleton had misread the political context: it was not polemic which was needed, but a rigorous and expansive

---

13   Jameson 2007, p. 11. This version of the interview is an anthologised reprint of the *Diacritics* original.

14   Jameson 2007, p. 13.

15   Ibid.

form of criticism which would convince the American intelligentsia that Marxism was a serious intellectual contender.

The second line of argument is related to the definitions of 'politics' and 'culture' implied by Eagleton's attack. 'As far as "the political" is concerned', he says, 'any single-shot, single-function definition of it is worse than misleading; it is paralyzing'.[16] Indeed, this 'mirage' of the single-shot notion of politics 'comes from impatience with the mediated, with the long term'[17] – precisely the retort Williams had made against Eagleton's voluntarism six years prior. Along with this monolithic conception of politics came an insufficiently nuanced definition of culture, not to mention an underestimation of the extent to which, in this latest stage of capitalism, culture itself had become coterminous with the social field as a whole: 'it is hard to see how *any* politics could be projected or conceived which is unwilling to take into account the structure of this actual moment of capital; which is unwilling – at least provisionally, experimentally – to take into account the possibility that our older models of both politics and culture may no longer be completely relevant'.[18] Again, just as Williams had criticised Eagleton's underestimation of the new status of culture within the capitalist economy, so Jameson pinpoints a certain ahistorical orthodoxy which transforms Marxism into the very type of metaphysical discourse it was supposed to dispel. For all of his materialist posturing, the implication goes, Eagleton's call to arms was not based on a coherent analysis of the present political conjuncture.

This is not to say, however, that Jameson's commendably flexible and adaptable approach was always and everywhere superior to Eagleton's. As we shall see, Jameson's radical openness to the present is coupled with an epic purview which implies a temporality curiously alien to the time of political intervention. Even while one accepts the unsatisfactory nature of Eagleton's occasional descriptions of Marxism, then, he nonetheless locates a series of very real problems in Jameson's work. As one would expect of a tradition premised upon the primacy of social being over consciousness, the work of all three of these Marxist thinkers was itself marked by the practical and political situations in which they found themselves. Indeed, it has been the point of the overture and of this intermezzo to demonstrate precisely this – and to show that the ideas of style which each critic developed cannot be abstracted from the struggles out of which they emerged.

---

16   Jameson 2007, p. 16.
17   Ibid.
18   Jameson 2007, p. 19.

In the two chapters that follow, I shall trace the precise political and intellectual origins of Eagleton and Jameson's approaches to literary style. If in many ways they can be seen as inheritors of Williams's work, they can also be seen as offering alternative approaches to the problems he dealt with. Though neither achieves the nuanced richness of Williams's theory of style, both contribute important insights for a Marxist poetics that are not to be found in Williams's work.

Terry Eagleton: The Political Theology of Style

Of the three thinkers considered in this book, it is Eagleton who has most consistently emphasised the importance of style. His work offers a powerful addition to the Marxist poetics being developed here: a renewed attention to the political nuances ingrained in verbal texture, and a sense of the joy that such verbally inventive language can produce. Yet there are certain contradictions in Eagleton's approach to style and language – notably those between the secular and the divine – which may well prove irresolvable. This is not, however, to deny the moral and intellectual grandeur of his vision of 'tragic humanism'. On the contrary, the latter constitutes a major historical materialist research programme. This chapter is thus less a critique of 'tragic humanism' as such, than a critical consideration of one localised element within it.

1   The Body as Language

For a man who has said that when he comes across a copy of his early work, *The Body as Language* (1970), he burns it, Eagleton's late work draws a surprising amount on what that book contained.[1] As he himself has remarked of his work including and following *Sweet Violence* (2002) – that 'titanic tryst with the Tragic muse', as Homi Bhabha put it –[2] it constitutes not so much a 'metaphysical turn' as a *return* 'full circle' to the concerns of his earliest theological writing.[3] It is to this work, I claim, that we must look if we are to grasp the core presuppositions of Eagleton's theory of language and, by extension, style.

The context of his early theological writings is now well known.[4] They occurred at the juncture of the British New Left and the institutional upheavals in the Catholic Church following Vatican II, and were published principally in the short-lived journal *Slant*, which Eagleton went on to edit from 1969 to its conclusion in 1970. They were also informed by the writings of the late Dominican friar Herbert McCabe, a man whose influence on Eagleton he

---

1   This anecdotal curiosity is recounted in Boer 2007, p. 279, n. 9.
2   In the blurb on the dust jacket of Eagleton 2002.
3   Eagleton 2005c, p. vi.
4   Cf. Smith 2008, pp. 9–31 and Eagleton and Beaumont 2009, pp. 29–64.

himself has admitted is 'impossible to localize'.[5] Given that McCabe himself, in such works as *Law, Love and Language* (1968), combined the thought of Marx, Wittgenstein and Thomas Aquinas, one can well imagine the inherently eclectic nature of much of Eagleton's work at this time.

The opening chapters of *The Body as Language* are structured around the tragic Christian paradox of the *felix culpa* or 'happy Fall'. Unlike most animals, writes Eagleton, '[m]an ... is not passively trapped within the determining limits of his "species-life": language, by distancing and objectifying man's animal nature, allows him to enter into transformative relationship with it'.[6] For Eagleton, with the rise of linguistic consciousness, history and freedom are born. Yet this distancing and objectification which human language enables is at the same time the source of human destructiveness: 'Linguistic consciousness allows man to transcend the biological limits of his sensuous life, but the result is tragedy and violation'.[7] The problem is that the body for Eagleton is the source of authenticity, in that it is a solid, fleshly reminder of our in-built natural limits, those very limits which linguistic consciousness, by definition, transcends. If language enables us to overstep our natural bounds, the body reels us back in.[8]

It is this contradiction which is the source of what I take to be the central problematic of Eagleton's life's work: to aestheticise and somatise emancipatory discourse whilst leaving enough of a rational subject intact so as to enable political agency. From *The Body as Language*, through *The Ideology of the Aesthetic* (1990), all the way to his more recent *Trouble With Strangers* (2008), Eagleton seeks a resolution of the antitheses that open up in modernity (the Kantian tripartite architectonic stands as its allegory) between truth, morality and the body. In *The Body as Language*, an early work, this resolution is formulated in a relatively undeveloped manner: 'For the body to achieve the expressive flexibility and communicatory power of language, or for language to attain the permanent, sure, solid relationships possible to the body, would then be a healing of that dislocation inherent in the life of an animal constituted by both body and language, closed and open, bound and limited'.[9] What would such a 'healed' humanity look like? Eagleton gives two metaphorical

---

5 Eagleton 2003, 'Prefatory Note'.

6 Eagleton 1970, p. 3.

7 Eagleton 1970, p. 4.

8 This line of argument reappears constantly throughout Eagleton's oeuvre, usually accompanied by the same quotations from *Macbeth* and *King Lear*. See, for example, Eagleton 2003, pp. 140–207.

9 Eagleton 1970, pp. 6–7.

examples: the dance and the meal. In the former 'the form and structure of the community – the law of the dance – has been so fully interiorised by each member that each acts spontaneously in terms of the others – each acts *gracefully*',[10] whilst in the latter 'human interpersonal presence is mediated through, and in terms of, the material world of food and the body: these elements become, as it were, the language by which that human presence is given structure'.[11] These are early precursors to Eagleton's more recent metaphor of a healed humanity, which takes the form of a jazz band.[12] What each of these metaphorical resolutions conveys is the harmonious integration of spontaneous self-hood and community: body and language.

There are, however, two problems with this early work which continue to haunt Eagleton's project to this day. Firstly, all three metaphors of a healed humanity – the dance, the meal, the instrumental jazz band – are *non-verbal*. It will be recalled, in contrast, that one of Williams's primary concerns was the creation of a common *verbal language*, something which could not be achieved until the underlying contradictions of class society had been resolved *in practice*, precisely because language was nothing but the practical consciousness of those practices (albeit with a partial efficacy of its own). Until that happened, we would all to some extent be condemned to share the cleft tongue of a Thomas Hardy, torn between the cognitively and affectively opposed idioms of conflicting classes.[13] Eagleton's conception of language is thus too abstract and idealist (and this despite his constant citing of Wittgenstein that language is a 'form of life');[14] his concern for its bodily integration comes at the cost of his neglect of its internal historical and political contradictions. Whilst he is well aware that language is a way of being together, he nonetheless fails to link this insight to the political and historical analyses that feature elsewhere in his work.

This is then coupled with a second, perhaps even more serious problem. The source of the resolution between body and language in his early work is the resurrected Christ, whose eternal victory is ritually reenacted in the Eucharist:

---

10   Eagleton 1970, p. 9.
11   Eagleton 1970, p. 11.
12   Eagleton 2007c, pp. 99–100.
13   It is also worth noting, as Higgins has perceptively observed, that for all of Williams's admiration for German Expressionist cinema, one of his overriding reservations was that it was *silent*, 'achieved at the cost of a radical neglect of speech' (cited in Higgins 1999, p. 36).
14   See, for example, Eagleton 1986, pp. 99–130.

The bread and wine of the liturgy operate as a discursive language, like any other human product as sign: they are shared out, handled, exchanged, passed round, in a visible, concrete, durational interchange of symbols. But the eating of the bread is a participation in the body of Christ – a participation which, in Paul's thought, has all the direct, sensuous, dialectical quality of sexual knowledge: a communion of being established through a discursive communion of sign ... In the eucharist, then, that disjunction of sign and reality which I have argued to be endemic in human history is abolished ... The whole eucharistic action, incarnating within history the meaning of historical meaning, is a ceaseless returning of history onto its authentic reality, an insertion into the present of the pivotal event where past, present and future interlock.[15]

What for Williams had to be historically achieved – the integration of the immediacy of speech and the body with the abstract universalism of prose – has, for this Catholic Eagleton, always already been achieved by Christ's death and resurrection.[16] This proleptic, yet present, victory could even be seen as the source of the ambiguity which structures Eagleton's own style: he tries to reconcile a perennial political hope and self-righteousness (which Derrida once famously read as arrogance)[17] – an index of his Catholic faith that the divine has healed the human rift – with the quite patent fact that historically, if one takes a look around, this does not appear to be the case. Eagleton's work is then structured by syncopations between these two styles, which are also the verbal modes of two (sets of) temporalities: the hopeful and corporeal joyfulness associated with the (divine) comedy of Catholic eternity (the 'pivotal event where past, present and future interlock') and the more austere, secular temporalities of historical materialism. Taken together, his abstract conception of language and his ambiguous relation to Roman Catholicism are at the core of his problematic politics of style.

---

15   Eagleton 1970, pp. 29, 48–49.
16   Cf. McCabe 2003, p. 153: 'through the resurrection of Christ the future world is already with us as a disruptive force disturbing the order of the world'.
17   Having accused Eagleton of being a 'proprietary' Marxist, Derrida continues in uncharacteristically combative mode: 'One can only rub one's eyes in disbelief and wonder where he finds the inspiration, the haughtiness, the right. Has he learned nothing?' (2008, p. 222).

2   Leavis 2.0?

These metaphysical concerns directly inform Eagleton's ongoing attempts to revive the art of practical criticism. There is far more of an overlap between the predominantly literary works he has produced over the last 15 years (*The English Novel: An Introduction, How to Read a Poem, The Event of Literature, How to Read Literature*) and the more theological ones (*Sweet Violence, Holy Terror, Reason, Faith and Revolution,* and *On Evil*) than immediately meets the eye. The theological works began as an attempt to respond to a new post-9/11 political conjuncture – one in which 'terrorism itself is not political in any conventional sense of the term, and as such poses a challenge to the left's habitual modes of thought' –[18] by developing a 'tragic humanism' that 'shares liberal humanism's vision of the free flourishing of humanity … but … holds that this is possible only by confronting the very worst'.[19] The literary works respond to a new intellectual conjuncture in which attentiveness to the ideological implications of verbal texture has given way to an assortment of sophisticated modes of content analysis. Both sets of works, however, draw on the young Eagleton's Roman Catholic writings. The former elaborate on the tragic paradox of the happy Fall and develop the alarming claim that man must be dismembered in order to be renewed (thereby challenging secular conceptions of revolution, which are seen as simply not revolutionary enough)[20] whilst the latter draw on the concern with language and linguistic materiality as the proper of humanity. Here, I shall be concerned primarily with the latter, though, as we shall see, a possible contradiction between the imperatives of each soon comes into view.

It will be recalled from the first chapter that one of the reasons style became such an overdetermined category in the work of Williams and Eagleton was because of the tradition of 'practical criticism' or 'close reading' which they inherited from I.A. Richards and F.R. Leavis; any attempt to challenge the latter's institutional prestige would have to go by way of the now mythical

---

18   Eagleton 2005c, p. vi.

19   Eagleton 2009, pp. 168–9.

20   Cf. Eagleton 2007b: 'Was Jesus, then, a revolutionary? Not in any sense that Lenin or Trotsky would have recognised. But is this because he was less of a revolutionary than they were, or more so? Less, certainly, in that he did not advocate the overthrow of the power structure that he confronted. But this was, among other reasons, because he expected it to be soon swept away by a form of existence more perfected in its justice, peace, comradeship and exuberance of spirit than even Lenin and Trotsky could have imagined. Perhaps the answer, then, is not that Jesus was more or less a revolutionary, but that he was both more and less'.

'words on the page'. Eagleton, in perhaps his best-known work, provided a succinct critique of 'close reading':

> To call for close reading, in fact, is to do more than insist on due attentiveness to the text. It inescapably suggests an attention to *this* rather than to something else: to the 'words on the page' rather than to the contexts which produced and surround them ... [I]t encouraged the illusion that any piece of language, 'literary' or not, can be adequately studied or even understood in isolation. It was the beginnings of a 'reification' of the literary work, the treatment of it as an object in itself.[21]

It comes as somewhat of a surprise, then, to find Eagleton 25 years later apparently calling for a return to the very close reading he had once criticised:

> Literary criticism as I understood it and as the discipline in which I was trained – the close analysis, the alert, responsive analysis of literary works and language – is in many senses becoming a kind of moribund pursuit. And this is really very worrying because it works upon language which is part of the stuff we're made of. To encourage a sensitivity to the shiftingness and strategies of language I think is vital and that's what a literary education usefully did. I think that's much less so today in English courses and literary courses.[22]

How to explain this apparent discrepancy? Is there some larger context within which one can demonstrate that what appears to be a contradiction between the middle and late Eagleton is in fact nothing of the kind? Or has Eagleton's conception of literature become nothing but Leavis 2.0? The truth, I suspect, lies somewhere in between.

Firstly, we must recall the strategic importance of rhetoric for Eagleton's conception of a political criticism. He first made the case for an affinity between Marxist criticism and rhetoric in 1981. What classical rhetoric provided was a fusion of what Eagleton takes to be the two traditional functions of the critic: sensitivity to literary form and political critique.[23] 'The point of studying liter-

---

21 Eagleton 1996, p. 38.

22 Eagleton 2012. Cf. Eagleton and Beaumont 2009, p. 293: 'Criticism investigates the thickness and intricacy of the medium in which we come into our own as subjects: language'.

23 Eagleton reiterates this dual function in several places: Eagleton 1981, pp. 101–2; Eagleton 1985; Eagleton 1996, pp. 179–80; Eagleton 2007a, p. 16; Eagleton and Beaumont 2009, pp. 179–80.

ary felicities and stylistic devices', he writes, 'was to train oneself to use them effectively in one's own ideological practice ... Textual "beauties" were not first of all to be aesthetically savoured; they were ideological weapons whose practical deployment was to be learnt'.[24] Not only does rhetoric include and transcend Leaviste 'scrutiny', but it also offers a solution to the principal modern problem with which Eagleton is constantly concerned: it de-aestheticises the aesthetic, reinscribing it into a field of shifting political forces, whilst simultaneously retaining a literary sensitivity to style. Significantly, however, Eagleton's call for a return to rhetoric bypasses that other ancient discipline with which it was closely associated: poetics. He mentions it only in passing: 'If "poetics" was dedicated to the "beauties" of certain fictional uses of language, rhetoric subsumed such discussion in a transdiscursive gesture, indifferently engaged with the written and spoken, text and practice, "poetic" and "factual"'.[25] The rub, of course, is what exactly 'transdiscursive' might mean in this context. If the horizon of rhetoric is 'nothing less than the field of discursive practices as a whole',[26] then the peculiarity of the *literariness* of literary discourse is in danger of being 'subsumed' out of existence. Indeed, it is precisely because Eagleton disregarded poetics for rhetoric (not to mention misrepresenting it)[27] that he was forced, later in his career, to return to the precise nature of the literary in such works as *The Event of Literature* (2012).[28] This is one of many symptoms that Eagleton has never entirely managed to fuse what one might call his intra- and meta-critical ambitions: nuanced literary readings with direct political intervention. Seen from this angle, the return to Leavisite sensitivity to literary style is not so much a regression as an attempt to undo some of the problems which his resorting to an all-subsuming rhetoric produced in the first place.

Secondly, having noted that Eagleton was heavily influenced by the work of Herbert McCabe, it is perhaps worth indicating that there are two aspects of this influence that tend to be overlooked. For McCabe, 'ethics is the study of human behaviour in so far as it is a piece of communication, in so far as it says something or fails to say something'.[29] Ethics for McCabe is thus *paral-*

---

24   Eagleton 1981, pp. 101–2.
25   Eagleton 1981, pp. 102–3.
26   Eagleton 1996, p. 179.
27   Given the importance Aristotle attributes to *muthos* – at the direct expense of verse-form and *lexis* – it is, to say the least, problematic to reduce the *Poetics* to 'the "beauties" of certain fictional uses of language'.
28   This is one of the reasons I am attempting to develop a Marxist *poetics* rather than a Marxist rhetoric.
29   McCabe 2003, p. 92.

lel' to literary criticism;[30] it is not a matter of classifying deeds or intentions as good or bad, but a never-ending search for the deeper meaning of a human act, and in this it shares the same open-endedness as literary criticism itself. Eagleton's return to literary criticism is thus, from this perspective, inseparable from his recent investigations of ethics more generally. (It was McCabe, after all, who once wrote: 'In a piece of bad writing a man has not lived into his medium').[31] Moreover, the usual narrative which is recounted regarding Eagleton's relationships with McCabe and Williams is that, broadly speaking, the former was responsible for his theology and the latter for his first forays into literary and cultural theory.[32] On closer inspection, however, this is not strictly true. McCabe's conception of language and literature betrays an elective affinity with the work of Williams. When, for example, he rejects the existence of 'mankind' as a concept because it 'does not yet exist',[33] he develops his argument thus: 'Mankind does not form a single linguistic community and this implies a defect of human communication not only in extension but also in intensity'[34] – a possible reiteration of Williams's social reinterpretation of I.A. Richards's individualist and psychologistic understanding of miscommunication. Likewise, McCabe writes of literary composition that '[t]he poet discovers in his experience ... new forms of communication which he can offer to the larger community who use the language. Such an offer may be accepted or rejected as meaningless'.[35] This argument is surprisingly similar to Williams's understanding of communication, as set out in the first chapter of *The Long Revolution*, which was published seven years prior to McCabe's own book.[36] Eagleton's return to close reading is thus bound up with McCabe's correlation of ethics and literary criticism, which was itself potentially influenced by Williams's early understanding of communication. Significantly, however, Eagleton does not reproduce from their work the sense of the historical effort required to *produce* a single humanity that shares a 'common language' in the broadest

---

30   McCabe 2003, p. 94.
31   McCabe 2003, p. 100.
32   The exception to this rule is James Smith (2008, p. 30) who recognises in Eagleton's jocular style the influence of McCabe's ludic turns of phrase.
33   McCabe 2003, p. 98.
34   McCabe 2003, pp. 98–9.
35   McCabe 2003, pp. 89–90.
36   Cf. Williams 1965, p. 49: 'The "creative" act, of any artist, is in any case the process of making a meaning active, by communicating an organized experience to others. We have to see the process as one of many meanings being offered, by particular means, and only some of these meanings being received'.

sense of that term. He lacks their politically vital implication that good style is, at root, good social relations, and that you cannot have one without the other.

This failure to inherit the political imperatives of Williams's writing on style is then compounded by a return in his recent work to a barely disguised Leavisite explanation of the relation between language and (post)modernity. As we saw in the previous chapter, *Scrutiny* claimed that as a result of modern 'industrialism' language itself had undergone a degradation, one which had quite literally sapped it of its expressive capacities. Literature for Leavis was one of the few places where 'life' and language could still be fused in all their primal vitality; close reading was then the activity by which one accessed this soothing balm in the midst of the desiccated condition of contemporary language. It should thus be seen as symptomatic when Eagleton pens such phrases as this:

> Close reading for Nietzsche is a critique of modernity. To attend to the feel and form of words is to refuse to treat them in a purely instrumental way, and thus to refuse a world in which language is worn to a paperlike thinness by commerce and bureaucracy. The Nietzschean Superman is not an e-mail user ... What threatens to scupper verbal sensitivity is the depthless, commodified, instantly legible world of advanced capitalism, with its unscrupulous way with signs, computerised communication and glossy packaging of 'experience'.[37]

The point is not that this observation is wrong, but that there is nothing intrinsically Marxist about it: as one perceptive interviewer put it, 'someone like ... Geoffrey Hill would agree with lots of what [Eagleton is] saying, but is an Anglican Tory'.[38] The real problem is the type of politics it implies. It is obvious that any coherent Marxist stance will include a certain will to deinstrumentalise language – an element of autotelic linguistic joy –[39] but if it is incapable of integrating this stance into a broader, more contemporary and creative inter-

---

37   Eagleton 2007a, pp. 10, 17.
38   Eagleton, Barker and Niven 2012. Eagleton responded: 'But of course what one shares with someone like Hill there is rather formal: an agreement for a certain procedural way of reading. But then all the differences start. All the differences about the point of this, its place within culture'.
39   For a sophisticated defence of aesthetic autonomy – defined as 'the struggle to develop and secure the means for articulations of creativity that are separable from capital in some authentic measure' – as part of a Marxist critique of the neoliberalisation of the university system, see Brouillette 2013.

Micro-structures of feeling

vention into the present historical conjuncture, it is in danger of resorting to a conservative nostalgia and organicism which the Althusserian Eagleton would have rejected as the purest compensatory ideology.[40] The key difference between Eagleton on the one hand and Williams and Jameson on the other is that the latter are characterised by a constant openness to literary, linguistic and technological innovation, whereas the former, despite his penchant for the revolutionary avant-garde, has become a traditionalist – and not always in the progressive sense by which he understands that term.[41]

My criticism of Eagleton's project to resurrect close reading should not, however, be taken as an outright rejection of its relevance for a Marxist poetics. On the contrary, one of the original impetuses of this book was precisely to take account of the problem which Eagleton has indicated: the current predominance, within the fields of cultural and literary studies, of politically informed content analysis at the expense of critical attention to style and form.[42] But where Eagleton sees both artful stylistic composition and close reading as in and of themselves acts of political critique,[43] and therefore as *primary*, I see sensitivity to verbal texture as simply one, initial element of a political criticism. These micro-structures of feeling must be connected, in any careful analysis, to the other literary elements which inform and limit them: generic, formal and narratological. These elements act as mediating categories between text and history, verbal texture and political conjuncture.

Furthermore, whilst it is crucial for any materialist theory of style to recognise and account for that element of joy that we experience in the reading and writing of verbally inventive literature, I suspect that the specific quality of that joy is historically variable, depending on the range of linguistic-affective needs and expectations in existence and on their relative levels of satisfaction. A Marxist poetics would historically situate the specific quality of that joy whilst refusing to cede the subjective excitements it elicits to those critics who claim them as an unchanging feature of literature and human life alike.

---

40   I write this in full recognition of the potentially politically progressive functions which nostalgia may have elsewhere, as Eagleton – via Walter Benjamin – often reminds us.

41   For the 'revolutionary' conception of tradition see Eagleton 1981, Chapter 3.

42   I take it that the so-called 'new formalism' is motivated by similar concerns, albeit comprising a range of political and theoretical positions.

43   Cf. '[T]he emergence of an art-form concerned simply with registering the world in its rich integrity of being is itself a political event' (Eagleton 1970, 22, n. 4).

3   The Close Reading of Styles

I now wish to demonstrate some of the problems with the practical results of the close readings Eagleton performs. Only then will the weaknesses of his conception of style become clear in practice, rather than in theory. The following passage is indicative of what Eagleton takes to be the perfect fusion of attention to style and political critique:

> You can tell that George Eliot is a liberal by the shape of her sentences. Whereas Dickens's prose is declamatory and impressionistic, Eliot's sentences unroll like undulating hills, full of wry asides and scrupulously qualifying sub-clauses. There is an equipoise and authority about her prose style which is very far from the panache and hyperbole of a Dickens ... Her writing is mellow yet incisive ... This is not an author who is likely to be impulsive or one-sided.[44]

Eagleton proceeds to extrapolate from these observations an entire moral ideology: Eliot's 'supple, coolly rational prose style' is the index of her liberal conviction that egoism is the worst that can beset mankind and that its cure is imagination, which 'allows us to rise above our own interests and feel our way sympathetically into the lives of others'.[45] Eagleton's method here is threefold: firstly, he has (presumably) selected passages of Eliot's prose for close analysis, noting the syntactical, rhythmic and tonal peculiarities of her style; secondly, he has correlated those stylistic features with a moral outlook (e.g., the 'scrupulously qualifying sub-clauses' correspond to a writer who is attentive to individual differences and who avoids abstract stereotypes or hyperbole); finally, he configures these correlations such that the style and the moral outlook can be seen as part of a larger political ideology: in this case, liberalism. The power of this analysis is undeniable, since it does exactly what Eagleton claims all good criticism should do: it attunes itself to the unique verbal textures of the writing and uses these as an entry point into the implicit politics of the style.

The most striking difference between the respective approaches of Williams and Eagleton to the analysis of prose, however, is that where Williams was concerned with what we have come to know, via Bakhtin, as dialogism – the hierarchised interrelation of multiple idioms and intentions within a work

---

44   Eagleton 2005a, p. 163.
45   Ibid.

of prose fiction – Eagleton focuses almost exclusively on the monological, narratorial idiom – what, following Walsh, I have chosen to call diegesis.[46] The immediate upshot of this is that Eagleton is a far superior 'close reader' than Williams; indeed, I would go as far as to say that Eagleton is one of the great close readers of our age. This is a result, not only of his well-honed ear for verbal nuance, but also of his capacity to transform this aural sensitivity into perfectly articulated verbal descriptions. Yet the supreme skill with which he reads serves only to emphasise how limited close reading as a practice really is. For it fails the basic test that Bakhtin set literary scholars in the first half of the twentieth century when he criticised traditional stylistics for having failed to grasp the constitutively polyphonic nature of the novel:

> All attempts at concrete stylistic analysis of novelistic prose either strayed into linguistic descriptions of the language of a given novelist or else limited themselves to those separate, isolated stylistic elements of the novel that were includable (or gave the appearance of being includable) in the traditional categories of stylistics. In both instances the stylistic whole of the novel and of novelistic discourse eluded the investigator.[47]

By treating style in prose fiction as simply a matter of diegesis (the author's style under the regime of fictionality) Eagleton, in practice, overlooks its inherently threefold relational nature: as a linguistic mode of social relation between the author and the (perceived) reader, as the artistically organised totality of inter-relating sub-styles (level 3 of my working definition of style in Chapter 4), and as one of several formal elements which constitute the formal constellation of each and every literary work (as we saw in the previous chapter on drama). This is somewhat ironic since the recognition that verbal elaboration is informed and internally limited by the structural and formal elements of a literary text is the equivalent in the literary realm of the *social* recognition – which Eagleton constantly stresses – that the individual exists in his or her full individuality only by virtue of certain institutional structures, and not despite them. Like the social individual, the freedom of the individual sentence depends upon the formal, generic and narratological structures by which it is informed. (If this analogy with the *polis* seems out of place, the reader should recall that Aris-totle himself thought *lexis* via analogy with the structural relations of the Greek

---

46   See Chapter 4.
47   Bakhtin 1981, p. 261.

(city state:[48] the republic of letters has always understood itself using metaphors drawn from the political republic *tout court*.)

This is by no means to suggest that when it comes to truly polyphonic works of literature Eagleton has nothing to offer. He consistently recognises instances of significant polyphony, usually even celebrating them,[49] but his non-systematic criticism, unlike that of Williams and Bakhtin, is incapable of building a coherent theory of style which does not see polyphonic prose texts as somehow exceptional. Take this passage on Joyce, for example:

> What ... is James Joyce's style? The question is almost impossible to answer, as it is not in the case of Jane Austen or William Faulkner. *Dubliners* is less a plain style than a parody of a plain style . *Ulysses* includes tabloid journalism, metaphysical reflection, interior monologue, catechism, mock-heroic, scientific jargon, women's magazines, pastiches of English literature ... Joyce's writing reflects a linguistically unstable situation, not just in Ireland but in a newly cosmopolitanized world in which it is less and less obvious that there is a master or a mother tongue ... Words are shot through with other words, one style is bounced off another, one language folded within a second.[50]

The reason Eagleton cannot answer the question he poses at the outset is because his conception of style is fundamentally monological and non-relational. Whilst he makes some genuinely insightful comments on the linguistic situation in Ireland and advanced capitalist societies more generally,[51] and on the ways in which these affect literary style, he nowhere develops these insights with systematic rigour. He hints at Jameson's thesis that postmodernism spells the end of style, but never pursues it. Were we to offer a provisional reading of Joyce's style in *Ulysses* based on the working definition of style in prose fiction in Chapter 4, however, we might say that it is less a matter of diegesis than of the ambiguous relation between, on the one hand, the vast multiplicity of English idioms which are parodied (level 2 of my definition) and, on the other, the total configurational unity of these sub-ensembles (level 3). For the mastery of Joyce's overall configurational unity has no diegetic, idiomatic equivalent; it is a collage-like orchestration of a series of carefully crafted idiomatic parodies, but ones whose uncanny accuracy betrays a keen attentiveness to their verbal

---

48   See Chapter 2.
49   Eagleton 2007d.
50   Eagleton 2005a, p. 188.
51   Albeit ones that draw silently on Jameson 2007 (pp. 137–206) and Williams 2007.

nuance. This produces a triangulated ambivalence – between an absence of a controlling diegetic idiom, an almost loving sensitivity to that which is parod- ied, and yet a defiant will to master the totality of English idioms – which could be read as Joyce's attempt to negotiate his position as a British colonial subject, as someone who is at once both inside and outside, for and against English high culture.[52]

It is not that Eagleton is unaware of such ambiguities; it is that his theory of style, such as it is, cannot coherently accommodate them. Thus, whilst close reading as Eagleton understands and practises it will be a vital aspect of any self-respecting theory of style, it must be coupled with the threefold relational theory of style summarised above and a more elaborate set of concepts for thinking the relation between what I shall call the 'linguistic situation' of a writer (see part III) and the literary texts she is able to produce.

4   The Problems of Stylistic Ideals

The contradictions in Eagleton's position extend to his implicit and explicit stylistic ideal. It will be recalled that for the young Eagleton, the metaphysical and historical apotheosis he sought was for 'the body to achieve the express- ive flexibility and communicatory power of language, or for language to attain the permanent, sure, solid relationships possible to the body'.[53] It is this same metaphysical ideal which constitutes the central criterion of his critical evalu- ations of literary styles. It also has a political element, as is evident in his great essay on Hazlitt's prose:

> Forms of eloquence which violate the concrete breed political deception, swaddling the facts in distracting fancy ... But at the same time ... Hazlitt rejects those forms of pragmatism which cling cravenly to the 'real'; and it is in this dialectic that the true power of his radicalism lies. What renders his political case so forceful is its fusion of a reverence for the specific with an adherence to the necessarily abstract.[54]

Translated into the literary realm, this becomes an ideal of aesthetic harmony between the word and that which it represents, a playful revelling in the mater-

---

52   I draw here on Gaipa 1995, though I have rearticulated and supplemented his argument to suit my own critical vocabulary.

53   Eagleton 1970, pp. 6–7.

54   Eagleton 1973, p. 113.

iality of language but one which is internally limited by a cool-headed fidelity to that which it describes or narrates: 'the finest English novels manage to combine a convincing representation of the world with a verbal virtuosity which is neither too sparse nor too self-regarding'.[55] All three aspects – the theological, the political and the literary – are permutations of the abovementioned central problematic of Eagleton's oeuvre: the limited aestheticisation of reason.

   The relation to style is nowhere clearer than in his latest introductory work, *How to Read Literature* (2013).[56] The final chapter, entitled 'Value', deals with the problem of what counts as good or great literature. It was a problem Eagleton originally dealt with in a much different manner in *Criticism and Ideology*.[57] What interests me here, however, is both the implicit stylistic ideal by which he has come to judge literary styles and the problems it poses, not only for a Marxist poetics, but also for a coherent theory of literary value. Having demonstrated the problems with each of the usual modes of evaluating literary quality, Eagleton goes on to '[analyse] some literary extracts with an eye to how well they do'.[58] In total, he analyses seven excerpts of prose fiction and three poetic extracts (I shall focus here on the prose).[59] Four of the excerpts are predominantly descriptive in mode; one (by Shields) is analytic or philosophical; and two (by Nabokov) are predominantly narrative in nature. Only one of them includes speech. This is significant, firstly, because Eagleton has chosen to focus on diegesis at the expense of the multiplicity of idioms which are characteristic of the novel more generally and, secondly, because description is a structural feature of narratives which often acts as the motivation for various degrees of verbal elaboration.[60] That is, he has focused predominantly on those moments in prose fiction when the practical subordination of verbal texture to narrative action is momentarily relaxed, giving style free rein. By either masking

---

55   Eagleton 2005a, p. 21.

56   This is not one of Eagleton's strongest works. It includes no footnotes, no bibliography, and no attempt to systematise his insights or to link them to his previous work in a coherent manner. It features a chapter on narrative that fails to mention narratology, and suffers from a general scholarly laxness saved only by occasional brilliant close readings of individual sentences.

57   Eagleton 1976, pp. 162–87.

58   Eagleton 2013, p. 193.

59   Written by the following authors, from some of whom more than one extract is taken: John Updike, Evelyn Waugh, William Faulkner, Vladimir Nabokov, Carol Shields (all prose); Swinburne, Amy Lowell, and William McGonagall (all poetry).

60   Cf. Hamon 2004.

or simply ignoring the partiality of these selections, it is difficult to see how Eagleton could build a convincing picture of stylistic virtue based on them alone.

But this he tries to do, and he enlists a whole array of problematic adjectives in support. There is no real middle ground here. Bad writing is: too calculated; too clever; too *voulu*; artful but lifeless; it consists of language which draws too much attention to itself and its own cleverness; self-consciously fine writing; it is contrived (which seems to mean that it is essentially *reified*); and it is writing which tries to appear artless but does not quite manage it.[61] Good writing, by contrast, is: spontaneous; it draws no excessive attention to itself; it is crisp and pure; it is economical and every word pulls its weight; it is quietly efficient; it is honest; it possesses tact and reticence; if it is self-consciously 'literary', it is nonetheless *playfully* so; and it gives the object its due.[62] In short, the later Eagleton's literary stylistic ideal is a mixture of the efficient bourgeois, the roguish aristocrat, and the Victorian child who should be seen and not heard. We have come a long way from the critic who once wrote: 'It is not a question of whether Hardy wrote "well" or "badly"; it is rather a question of the ideological disarray that his fictions, consciously or not, are bound to produce within a criticism implacably committed to the "literary" as a yardstick of maturely civilized consciousness'.[63] Not that we should simply disregard Eagleton's pronouncements. As we saw above with respect to Joyce, the ideal of stylistic excellence which Eagleton develops in *How to Read Literature* does not in fact faithfully represent his own published evaluations of many literary works. His myriad literary reviews in *The Guardian* and the *London Review of Books* show that his real delight lies precisely in those works that combine moral and metaphysical seriousness, tragedy, comedy and excessive verbal virtuosity (not to mention his basic bias for Irish authors, most of whom just happen to combine all of these virtues).[64]

The real problem is that, as the Eagleton of *Criticism and Ideology* was well aware, any absolute aesthetic ideal runs the risk of becoming abstract and ahistorical. The above logic, for example, simply cannot accommodate Williams's crucial historical insight that those writers who responded most deeply to the fundamentally unsettled life of the nineteenth century 'had no unified form, no unity of tone and language, no controlling conventions, that really answered

---

61   Eagleton 2013, pp. 193–6.
62   Eagleton 2013, pp. 193–204.
63   Eagleton 1981, p. 129.
64   See, for example, Eagleton 2007d.

their purposes'.[65] For such an insight requires at least a minimally historicist logic, one which recognises that the criteria of aesthetic judgment are historically and contextually variable, and thus that our own judgements must be inherently self-reflexive. Here the split we noted earlier between the two styles and their concomitant temporalities which structure Eagleton's work – the Catholic-hopeful and the duty-bound historical materialist – return with a vengeance. For the Catholic Eagleton upholds the eternal truth of the Incarnation, the Crucifixion and the Resurrection, all of which are celebrated in the Eucharist, which is a sacramental form of the stylistic ideal he propounds: body and language, affect and cognition, materiality and spirituality harmoniously fused. The Marxist Eagleton, by contrast, even the Althusserian avatar for whom 'science' possesses its own speculative temporality, must hold that literary value, if it exists at all, 'is the function of a particular process of textual production which is itself a sustained relation (overdetermined by the ideological sub-ensemble with which the texts are held) to ... an ideological formation'.[66] This contradiction is never resolved. Not that this is entirely negative: it is often the source of some of Eagleton's most original insights, the two discourses – the divine and the secular – striking off one another to produce brilliant sparks. But when it comes to style, that topic to which Eagleton so frequently returns, one simply cannot have one's cake and eat it. There comes a moment when the drive practically to bring about a 'common language' is simply incompatible with a divine assurance that it has already been achieved.

5   Tragic Styles

This contradiction takes on a wholly different form in Eagleton's recent theological and metaphysical work. If I earlier stressed the overlap between this body of work and the neo-Leavisite texts calling for the resurrection of close reading, I now wish to demonstrate one important way in which they differ. For the deafening silence that resounds throughout such works as the stunning *Sweet Violence* or *Holy Terror* is precisely the voice of the Eagleton for whom formal and stylistic analysis must be renewed. One of the characteristic traits of this work, aptly dubbed 'encyclopaedic' by Roland Boer,[67] is what the latter calls 'a perpetual gliding from one reference to another'.[68] The mode of argu-

---

65   Williams 1970, p. 85.
66   Eagleton 1976, p. 185.
67   Boer 2007, pp. 278–82.
68   Boer 2007, p. 281.

mentation is one of quantity rather than quality, accumulation of quotations rather than judicious selection. Boer even reads this as an example of Eagleton's 'catholicity' in the strict sense: 'seeing the hand of God in the most unlikely of places'.[69] But what is striking about the majority (though not all) of his literary references is that they entirely eschew stylistic and formal analysis, abstracting the themes, moral lessons or suggestive *aperçus* and incorporating them into the collage of his own sprawling argument.[70]

It is worth remarking in passing, however, that the principle behind this (if not the precise method) is not entirely unusual in the tradition here under discussion. Unlike the German *Literaturwissenschaften*, though akin to the more radical strains of the French *critique littéraire* (from Sartre to Derrida), the British tradition of literary criticism is characterised by a mode of argumentation which is not purely analytic or explicatory. It does not always assume as its sole task the critical analysis or explanation of literary works, but draws on the contents – and occasionally the forms and styles – of such works in the elaboration of a broader moral or political argument. This was very much the point Eagleton tried to make in *The Function of Criticism*:[71] that those literary-critical conservatives who called for attention to the text alone, rather than to its broader moral or political implications, were in fact the upstarts, whereas the radicals were the true conservatives, upholding a critical tradition which began with Addison, Steele and Johnson.

Nonetheless, *Sweet Violence* and the works which follow from it give this generic attribute a quite specific valence. In one sense these works are a continuation of Eagleton's ongoing research programme, which aims to develop a non-historicist but nonetheless politically radical materialism. He writes:

> Materialism is concerned with the sudden shock of political conjunctures, dramatic shifts in the balance of political forces ... But a genuine materialism, as opposed to an historicist relativism or idealism, is also attentive to those aspects of our existence which are permanent structures of our species-being.[72]

Against those adherents of the immediate political conjuncture, Eagleton is arguing for the recognition of the biological and innate features of humanity

---

69   Boer 2007, p. 282.

70   The major exception to the rule is the brilliant chapter on 'Tragedy and the Novel', in Eagleton 2002, pp. 178–202.

71   Eagleton 2005b.

72   Eagleton 2002, p. xii.

whose scope is that of the *longue durée*. Yet, in *Holy Terror*, his justification of this metaphysical turn (as we saw above) is nothing if not conjunctural:

> ... terrorism itself is not political in any conventional sense of the term, and as such poses a challenge to the left's habitual modes of thought. The left is at home with imperial power and guerrilla warfare, but embarrassed on the whole by the thought of death, evil, sacrifice, or the sublime. Yet these and allied notions, I believe, are quite as germane to the ideology of terror as more mundane or material conceptions.[73]

So we are faced with the curious situation of an *intra-conjunctural* justification for attending to the *non-conjunctural* (or *trans-conjunctural*) permanent elements of our species-being.

Terrorism aside, however, one might well ask whether this return to metaphysics is really all that different from Eagleton's early Catholic theology. According to James Smith, there is one crucial difference:

> ... [the early] Eagleton's writing was aimed towards a direct and specific political conjecture [*sic*]: the state of the Catholic Church, as it went through a time of fundamental structural and political change, and an overall political culture in which progressive politics was in the ascendancy. Eagleton's interventions at this point thus had a clear and manifest political aim, that being forging a direct link between the discourse of the Catholic Left and that of the wider New Left, and his work had a defined audience, stemming from the *Slant* groups ... [I]t was a discourse that intersected with an already existing counter-public sphere. In this second incarnation, however, when such a specific counter-public sphere is manifestly lacking, the question is as to whether this metaphysical discourse ... will inform a similar mode of practical politics ... or whether it will only serve to further sever cultural theory from interventionist institutional debates.[74]

Roland Boer makes the remarkable suggestion that Eagleton's borderline repression of the politically charged context of his early theology – the way in which his metaphysical musings suddenly emerge in *Sweet Violence* as if *ex nihilo* – has resulted in his increasingly prominent use of the notion of autotel-

73   Eagleton 2005c, p. vi.
74   Smith 2008, p. 154.

ism (poetry as an end in itself, evil as an end in itself, Creation as inherently useless, love as autotelic, or the virtuous life as intrinsically worthwhile).[75] If theology is, in one sense, nothing but the ideology of the Church, then it bears within it traces of the institutional history and internal struggles of that collective body; by disembedding his earlier theology from its fractious post-Vatican II context, Eagleton idealises it – in the precise sense that he *celestialises* it, rendering it transcendent of the terrestrial struggles from which it emerged.

Yet what does this have to do with the relative absence of stylistic and formal analysis in the metaphysical works? We must recall that one of Eagleton's major aims is to remind the Left that '*longues durées* are quite as much a part of human history as pastoral verse or parliaments'.[76] We must then correlate this with Eagleton's claims for the importance of formal analysis: 'It was Roland Barthes who remarked that to push form all the way through is to emerge into the domain of the historical ... Form always comes saturated in historical and ideological content, and historical or political content is always already formed, shaped, significantly organized, before either the artist or the critic comes to lay their hands on it'.[77] Given that both of these quotations, in their own way, claim a unique mode of access to history, one would expect to find them combined in those metaphysical works which see themselves as important interventions into the current historical conjuncture. But we do not, and the very fact that we do not is a symptom of their incipient idealism: by extracting the morals, themes, and *aperçus* from the formal and stylistic matrices in which they are embedded, Eagleton removes them from precisely that 'historical and ideological content' it was the supposed aim of formal analysis to locate. Just as the later Eagleton conceals the intra-ecclesiastical battles from which his theology emerged, so he predominantly extracts the literary supports for his theological insights from their formal and ideological contexts. Their transcendence of specific historical conjunctures is then perhaps an index of the absent counterpublic sphere to which they are addressed.

Another way of articulating this problem is to say that Eagleton's conception of tragedy is non-immanent: it fails to dwell (im*manere*) within (*im*manere) the historical situation. This was not a problem for the early Eagleton since at this point there was a mediator between the transcendent and the immanent: Jesus Christ himself. The crucial passage from *The Body as Language*, which at once

---

75   Boer 2007, pp. 324–33.

76   Eagleton 2002, p. 12.

77   Eagleton and Beaumont 2009, pp. 295–6.

agrees and breaks with the immanent conception of tragedy found in Raymond Williams's *Modern Tragedy*, is the following:

> It *must* be true that irredeemable, local and personal breakdown is genuinely tragic, and it *must* be true that tragedy can be overcome. To deny either proposition is at the deepest level unthinkable, as *Modern Tragedy* brilliantly shows. But it is only by the self-transcendence of history itself that the *either/or* of this tragic contradiction can be converted into a *both/and*. The Jesus who confronted and conquered tragedy in the world-historical action of the cross was also the Jesus who wept over the death of an historically insignificant friend; it is only in the kingdom of heaven ... that the redemptive power of that first tragic action will penetrate the darkness of the second with its own victory.[78]

By the time of *Sweet Violence* the religious certainty of this victory has disappeared.[79] Without it, and without its crucial mediatory function, Eagleton's entire argumentative apparatus is condemned to hover at the level of the impossible *either/or*. This is not to deny the power of his 'tragic humanism' – on the contrary, it is an incredibly compelling ethico-political vision – but it is certainly to suggest that one cannot continue to propagate Catholic ideas when the animating heart of those ideas – Jesus Christ – has been demoted to simply 'one of many tragic scapegoats'.[80] This may well be the case, of course, but there is then an obvious disjunction between an argument whose crux is the Resurrection – the victory of divine love – and a superficially identical argument for which that crux is no longer held to be actual. Eagleton's political theology of style hovers on the brink of that spectral actuality.

This, then, is the final break that began as a hairline fracture, splitting Eagleton off from Williams: the absence of an emphasis on the historical effort required to *produce* a single humanity that shares a 'common language' in the broadest sense of the term. This, according to Williams, was the conception of language of those avant-gardists who were modernist in both theory and practice, who were willing to '[engage] with received forms and possibilities of new practice' and to '[treat] language as material in a social process'.[81] It was this same insight which linked Williams's social-formalist understanding

---

78   Eagleton 1970, p. 113.
79   James Smith, whose work drew my attention to this passage, makes a similar observation: Smith 2008, pp. 149–50.
80   Eagleton 2002, p. 283.
81   Eagleton 2007, p. 77.

of revolution as the modern incarnation of tragedy – 'The tragic action, in its deepest sense, is not the confirmation of disorder, but its experience, its comprehension, and its resolution. In our time, this action is general, and its common name is revolution' –[82] to his drive towards the production of new forms that would embody new social relations. If it was Eagleton who originally penned the provocative phrase 'the politics of style', I suspect it was Williams who most fully developed the true range of its implications.

---

82   Williams 1979, p. 84.

CHAPTER 7

Fredric Jameson: Epic Poet of Postmodernity

Like a jazzman riffing on a phrase, Jameson's work consists of variations on a broad but fixed range of topics: narrative, the problem of periodisation, representations of totality, mediation, figuration, Utopia, the ideology of form, the visual, and space – to name but the principal ones. Central to the constellation of Jamesonian themes, connecting almost all of them simultaneously, is the rise and fall of style as a dominant literary category. The methodological importance of style for Jameson's theories of modernism and postmodernism cannot be overstated: without it he could not have developed those theories.

1   Narrative and Praxis

No account of Jameson's theory of style can avoid a preliminary reckoning with his conception of narrative. In the wake of Jean-François Lyotard's *The Postmodern Condition* (1979), Marxism came to be seen as a 'grand narrative': an overarching story through which the totality of smaller narratives and conflicts of human history could be understood. The irony of this was that, until Jameson, few Marxists had ever made any grand claims about Marxism as a narrative: it was generally taken to be an analytic.[1] Yet, for Jameson, Marxism is only *possible* if narrative as such is possible. To understand why this is so, we must first reconstruct Jameson's unique understanding of narrative.

If he has always drawn heavily on structuralist narratology, his conception of narrative has little in common with prevailing narratological theory.[2] Where the latter defines the elements of narrative as situatedness, event-sequencing, worldmaking/ world disruption and experientiality,[3] Jameson's implicit definition has far more in common with Aristotle's notion of *muthos* as 'the organization of the events' [*è tōn pragmatōn sustasis*] which is the 'soul' of tragedy, this latter itself an 'imitation of action' [*mimēsis praxeōs*] whose correlate is human praxis as such. For Aristotle, praxis has a narrative structure: it is a

---

1 Anderson 1998, pp. 53–4. Anderson's claim that *no* Marxists had ever made grand claims regarding Marxism as a narrative is dubious when one considers such works as Engels's *Dialectics of Nature*.
2 I take David Herman's *Basic Elements of Narrative* (2008) to constitute a *summa* of this theory.
3 Herman 2008, p. xvi.

temporal process which passes from a beginning, through a middle, towards an end or 'limit' [*peras*]. Given this immanent relation between narrative and praxis – always hinted at by Jameson, but never categorically stated – it is clear that narrative in Jameson's work, as in that of Lukács,[4] is neither a type of object or text nor a genre: it is a mode of apprehending the world.[5] It is that mode of mimetic activity capable of transposing the processual, practical nature of social reality into the immanent totality of a finished work, be it fictional or non-fictional. Unlike Lukács, however, for whom narrative and its principal generic mode, realism, became an ahistorical categorical imperative, Jameson recognises that this mode of apprehending reality is not always historically possible. There are two factors which can diminish reality's innate narratability: in the economic sphere – rationalisation, reification and commodification; and in the political sphere – the experience of subalternity. With the increasing rationalisation and commodification of social reality, the world becomes reified, a shimmering field of surfaces whose origins in human praxis have become masked. Such reified reality is impervious to the narrative mode of apprehension precisely because the temporal and narrative structure of praxis has been concealed from view. At the same time, there are also distinct political factors which produce denarrativisation: political subjection has the effect of disintegrating the time of praxis, of disaggregating the link between past, present and future necessary to any narration:

> The narrative time of epic is ... the time of the project: it is in other words the time of the victors, and the temporality of their history and their worldview. Epic is therefore very precisely the generic expression of empire and imperialism, understood as the intent and project of overcoming and subduing other groups ... But who are the subjects of those anti-narrative and anti-epic tendencies? They are ... the losers in this imperial triumph ... '[R]omance' somehow expresses the experience of defeat, a shattering experience that annuls historical teleology: it is an end of history which is an end of narrative as well.[6]

---

4   See, in particular, Lukács's essay 'Narrate or Describe?' in Lukács 1970, pp. 110–48.
5   In this sense, Jameson shares with the modernists that sense of art and literature 'not as a commodity to be consumed by a public and in a pinch to change and modify its views or actions, but rather as a vehicle for revealing new zones of being and for churning up the sedimented levels of the world itself, whether social or natural' (Jameson 1992, p. 164).
6   Jameson 2009, p. 556.

If you can narrate, you have either won or have given yourself a fighting chance. If you can't, you've lost.

The upshot of this expansive conception of narrative is Jameson's almost visceral horror of 'contemplation'. What for Thomas Aquinas was the acme of human spirituality is for Jameson, after Lukács, the pit of human despair: the very contrary of narrativity. The contemporary nightmarish vision of a life without narrative is that visited upon 'those massive populations around the world who have, as it were, "dropped out of history" ... confined in camps of various kinds, and ministered to by NGOs ... [this is] naked life in all the metaphysical senses in which the sheer biological temporality of existences without activity and without production can be interpreted'.[7]

What is to be done? If it is true for Jameson that narrative as a mode of apprehension presupposes a world which is visibly the product of human praxis, then it is also true that to narrativise at a time when social reality no longer offers itself as easily narrativisable is, potentially at least, to rekindle the flames of human praxis in reality itself. Here, however, 'human praxis' no longer signifies Marx's 'fire of labour',[8] but a collective *political* praxis capable of translating the illegible ideograms of Capital into the language of human deeds. Jameson thus dialecticises the relations between mimesis, *muthos* and praxis. If the writer transforms the narrative or non-narrative structures of the world into a literary object, then narrative itself informs the potential for collective political praxis – a politically radical version of the relation between refiguration and prefiguration in Ricoeur's threefold mimesis. Like pin pricks in a temporarily paralysed limb, the textual narrativisation of a denarrativised world reminds readers that historical reality is the product of collective action – *their* action.

Hayden White has stressed the overtly political aspect of this idea:

> [Jameson distinguishes] less between ideology and truth (because all representations are ideological in nature) than between the ideologies that conduce to the effort to liberate man from history and those that condemn him to an 'eternal return' of its 'alienating necessities'. In those works of literature in which narrativity is either refused or breaks down, we are met with the traces of despair that is to be assigned, not to the moral weakness or lack of knowledge of their authors, but rather to the apperception of a shape of social life grown old. The breakdown of narrativity in a culture, group or social class is a symptom of its having

---

7   Jameson 2011, pp. 149, 151.

8   Marx 1990, p. 289.

entered a state of crisis. For with any weakening of narrativizing capacity, the group loses its power to locate itself in history, to come to grips with the Necessity that its past represents for it, to imagine a creative, if only provisional, transcendence of its 'fate'.[9]

We shall see shortly that the rise of style as a dominant literary category was coeval with just such a period of the demise of narrativity, in many ways becoming its chief linguistic index. The point to note here, however, is that, as White rightly sees, the capacity to narrate – in the precise Aristotelian sense of the dual operation of emplotment and *mimēsis praxeōs* – is both an index *and* an enabler of practical vitality.[10] It is at once an indication of hegemony and, in times of political defeat, a unifying force which increases one's capacity to act. Consequently, the converse is also true: those forms of representation which subvert or deny narrativity are potentially detrimental to one's coming to consciousness of the practical processes which produce the historical reality in which one is an agent. One way of describing Jameson's critical methodology would thus be that he translates those literary and cultural phenomena which deny narrativity into the narrative of History provided by the Marxist framework; in doing so, he hopes to resurrect his readers' sense of History as a single, collective project of which they are a part.[11]

2   Jameson as Epic Poet of Postmodernity

It is in this precise context that I wish to extend the argument of Georg Lukács's *The Theory of the Novel* (1920), by claiming that we must understand Jameson

---

9   White 1987, pp. 148–9.

10   'That the possibility of plot may serve as something like a proof of the vitality of the social organism we may deduce, negatively, from our own time, where that possibility is no longer present' (Jameson 2008, p. 11).

11   '[Past cultural phenomena] can recover their original urgency for us only if they are retold within the unity of a single great collective story; only if, in however disguised and symbolic a form, they are seen as sharing a single fundamental theme – for Marxism, the collective struggle to wrest a realm of Freedom from a realm of Necessity; only if they are grasped as episodes in a single vast unfinished plot' (Jameson 1981, pp. 19–20). Cf. also: 'In a society like ours, not stricken with aphasia so much as with amnesia, there is a higher priority than reading and that is history itself: so the very greatest of critics of our time – Lukács, for example, and to a lesser degree, Leavis – are those who have constructed their role as the teaching of history, as the telling the tale of the tribe, the most important story any of us will ever have to listen to' (Jameson 2008, p. 159).

as the 'epic poet' of postmodernity. I should stress immediately that this grand epithet is not intended as an empty rhetorical flourish, but as a way of capturing the political and theoretical ambiguities of Jameson's work, as will become clear. It will be recalled that Lukács saw the novel as the 'epic of an age in which the extensive totality of life is no longer given, in which the immanence of meaning in life has become a problem, yet which still thinks in terms of totality'.[12] The empirical world, he argued, in stark contrast to the 'integrated civilization' of Homeric Greece, had come unhinged from all transcendence, all substance had been dispersed in reflexivity. The most characteristic attribute of the novel was that it was a created form, a false totality that had been conjured up by fiat by the author, as opposed to the authentic epic which was effectively the social totality forming itself through the poet.[13] The overarching term Lukács uses to describe this state of modern being is *irony*. In a crucial passage of *The Theory of the Novel* he writes that irony is the 'highest freedom that can be achieved in a world without God'.[14] Man himself has become the source of all foundations, but the price he has had to pay is his world's ultimate foundationlessness. Yet, irony is, in Lukács's words, 'the sole possible *a priori* condition for a true, totality-creating objectivity'.[15] There is here, then, no simple nostalgia for Homeric Greece: Lukács seems to suggest that the only way out of secular modernity is all the way through it and out the other side. If man has become the source of his own meaning, and if the crisis of irony is simultaneously the foundation of his total freedom, then irony and man's self-creation will constitute part of any possible solution to this fundamental homelessness. Such a solution would require that the form-creating freedom of the individual novelist be mirrored in the objective foundations of the totality; for the novel's dilemma to be overcome, the alien world which is impervious to man's consciousness must somehow be found to be subject to the same laws of creation as the novel itself.

The pre-Marxist Lukács of *The Theory of the Novel*, however, could not solve this dilemma; only in *History and Class Consciousness* (1923) would he square the circle by naming the proletariat as the epic poet of modernity. For Lukács, the standpoint of the proletariat is that of the commodity as such, and since

---

12   Lukács 1971, p. 56.
13   'Totality of being is possible only where everything is already homogeneous before it has been contained by forms; where forms are not a constraint but only the becoming conscious, the coming to the surface of everything that had been lying dormant as a vague longing in the innermost depths of that which had to be given form' (Lukács 1971, p. 34).
14   Lukács 1971, p. 93.
15   Ibid.

the commodity form itself contains the secret to the whole capitalist system, the self-consciousness of the worker is both the self-consciousness of the commodity form and the self-revelation of capitalist society as a whole. Once the proletariat achieved self-consciousness, Lukács believed, it would be able to *dereify* (that is, for Lukács, to *renarrativise*) all forms of knowledge and to tear away the veil of commodity fetishism to reveal the historical class struggle. It was that class capable of aspiring towards and realising *in modernity* the living narrativity of the lost epic totality. The standpoint of the proletariat was the solution to the problem that the novel was born to fail to solve.

There is no space here to chart how in Lukács's later work these suggestive, if problematic, insights degenerated into a dogmatic defence of 'realism' and a wholesale repudiation of the various literary modernisms. Suffice it to say that Jameson was able to think what, for the mature Lukács, remained unthinkable: that the category of totality is not always historically achievable. Consequently – and this is Jameson's ingenious twist – rather than considering totality in terms of its validity, he suggests thinking of it in terms of its very historical conditions of possibility. Where, when and how, in other words, does a total understanding of society become possible? His basic answer is that totality emerges into view only when two modes of production exist side by side during a process of transition;[16] there is something about the co-presence of differing temporalities, of conflicting value-systems and ways of life that generates that fundamental sense of historicity which is a prerequisite to any totalising insight. Thus, according to Jameson,[17] the very concept of a 'mode of production' – the totalising concept par excellence – was born in pre-revolutionary France, when feudal forms stood out more starkly against the background of rising bourgeois culture and class consciousness.

We shall see below that for Jameson the chief feature of the shift from modernism to postmodernism is the relative completeness of the process of 'modernisation'.[18] Where modernism corresponds to a situation of incomplete modernisation under monopoly capitalism, the co-existence of two socioeconomic temporalities (residual feudalism and increasingly dominant transnational capitalist metropolises),[19] postmodernism corresponds to complete

---

16   Jameson 1991, pp. 404–5.

17   Ibid.

18   Here, 'modernisation' means little more than the increasing dominance of capital's rule
—   and the subsumption of increasingly large tracts of the socius under processes of commodification.

19   Cf. Jameson 2002, p. 141ff., and Jameson 2008, pp. 636–58.

modernisation under 'late capitalism' (the term is Ernest Mandel's),[20] an existence devoid of that experiential differential between the archaic and the modern. One of the principal features of the postmodern is the universalisation of reification: for Jameson, this includes those classic topoi of 'the transformation of social relations into things' and 'the effacement of traces of production',[21] but also extends – in the realm of cultural products – to the 'radical separation between consumers and producers'.[22] This latter involves a sense in the consumer that the production process behind the objects they encounter in day-to-day life is either totally irrelevant to them or quite simply beyond their capacity of comprehension. This arises when people's 'relations to production are blocked, when they no longer have power over productive activity'.[23] Taken together, the disappearance of differential socioeconomic modes of experience within a single lifeworld and the radical separation of consumers from the processes of production effectively eliminate all those signs of human praxis which are necessary for narrativisation. Postmodernism is nothing less than a vast process of denarrativisation of social existence.[24]

Given that, as we have seen, narrativity is essential in Jameson's view to any hegemonic project, such denarrativising tendencies pose serious problems for any political Left which wishes to organise a coherent counter-hegemonic project. This is why he can claim that 'an aesthetic of cognitive mapping in this sense is an integral part of any socialist political project'.[25] By 'cognitive mapping', a term he takes from Kevin Lynch, he means essentially any mode of representation which enables the individual political subject to articulate his or her individual position in the world system with 'the vaster and properly unrepresentable totality which is the ensemble of society's structures as a whole'.[26] Jameson explicitly links 'cognitive mapping' to Althusser's definition of ideology:[27] 'the representation of the subject's Imaginary relationship to his or her

---

20   Though it should be noted that for Mandel 'late capitalism' refers primarily to the long boom of the immediate postwar period, which enters its historical demise with the conjoined social and economic crises of the late 1960s and early 1970s.

21   Jameson 1991, p. 314.

22   Jameson 1991, p. 315.

23   Jameson 1991, p. 316.

24   Cf. Jameson's observations on the breakdown of the 'syntagmatic' in the postmodern: 'the breakdown of temporality suddenly releases this present of time from all the activities and intentionalities that might focus it and make it a space of praxis' (Jameson 1991, p. 27).

25   Jameson 1991, p. 416.

26   Jameson 1991, p. 51.

27   'There is ... a most interesting convergence between the empirical problems studied by

Real conditions of existence'.[28] For Jameson 'ideology must always be necessarily narrative in its structure, inasmuch as it not only involves a mapping of the real, but also the essentially narrative or fantasy attempt of the subject to invent a place for himself/herself in a collective and historical process which excludes him or her'.[29] Thus, it is obvious that Jameson sees his task – both critical and political – as the attempt to renarrativise postmodernity as such. In doing so, he aims to rehistoricise the present, to render it recognisable as the result of collective political action and thereby increase the Left's capacity to organise and act within it.[30] If the novel was the epic of modernity, that which aspired to the lost totality of Homeric Greece, then Jameson's precise blend of theory and criticism is the epic poetry of postmodernity.

Already in a 1977 essay on the realism-modernism debate, Jameson's programme was clear: the invention of a post-modernist (that is *after* modernist) realism.[31] Like Brecht's, it would be a 'realism achieved by means of Cubism';[32] and like Lewis, it would '[bury] Euclid deep in the living flesh'.[33] Part of Jameson's attraction to Sartre, Brecht and Lewis (the subjects of three of his monographs) – the latter an otherwise unlikely figure for a Marxist pantheon – is that all three of them combine 'linguistic optimism',[34] the force to make language speak even when those around you believe it condemned to silence, with a bric-a-brac narrative flair. Even in times of profound reification or political subjection, times when narrative is no longer organically available as a mode

---

Lynch in terms of the city space and the great Althusserian (and Lacanian) redefinition of ideology' (ibid.).

28 Cited in Jameson 1991, p. 51.

29 Jameson 1979, p. 12.

30 'The rhetorical strategy of the preceding pages has involved an experiment, namely, the attempt to see whether by systematizing something that is resolutely unsystematic, and historicizing something that is resolutely ahistorical, one couldn't outflank it and force a historical way at least of thinking about that' (Jameson 1991, p. 418).

31 'Under these circumstances, the function of a new realism would be clear; to resist the power of reification in consumer society and to reinvent that category of totality which, systematically undermined by existential fragmentation on all levels of life and social organization today, can alone project structural relations between classes as well as class struggles in other countries ... Such a conception of realism would incorporate what was always most concrete in the dialectical counter-concept of modernism – its emphasis on the violent renewal of perception in a world in which experience has solidified into a mass of habits and automatisms' (Jameson 2010, pp. 212–13).

32 Jameson 1998, p. 59.

33 Cited in Jameson 1979, p. 33.

34 Jameson 1984, p. 208.

of apprehending reality, such figures root around in the dustbins of literary history and daily life to gather together enough narrative materials to spin a decent yarn. It is just such a combination of the *bricoleur*'s opportunism with a subjective and political will-to-style that informs Jameson's own writing. All of these writers, though especially Sartre and Lewis, combine the verbal intensity of the high modernists with an obsession with the visual typical of the post-modern. Terry Eagleton's canny analysis of Jameson's style picks up on yet more two-sided features of his writing: Jameson combines sensory immediacy with conceptual reflection,[35] investing the energies that one would normally asso-ciate with argument into what the anthropologists call 'thick description'; his style is poetic in texture but discursive in structure, 'providing us with object-ive correlatives for our knowledge';[36] finally, Eagleton notes 'a kind of subject-iveless affectivity' at work in Jameson's style: 'he is modernist in so far as he deploys a high, uniquely individuating style, but ... this style is ... a mode of self-masking; and ... he is postmodernist because he is allured by the idea of being freed from the tyranny of deep subjectivity'.[37] Jameson's style thus has a foot in both camps: it maintains allegiance to the great modernist desire for totality, to its stylistic elaborations, and to its poetics of the epiphany, but it also demon-strates a bias for the visual and the affective (as opposed to the subjective) more commonly associated with the postmodern. In the shift from the novel as the epic poetry of modernity to Jameson's unique blend of postmodern The-ory – combining narrative, discourse and style – epic poetry has not emerged unscathed. This truly is a 'new realism': a narrative machine which fuses struc-tural, sociological and theoretical abstraction with defamiliarising phenomen-ological descriptions worthy of the greatest science fiction writers. Jameson has merged theory and storytelling into a qualitatively new kind of writing.

3   Jameson, the Epic Contemplator?

Yet, there is a fundamental ambiguity in the entire Jamesonian project. For if, as I have claimed, Jameson's mode of theory is the postmodern heir to the novel in

---

35   Eagleton 2009, p. 125.
36   Eagleton 2009, p. 127.
37   Eagleton 2009, p. 130. Eagleton might well have added to this list Jameson's penchant for the modernist epiphany. What attracts him to Adorno's 'historical tropes', for example, is that 'for a fleeting instant we catch a glimpse of a unified world, of a universe in which discontinuous realities are nonetheless somehow implicated with each other and intertwined' (Jameson 1971, p. 8).

its attempt to achieve epic totality in an age in which it is no longer historically possible, then it is also heir to the idealism and contradictions of this novel-istic undertaking. It was Lukács's great strength to have short-circuited the two apparently unrelated problems of literary form and social revolution. In show-ing that the structural categories of the novel coincide with those of the modern world, Lukács fused the fate of the novel with the fate of capitalist modernity as such.[38] When he discovered the proletariat to be the collective subject of history (according to a logic long since criticised by Althusser), he discovered the social force in the present which could sublate capitalist modernity. But if we pursue the implicit logic of this argument, which he did not, we would have to conclude that the sublation of capitalist modernity would also bring about the end of the novel which was its offspring. The demise of the capitalist world would entail the disappearance of the structural categories of the novel. Ultimately, then, Lukács hit upon a kernel of truth essential to any Marxist poet-ics: at their extremes, poetics and political praxis coincide. Problems of literary form and stylistic innovation become, at their outer limit, *political* problems.

It is here that Jameson's ambiguity becomes clear. On the one hand, as we have seen, he takes cognitive mapping to be part of any socialist political project under postmodernity: epic representations of the social totality play a politically strategic role that they did not possess in prior historical periods. On the other hand, he seems to believe that an attempt theoretically or fictionally to narrativise the social totality within the pages of a book (or on screen) is somehow in and of itself politically radical. Jameson's sense of narrativisation thus hovers between a political practice which aims to realise in actuality the dereification of social reality (thus extending the presuppositions of Lukács's *History and Class Consciousness*) and a purely textual, mimetic transformation of reality into a written narrative (thus inheriting the representational limits of the novel). The advantage of the former conception is that it takes narrativity as that which must be practically achieved, whereas the latter leads Jameson to his triumphalist proclamations on Marxism as offering the great collective plot of all human existence. The effect of this is to fall prey to precisely that 'contemplation' it was his express desire to avoid. J.M. Bernstein is quite right to argue that

> [t]o urge at this juncture [i.e., when the language and practices of a world systematically obscure the worldliness of the world as such] that there *is* a collective history, an unfinished plot, breaks the fundamental

---

38   Lukács 1971, p. 93.

connection between collective narratives and social identity; it makes the
Marxist narrative transcendent to concrete social practices, and therefore
transcendent to any particular world. Marxism thus becomes a collective
narrative which is no one's narrative, a narrative searching for an agent, a
hero to complete it.

It is inadequate simply to pose the Marxist historical narrative against
the anti-narrative of modernism, employing the theoretical terms of the
former to decode or decipher the historical meaning of the latter ... *Pace*
Jameson, no contemplation, no hermeneutical act of decipherment, can
restore to history its missing narrative dimension.[39]

Admittedly, Bernstein's argument cannot account for Jameson's claim that cognitive mapping has become a *precondition* for what we might call the 'practical
narratology' that Bernstein equates with political praxis.[40] Nonetheless, the
danger is clear: if the purely textual sense of narrativisation comes to usurp
the practical or strategic sense, then political praxis gives way to passive contemplation, even in its insistence on the primacy of the deed.

This danger is compounded by the poetics of Jameson's methodology.[41]
The *differentia specifica* of Jameson's Marxist method lies in that he 'sought
to replace the well-worn formula of reflexion, let alone determination, with
that of situation and response'.[42] In fact, he combines four quite different influences: the Sartrean notion of a 'situation' (itself inherited from Karl Jaspers),
the Marxist understanding of symbolic resolutions of historical contradictions
(also developed in the work of Lévi-Strauss), the 'logic of question and answer'
developed in the philosophy of R.G. Collingwood (and, later, in the hermeneutics of Gadamer), and Kenneth Burke's work on 'symbolic action'.[43] What the

---

39   Bernstein 1984, pp. 261–2.
40   'Marxist political practice can succeed only through the attempt to renarrativize exper-
      ience, to construct a narrative whose narrating would be the production of a narratable
      world' (Bernstein 1984, p. 266).
41   If it seems curious to suggest that a methodology can have a 'poetics', let us recall that
      Jameson himself often locates the strengths and weaknesses of theories in the implicit
      aesthetic structures which enable their theoretical insights. This is true of his comments
      on both formalism (Jameson 1972, pp. 78–9) and New Historicism (Jameson 1991, p. 188).
      Likewise, in an essay on Derrida, he argues that deconstruction is informed by what he
      calls a 'linguistic' (the verbal equivalent of an 'aesthetic') – 'that series of rules which
      govern the production of acceptable sentences ... in a given generic system' (Jameson
      2009, p. 135, n. 11).
42   Jameson 2008, p. x.
43   'Culture itself as a system, but also the individual texts and works of art and literature

first three influences emphasise is that no human artefact or act can be understood immanently, on its own terms; it must be seen as the response to a prior
situation, or as an answer to the 'question', or a solution to the contradiction,
which that situation posed. A situation is a problem-field,[44] full of contradictions and obstructions which one must overcome if one is to assert one's freedom.[45] Thus, the initial impetus of any critical reading is the reconstruction of
the underlying situation to which the text in question was a response.[46] Unlike
traditional criticism, however, this situation cannot simply be some neutral
'background' or 'context', but must possess a central and active dilemma which
the work attempts to *resolve* in some way. The critic must write with the eye
of the dramatist or the novelist, sketching out basic existential or social conflicts so as to frame writers and cultural producers as co-protagonists of the
situation.[47] Whilst the work of criticism is certainly not to be equated with
novel-writing, it is clear that Jameson's methodology draws on its poetics so as
to produce metanarratives capable of dereifying and renarrativising past symbolic acts.

There are, however, two factors which undermine the refreshing proactivity
incited by this methodological approach, which seems to avoid the reductive
mechanicity of its base-superstructure or 'reflection theory' forebears. Firstly,

---

that are "included" in it, are both best grasped as responses to situations, as solutions to
contradictions, as answers to questions' (Jameson 1987b, p. 19).

44   Jameson 1987b, p. 20.

45   'Agency constitutes both the agent and the situation. The situation only exists as a situ-
      ation for some agent. The agent only exists as an agent in some situation so to be in a
      situation is to choose oneself in a situation' (Priest 2001, p. 178).

46   For a clear example of this, see Jameson's essay, 'Modernism and Imperialism', in which
      the 'situation' to which modernist literature responds is the world of inter-imperialist
      rivalry, where the determinants of daily life now lie beyond the boundaries of the nation-
      state in the unseen barbarism of the colonies: 'daily life and existential experience in the
      metropolis ... which is necessarily the very content of the national literature itself, can now
      no longer be grasped immanently; it no longer has its meaning, its deeper reason for being,
      within itself. As artistic content it will now henceforth always have something missing
      about it, but in the sense of a privation that can never be restored or made whole simply
      by adding back in the missing component ... This new and historically original problem in
      what is itself a new kind of content now constitutes the situation, and the problem, and the
      dilemma, the formal contradiction, that modernism seeks to solve' (Jameson 2007, p. 157).

47   In another context Jameson praises the science fiction novelist, Kim Stanley Robinson,
      because he stages 'scientific facts and findings, presuppositions and activities' as 'data
      and raw materials for the solving of problems, rather than as abstract and contemplative
      features of an epistemology or scientific world picture' (2005, p. 394).

whereas Sartre saw situations as multiple and obtaining in hierarchies, from the smallest to the largest scale,[48] Jameson chooses to focus primarily on the *ultimate* situation – that which contains all the others. For Sartre, however, the situation of all situations was being-in-the-world as such,[49] but Jameson, via an unannounced sleight-of-hand, epochalises this situation. 'Situation' in Sartre's work categorically is *not* a 'code word' for the 'mode of production', as Jameson would have it.[50] In at once expanding and reducing Sartre's concept of the 'situation' to the 'mode of production' – which is, for Jameson, essentially synonymous with the 'period' – he voids it of the novelistic and dramatic (and hence *critical*) potential it initially seemed to possess, for if every individual act is a 'response' to a situation, then it is quite clear that any single individual act will register as but a drop in the ocean of the truly epic 'situation' which is the mode of production (or its current stage of development). What Jameson gives with one hand – a theory of literary and cultural production as proactive, non-reflective and constitutive social activity – he takes away with the other, transforming literary acts into the most insignificant of deeds. It is here that the full ambiguity of Jameson's misreading of Kenneth Burke's notion of 'symbolic action' – which he interprets as 'symbolic act' – comes to the fore: it is 'on the one hand affirmed as a genuine *act*, albeit on the symbolic level, while on the other it is registered as an act which is "merely" symbolic, its resolutions imaginary ones that leave the real untouched'.[51] One is tempted to read 'real' and 'symbolic' here as barely disguised substitutes for 'base' and 'superstructure'.

This is nothing less than a special form of dualism: Mallarméan dualism. One of the epigraphs to *Marxism and Form* invokes Mallarmé's dictum that 'only two paths stand open to mental research, where our need divides: aesthetics, and also political economy'.[52] The obvious missing term here is politics. This term does appear in Jameson's work but oscillates between two extremes. On the one hand, he can claim that 'there is nothing that is not social and

---

48   'Sartre's being about to smoke depends upon the existence of smoking as a practice in mid-twentieth-century France. Keeping an appointment depends upon friendships or meetings. These in turn depend upon the existence of human beings, their projects and situations' (Priest 2001, p. 178).

49   Cf. Priest 2001, pp. 177–8.

50   Cf. Jameson 1987a, p. 27.

51   Jameson 1981, p. 81. In Burke 'symbolic action' is almost always *practical*, even when used in fiction. Cf. Burke 1966.

52   I have taken the translation of this epigraph from Jameson (1991, p. 427), but have included what Jameson omits: 'where our need divides [*où bifurque notre besoin*]'. Cf. Anderson 1998, p. 125.

historical – indeed, that everything is "in the last analysis" political'[53] – which essentially inflates the political beyond all meaningful limits and conflates it with two other quite distinct and problematic concepts: the social and the historical. At the same time, as Perry Anderson has rightly observed,[54] the political is reduced in Jameson's Marxist hermeneutic to the sphere of what Braudel knew as *l'histoire événementielle*, that 'evanescent foam of episodes and incidents which he compared to the surf on the waves from Africa'.[55] Thus, Jameson's understanding of the political is at once too omnipresent to be of any practical or critical incisiveness and too superficial to produce any real effects. In that, it suffers from the same fundamental ambiguity as the poetics of his methodology: a 'situation' which is an entire mode of production, or one stage of its development, and a literary act so irrelevant as to be purely 'symbolic'. In such a framework, it is difficult to claim that literature or culture are in any way political, since they have been robbed of the specificity and effectivity required for even the most modest of political interventions.

This lacuna – the missing mediations between the totalising situation and the individual literary work, which is also the lack of politics as such – is one we shall encounter time and again as we outline and analyse Jameson's theory of style. Nonetheless, his blindness in this respect proves to be the source of some of his greatest insights. His theory of style constitutes one of the few convincing materialist explanations for the rise (and possible demise) of style as a dominant literary category. As we shall see, style in Jameson's sense is essentially what happens to literary language when narrative as a mode of apprehension is no longer available. It is a linguistic index of denarrativisation and reification, at once a signal of political defeat and a Utopian gesture of affective and verbal compensation.

4   Style and Modernity

From the first line of his first book, Jameson has associated style with modernity:

> It has always seemed to me that a modern style is somehow in itself intelligible, above and beyond the limited meaning of the book written in it,

---

53   Jameson 1981, p. 20.

54   Anderson 1998, pp. 127–8.

55   '... political history, in the narrow sense of punctual event and a chroniclelike [*sic*] sequence of happenings in time' (Jameson 1981, p. 75).

and beyond even those precise meanings which the individual sentences that make it up are designed to convey. Such supplementary attention to style is itself a modern phenomenon.[56]

This is why he claims that, strictly speaking, a 'general science of stylistics is a contradiction in terms':[57] if style as a dominant literary category only arises in modernity, then to read pre-modern (or postmodern) works in terms of this category would be anachronistic. Yet it could certainly be objected that style in the broadest sense of 'verbal phrasing' has existed for far longer than modernity: after all, we saw in a previous chapter that *lexis* was one of the components of the ancient rhetorical system. If Jameson's claims are to be made credible, it will be necessary to identify precisely what he means by 'style'. To do so, I shall separate out four overlapping strands of Jameson's argument: the split that occurs in modernity between style and rhetoric, the extinction of the narrative categories of experience, the split between style and narrative, and the Utopian element of stylistic practice.

4.1   *Rhetoric versus Style*

Jameson's clearest definition of style is contained in an essay from 1976, entitled 'Criticism in History'.[58] The passage in question, which spells out the difference between (pre-modern) rhetoric and (modern) style, is worth quoting at length:

> Rhetoric is an older and essentially precapitalist mode of linguistic organization; it is a collective or class phenomenon in that it serves as a means of assimilating the speech of individuals to some suprapersonal oratorical paradigm, to some non- or preindividualistic standard of *beau parler*, of high style and fine writing. A profound social value is here invested in spoken language, one that may be gauged by the primacy of such aristo-

---

56   Jameson 1984, p. vii. Note the dual vision of the dialectic at work even here at this early stage: the first sentence deals with the object – 'modern style' – whilst the second deals with the subjective appropriation of the object – 'attention to style'. In *The Political Unconscious* this would become the 'two distinct paths' of historicisation: 'the path of the object and the path of the subject, the historical origins of the things themselves and that more intangible historicity of the concepts and categories by which we attempt to understand those things' (Jameson 1981, p. 9). Jameson almost always pursues the path of the subject.
57   Jameson 1971, p. 397.
58   Jameson 2008, pp. 125–43.

cratic forms as the sermon and the verse tragedy, the salon witticism and the poetic epistle.

Style, on the other hand, is a middle-class phenomenon and reflects the increasing atomization of middle-class life and the sapping of the collective vitality of language itself, as the older collective and precapitalist social groupings are gradually undermined and dissolved. Style thus emerges, not from the social life of the group, but from the silence of the isolated individual: hence its rigorously personal, quasi-physical or physiological content, the very materiality of its verbal components.

We may put all this the other way around by reformulating it in terms of the literary public. Rhetoric would then reflect the existence of that relatively homogeneous public or class to which the speaker addresses himself/ herself and may be detected by the predilection for standardized formulas as codified in classical antiquity. Style is, on the contrary, always an individual and problematical solution to the dilemma of the absence of a public and emerges against the background of that host of private languages into which the substance of the modern work has been shattered.[59]

Jameson constantly repeats this story of the rise of modern style, making additions and slight adjustments where necessary.[60] Let us tabulate the basic binary opposition:[61]

RHETORIC	STYLE
Pre-capitalist	Capitalist
Collective/ class-based	Individualist/ social atomisation
Oratorical/ speech-oriented	Quasi-physical/ (written?)
Aristocratic	Bourgeois
Homogeneous public	Absence of public
Shared common language	Host of private languages

---

59   Jameson 2008, pp. 127–8.
60   See, for example, Jameson 1971, pp. 332–5; Jameson 2008, p. 40; Jameson 2002, pp. 148–9; Jameson 2007b, pp. 152–69, 208–9, 212–13, 227.
61   This opposition should not be equated with a clean-cut chronological shift from one to the other; as with periodisation more generally, uneven development will be key to understanding the transformation.

The description focuses on the historical variability of the experience of language and the relation between writers and their publics. The most controversial claim, yet perhaps the most important for the construction of a Marxist theory of style, is that the experience of language alters depending on the historical conjuncture. Here, the so-called collective vitality of language in pre-capitalist societies is sapped in the transition to capitalist social atomisation. From a methodological point of view, this poses some obvious problems. The general historical shift from pre-capitalist to capitalist modes of economic organisation can be reconstructed relatively easily, and the written forms prevalent in each still exist as documents for analysis. Yet Jameson's claims go beyond this empiricism to the realm of the phenomenological *experience* of language. The theoretical apparatus necessary to capture such experience will have to be nuanced indeed – far more nuanced than anything Jameson himself will provide.

The two principal sources of Jameson's theory of the rise of style are Sartre's *What is Literature?* (1947) and Barthes's *Writing Degree Zero* (1953): the first two paragraphs of the above-quoted passage draw on the latter, the third the former.[62] Sartre saw the birth of modern style as coeval with the break in

---

62 I say 'principal' because Jameson was also influenced by the work of Erich Auerbach and Leo Spitzer. For reasons of space and direct relevance, I have chosen to focus here on Sartre and Barthes. Nonetheless, it is worth briefly noting what Jameson takes from Auerbach and Spitzer respectively. Central to Jameson's inheritance of Auerbach is the latter's theory of form and style, of which we can locate three principal features. Firstly, in *Mimesis* (2003), Auerbach outlined a general history of 'style' and explained how its changing nature related directly to various shifts in value systems. Secondly, he inspired Jameson's attraction to formalism, sensing that the real importance of criticism was not to discover what a work means, but rather to demonstrate *how* it means and why that 'how' might be historically relevant. Finally, and most importantly, Jameson's reticence on matters of morality also finds its origins in Auerbach. For example, the latter is warmly sympathetic to the author-figure he himself constructs under the name of 'Cervantes' (Auerbach 2003, pp. 334–58), but this does not prevent him from suggesting that the author's 'devout wisdom' is a formal ruse to enable the production of startlingly eclectic tales and styles. Cervantes's lack of moral judgement at the level of content, which implies a devout deference to God's will ('Judge not, and you shall not be judged'), is *inseparable* from his formal desire to write in myriad styles which juxtapose high and low, tragic and comic styles, without ever finally opting for one over the other. This then leads us to ask: what are the consequences for morality if it is proved, in the realm of art, to be nothing but form under another name? Such are the types of questions to which Jameson has often returned, but which he translates into a more overtly Marxist vocabulary (e.g. the ideology of form).

    In Spitzer (1970), furthermore, we find three elements which would be important for Jameson. Firstly, his emphasis on style as betraying the absolute singularity of a given

relations between authors and their publics which arose in the nineteenth century. Literature had until this point been an unproblematic activity since the literary vocation had been at one with the writers' social position, but now the abstract universality of the bourgeoisie had been revealed to have been secretly particular all along.[63] In this state of existential schism, the greatest writers according to Sartre were those who wrote *against* their public, yet this was also the source of their bad faith:

> [The writer] lived in a state of contradiction and dishonesty since he both knew and did not want to know *for whom* he was writing [i.e., the bourgeoisie]. He was fond of speaking of his *solitude*, and rather than assume responsibility for the public which he had slyly chosen, he concocted the notion that one writes for oneself alone or for God. He made of writing a metaphysical occupation, a prayer, an examination of conscience, everything but a communication.[64]

This was, in Sartre's view, the social origin of modern – and modernist – literature: of Flaubert's maniacal search for *le mot juste* and his dream of a book without content.[65] This disjunction between the writer and his public would

---

writer is a non-materialist precursor to Jameson's notion of style, borrowed from Barthes, as exemplary of the bourgeois monad, an almost physiological uniqueness engrained into the very *stilus* of his handwriting. Secondly, there is a problematic, since unconvincingly theorised, link made between the 'mind' of the author and the 'mind' of a given place and time, and also between that of the period (sentence) and the period (era). Finally, Spitzer's dictum that the generation of categories for analysis should arise spontaneously out of the reading process feeds into Jameson's Hegelian tendencies, and would strongly influence his first attempt to outline a hermeneutical methodology in 'Metacommentary' (Jameson 2008, pp. 5–19).

63 Cf. Richard Terdiman 1994, p. 707: '... the generation of the 1848 revolution discovered a truth about their own society that they had hardly suspected before. The values of "fraternity" and "equality" inherited from 1789 had never been forgotten – particularly by middle-class idealists, intellectuals, and artists. But now the universalizing ideas that up to 1848 had undergirded *all* the French revolutions seemed to have been liquidated along with the working-class protestors'.

64 Sartre 2001, p. 95.

65 Cf. Flaubert's letter to Louise Colet, 16th January 1852: 'What seems beautiful to me, what I should like to write, is a book about nothing, a book dependent on nothing external, which would hold up on its own by the internal strength of its style, just as the earth, with no support, holds up in the air; a book which would have almost no subject, or at least in which the subject would be almost invisible, if such a thing is possible. The finest works are those that contain the least matter' (cited in Jameson 2007, p. xx).

not be resolved, claimed Sartre, until the social contradictions which had led to his alienation from that public had been practically overcome. Only then, in a classless society, could what he calls 'actual literature' be achieved:

> [T]he literary antinomy of lyrical subjectivity and objective testimony would be left behind. Involved in the same adventure as his readers and situated like them in a society without cleavages, the writer, in speaking about them, would be speaking about himself, and in speaking about himself would be speaking about them.[66]

For Sartre, the rise of style in the modern sense is coextensive with the alienation of bourgeois writers from their publics (both actual and virtual), itself produced by periods of active and passive revolution; metaphysical talk of the literary Absolute was the self-mystifying ideology of those writers caught in these divisions. The overcoming of 'style' – in the sense of a mode of communication which attempts internally to mask its very status as communication – can only be achieved by the overcoming of social alienation of writers and publics: that is, by social revolution.

If, for Sartre, the first of Jameson's inspirations, literature is a social act, for Barthes it is a type of language which emits 'literary signs'. A sign is an associative total of a signifier and signified, but in the sense in which he uses the term in *Writing Degree Zero*, he is referring to a second-order sign. This latter arises when a first-order sign becomes in its turn a signifier with a signified. Barthes would later call this second-order language, or 'meta-language', myth.[67] Such connotative second-order signs are only applicable to what Barthes calls *écriture* or 'writing'. Located between style, which is – and this is crucial – *strictly involuntary and thus apolitical*,[68] and 'language' [*langue*], which is simply the negative horizon of linguistic possibility imposed by a national language, *écriture* is the 'moral of the form' and is the sole locus of political engagement.[69] Where Sartre's conception of literary politics was based on the question 'For whom does one write?', Barthes's centres on the issue of the forms in and through which a writer addresses a public and the various social connotations they emit.[70] Writing for Barthes was thus inherently ambiguous: the words on

---

66   Sartre 2001, p. 120.
67   Barthes 1957.
68   Barthes 1953, p. 16.
69   Barthes 1953, p. 19.
70   Thus, for example, Barthes (1953, pp. 27–30) famously attacked the *écriture* of the bourgeois realist novel for using the preterite tense, which is the time of myth, and which

the page signified two things at once; the tones, timbres and forms in which they denoted something had a second-order meaning whose political significance was greater than the actual content.

The problem of *écriture* – a writing condemned to mean two things on two levels at once – has not always existed. It arose, says Barthes, in 1848, the year of the European revolutions. Only when the universality of bourgeois ideology was revealed as one more particularity did *écriture* become plural, Jameson's 'host of private languages' vying for the (abstract) universality that had once belonged to the liberal bourgeoisie. This was still, according to Barthes, the linguistic situation in 1953.

At this point a certain ambiguity creeps into Barthes's argument. We have seen that style was classed as apolitical because involuntary, a 'secret of the flesh'. Now, however, as Barthes explains writers' reactions to the post-1848 situation, style begins to be equated with *écriture* as such, thus becoming the very locus of the political. The ultimate example is what Barthes calls *écriture blanche* – white or blank writing. As we saw in the chapter on the history of style in the Marxist tradition, this is a type of writing which would transcend all connotations of literariness or political stance. It is a zero degree or amodal form shorn of all moral and political implication: an innocent writing – a 'style of absence which is almost an ideal absence of style'.[71] It is also, at least implicitly, a *willed* style, a linguistic neutrality for which writers can consciously aim. Thus, there is a contradiction: style is and is not voluntary, is and is not political. This means there are in fact *two* theories of style at work in Barthes's essay. Jameson, whose epic scope sweeps him up and away from the small-print,[72] conflates the two, leading to his curious conception of modernist style as somehow *both* 'physiological' *and* voluntary.

Nonetheless, there is a further point of which Jameson will make much use. When the institution of literature is thrown into turmoil in 1848, it puts an end to what Barthes calls 'the use-value' of form,[73] i.e., the writer's unproblematic inheritance and putting-to-work of pre-formed linguistic units. Prior to 1848, according to Barthes, there was no major emphasis on linguistic novelty; one's task was simply to rearticulate what everybody already knew in a manner that

---

reduced the time of experiential initiative and possibility to a fixed and ordered past, impervious to change.

71   Barthes 1953, p. 60.

72   Eagleton is quite correct in his judgment that '[Jameson] is not very interested in rigorous logical analysis – it works on both too abstract and too humdrum a scale for his epic turn of mind' (2009, p. 126).

73   Barthes 1953, p. 50.

was already communally recognised. Since this linguistic unselfconsciousness was at one with the 'universally' accepted worth of *belles-lettres*, casting the latter into doubt meant altering the former. To justify their 'vocations' writers began substituting the use-value of their work for its work-value – the labour it cost them to produce it. Thus was born in France the writer-artisan with his boasts of the agonies of creation.[74] In Jameson, this observation will be transformed into the fairly convincing argument that modernist works '[show] a far greater degree of conscious and unconscious *elaboration* on the basis of its primitive element or original content' and that this elaboration must itself be factored in to any analysis of style.[75] This is a useful corrective to Williams's ambiguous account of the potentially self-conscious *labour* of writing.[76]

By combining Barthes's ambiguous linguistic theory of style with Sartre's public-centred one, Jameson produces the embryo of a suggestive model with which to map the broad shifts in French prose style throughout the nineteenth and twentieth centuries. At its heart are the European revolutions of 1848. For Sartre the events of 1848 spelled the end of the writer's unproblematic relation to his public, for Barthes the explosion of *langue* into a multiplicity of *écritures*. For Jameson, however, the main relevance of this momentous political betrayal was that it put an end to what he calls 'rhetoric' – that predominantly oral mode of writing which presupposed the class homogeneity of the aristocracy in power or the 'rising' bourgeoisie – and gave birth to 'style': an individualist linguistic mode coextensive with social atomisation. In the passage immediately following the above quotation from 'Criticism in History', Jameson uses the events of 1848 as a criterion by which to compare the histories of the English and the French novels. He argues that the English novel is modernised at a far later date (around 1900) than its French counterpart; its linguistic priorities are predominantly oral – 'telling, digressing, repeating, exclaiming, rambling, and apostrophizing' – as opposed to the post-1848 French novel in which the individual prose sentence and prose paragraph have become 'dominant literary and stylistic categories in their own right'.[77] He attributes the continuance of the rhetorical strain in the English novel until a far later date to 'the British class compromise, in which the older feudal aristocracy is

---

74   'Gautier (impeccable master of *Belles-Lettres*), Flaubert (grinding out his sentences in Croisset), Valéry (in his bedroom in the small hours), or Gide (stood before his desk as if before a carpenter's bench)' (Barthes 1953, pp. 50–51).

75   Jameson 2008, p. 18.

76   I write 'ambiguous' because, as we saw in Chapter 5, he tends to hover between attributing to writers at once too little and too much self-consciousness.

77   Jameson 2008, pp. 128–9.

able to maintain its control of the apparatus of the state to the very middle of the First World War'.[78] By contrast, in France, with the publication of *Madame Bovary* in 1857, the novel had become 'the pretext for the forging of individual sentences, for the practice of style as such'.[79] The relative national shifts in dominant literary paradigms were coextensive with the uneven rhythms of historical development in the nations themselves.

The virtue of Jameson's theory is that it provides historically verifiable reasons for the stark contrast in stylistic practices in the novels of England and France, and it does so by providing precisely what Ricoeur's poetics could not: a theory of verbal language (that is, of language beyond the sense of Ricoeur's 'symbolism') and a gesture towards the notion that everyday experience undergoes profound historical mutations. The problem – which we have termed Jameson's Mallarméan dualism – is that it works on too grand a scale, with too few mediatory categories between the epochal historical situation and the individual works of literature themselves, and relies on a historiography which emphasises the break at the expense of continuity. As far as the '1848 thesis' is concerned, Tony Pinkney had it right when he wrote, in a different context, that it

> remains too external to the Modernism it aims to explain, merely tacking a political bloodbath onto the front of what otherwise remains an autonomous literary series. 1848 is not a genuine alternative to Modernism's ideologies of itself ... And whatever did change in European culture then will have to be thought through in models of temporality and the social formation much more complex than that 'expressive totality' which lets Lukács and others see every last tiny poetic image obediently mutating at the very instant the barricades are thrown up.[80]

What Jameson requires is a set of literary and sociological categories whose shifting constellations could be charted in more nuanced analyses. For example, any theory of style in the novel will inevitably have to study the development of voice, description and – if we take Flaubert as our model – tense

---

78   Jameson 2008, p. 129. This compromise entailed the aristocracy's '[appropriating] for itself the techniques of the [bourgeoisie's] commercial and productive activity' (ibid.). This thesis can be usefully compared with Perry Anderson's (1964; 1968) narrative of Britain's anomalous class compromise.

79   Jameson 2008, p. 129.

80   'Introduction' to Williams 2007.

usage.[81] As we saw in Williams's work, such categories provide the force-field within which certain types of linguistic elaboration become possible. In terms of sociological categories, Williams's concept of a 'formation' would be an obvious mediating term, denoting a range of organised and self-organised groupings within the sphere of cultural production (from guilds, to schools, to movements, to class fractions). The function of such a concept is to nuance, yet never ultimately to replace, the more unwieldy generalisations involving writers and their social classes – these latter undergoing constant historical mutation in relation to one another. In terms of the linguistic claims Jameson makes, I would then propose two new concepts: 'linguistic situation', by which I mean the critical reconstruction of the state of a language as a writer would have experienced it, including its internal tensions and social stratifications, and 'linguistic ideology' which denotes, on the one hand, the prevailing general understanding of what language is and how it works (always articulated with the general ideology), and, on the other, those formational or private theories of language developed by literary practitioners themselves (especially in the modernist and postmodernist periods). Developed at length in Part 3 of this book, these concepts provide the mediations necessary, not only for a nuanced *critical* analysis, but also for a more convincing *political* analysis of cultural production: one which *enables* it in the present.

4.2   *The Extinction of the Narrative Categories of Experience*

The break between rhetoric and style, however, is only the first aspect of Jameson's theory of style. The second is what he calls the 'extinction of traditional storytelling and of the narrative categories of experience'.[82] Projecting backwards the logic of Lukács's claim that 'the structural categories of the novel constitutively coincide with the world as it is today', Jameson equates the traditional narrative categories of 'fate, destiny, providence or fortune' with the actual structure of pre-modern, pre-capitalist experience itself.[83] When the structure of that experience starts to undergo transformation, there is no longer an 'organic' relation between it and the literary form of the tale. The traditional tale was a commemoration of the unique: the temporally irrevocable and the stroke of good or bad fortune. The uniqueness of the event presupposed 'the immemorial patterns of a hierarchical and traditional social order, in which your life path is laid out in advance by the caste, status or calling of

---

81   Flaubert's revolutionary use of the imperfect tense and its capacity to produce a sense of
       temporal *ennui* is well-documented. See Finch 2004.

82   Jameson 1984, p. 211.

83   Jameson 1984, p. 212.

the forefathers'.[84] But this 'immense frozen ice flow ... will split and crack thunderously under the warming dynamism of capital, releasing a new wealth of existential content which can no longer be organized in storytelling categories'.[85] The modern protagonist lacks the absolute definition of the *homme-récit*, Todorov's memorable term for the hero of the folk tale. For the moderns the 'absence of fate means perpetual possibility, lability, freedom, lack of ultimate definition'.[86] Capitalist modernity for Jameson is thus a narrative Fall, but a historically happy one.

Elsewhere, Jameson supplements these existential theories of narrative with alternative emplotments of literary modernity. When he discusses the shift that occurs from the novel of plot to the psychological novel (the substitution of the unity of personality for the unity of action), he claims that the technique of point of view 'expresses the increasing atomization of our societies, in which the privileged meeting places of collective life and of the intertwining of collective destinies – the tavern, the marketplace, the high road, the court, the *paseo*, the cathedral, yes, and even the city itself – have decayed and, with them, the vital sources of the anecdote'.[87] Another way of framing this is that 'in older societies and perhaps even in the early stages of market capital, the immediate and limited experience of individuals is still able to encompass and coincide with the true economic and social form that governs that experience'.[88] What appears with the rise of monopoly capitalism, according to Jameson, is 'a growing contradiction between lived experience and structure ... the truth of that experience no longer coincides with the place in which it takes place'.[89] Daily life in early twentieth-century London, for example, was secretly determined by what happened in the colonies, beyond the ken of any single inhabitant of the metropolis. Indeed, Jameson will see modernism as nothing less than a series of formal solutions to this basic problem: how to achieve aesthetic totality when one's social existence itself now lacks the immanent wholeness of the pre-modern lifeworld. If this spatial disjunction were not difficult enough to narrativise, however, it is compounded by the rise of a basic temporal disjunction in social life as well: 'The rhythms that appear in modernity are ... the great fifty year cycles of the Kontratiev [*sic*] wave ... such long waves are clearly out of

---

84   Ibid.
85   Ibid.
86   Jameson 1984, p. 213.
87   Jameson 2008, pp. 11–12.
88   Jameson 1991, pp. 410–11.
89   Jameson 1991, pp. 410, 411.

synchrony with the briefer periods in which the individual subject lives his or her "existential" experience'.[90] Such are the strands that form the bind of modernism under monopoly capitalism: the extinction of the narrative categories of existence, the demise of collective meeting places which offer the raw materials and situation of storytelling, and the spatial and temporal rifts between individual experience and structure. These are the historical preconditions for the autonomisation of style, for the sentence to free itself from the shackles of narrative representation.

Once again, we see here in practice Jameson's epic scope. A mind attuned to the shifts between modes of production or the transitions between stages within a single mode of production – the 'problem' to which writers offer 'solutions' – is sketched out on so vast a scale as to lose all sight of the more immediate formal and political configurations in which literary works arise. It becomes difficult to see how literature could be grasped as an ideological *Kampfplatz* if it is reduced to so many miniscule individual attempts symbolically to resolve fundamental problems in which it plays no constitutive role. That is not to say that the epic purview is useless; on the contrary, without such ultimate horizons, one would be forever condemned to the idealisms of the pedant – the rummager in the footnotes of history, blind to the towering monuments in whose shadows he works. At the same time, however, literary experimentation in the present is condemned almost before it has started, the stillborn infant of a situation to which it will have been, at best, a ghostly 'resolution'. In the context of a Marxist poetics, then, the epic mode of criticism is a necessary failure; its success relies on its being coupled with less sweeping modes of analysis.

4.3   *Narrative versus Style*

Nonetheless, the transformation of the existential parameters is a useful prologue to the third aspect of Jameson's theory of style: the split between style and narrative. Here, 'style' must be seen as that which occurs at the level of the individual sentence. 'Every serious practising critic', writes Jameson, 'knows a secret which is less often publicly discussed, namely, that there exists no ready-made corridor between the sealed chamber of stylistic investigation and that equally unventilated space in which the object of study is reconstituted as narrative structure'.[91] This split between style and narrative has not always existed: it is 'an event in the history of form':

---

90   Jameson 1984, p. 215.
91   Jameson 1979, p. 7.

... Flaubert is a useful marker for this development, in which the two
'levels' of the narrative text begin to drift apart and acquire their own relative autonomy; in which the rhetorical and instrumental subordination of
narrative representation can no longer be taken for granted. The plotless
art novel and the styleless bestseller can then be seen as the end products
of this tendency, which corresponds to the antithesis between what, following Deleuze and Guattari, we will call the *molecular* and the *molar*
impulses in modern form-production no less than in contemporary life
itself.[92]

What Jameson is suggesting is that in pre-modern literature individual sentences were, as a rule, subordinate to the overarching narrative representation;
'such sentences force us constantly to shift our gears back to the content level,
in order to understand their relationship to each other'.[93] The sentences of
a Flaubert, by contrast, possess an autonomy, an intrinsic wholeness, which
exceeds their mere instrumental subordination to the plot: 'In Flaubert ... you
can remain on the micro-level, and live as fully in a single page as in the novel's
"unity of action"'.[94] Jameson then equates this moment in literary history with
'the twin birth of modernism and mass culture'.[95] This is the origin of the split
between the literature of a 'high culture' in which every sentence or phrase is
sculpted as if the writer's life depended on it (Flaubert's *mot juste*; Proust in the
darkness, weaving arabesques) and that mode of writing in which the sentence
is a mere means to an end: the Dan Browns of this world.[96] The ratio of style to
plot is inversely proportional: the art sentence is sculpted in the void of action
as the potboiler shucks off elocution.

What gave rise to this 'event in the history of form'? Jameson's answer is the
antithesis which arises in capitalist society between what Deleuze and Guattari
call the 'molecular' and the 'molar', which is reproduced within the literary text
itself. In *Anti-Oedipus*, Deleuze and Guattari write that under capitalism there

92   Jameson 1979, pp. 7–8.
93   Jameson 2007, p. 260.
94   Ibid.
95   Ibid.
96   John Banville could then be seen as the *reductio ad absurdum* of this position, a writer
      whose meticulously crafted art novels drove him to reinvent himself as Benjamin Black, a
      mediocre writer of crime fiction. He himself has spoken publicly, in a televised interview
      with the US host Charlie Rose, about a split in his writing habits between the sculpted
      prose of his 'literary' novels and the speed-written, plot-driven nature of his crime nov-
      els.

exist 'two poles of social libidinal investment':[97] paranoia and schizophrenia. At once psychic and social, schizophrenia is that free-form desire which has been 'deterritorialised' from all (pre-modern, religious) coded representations; paranoia, by contrast, is that which attempts to fix or 'reterritorialise' desire in determinate, socially sanctioned representations.[98] If the former are anarchic drives and cathexes, the latter are those social and psychic forms which capture and subject them. Jameson wishes to use this aspect of the *Anti-Oedipus* as 'an *aesthetic*, that is, as the description of and apologia for a new type of discourse: the discontinuous, "schizophrenic" text'.[99] By 'molecular level' he will understand 'the here-and-now of immediate perception or of local desire, the production-time of the individual sentence, the electrifying shock of the individual word ... of the regional throb of pain or pleasure'.[100] The molar level is its counterforce:

> all those large, abstract, mediate, and perhaps even empty and imaginary
> forms by which we seek to recontain the molecular: the mirage of the
> continuity of personal identity, the organizing unity of the psyche or the
> personality, the concept of society itself, and, not least, the notion of the
> organic unity of the work of art.[101]

Thus the stage is set for the schizophrenic modernist work of art, torn between the centrifugal thrusts of sentence production and the centripetal pull of the narrative frame.

It should be obvious that, in this context, 'narrative' means something different to 'mode of apprehension' (the definition I introduced above). Here, it denotes rather that structural principle immanent to a work which is the source of its unification. Nonetheless, there are certain similarities between the two. If narrative as an operation of apprehension always aspires, in Lukácsian fashion, to totality, it is one of the assumptions of Jameson's theory of representation that it 'is governed by "an intention towards totality"', one whose 'limits must also be drawn back into the system' in order to achieve closure.[102] The point,

---

97   Deleuze and Guattari 1983, p. 366.
98   For an excellent overview of these two modes of libidinal investment, see Holland 1999,
     pp. 93–6.
99   Jameson 1979, p. 7, n. 6.
100 Jameson 1979, p. 8.
101 Ibid.
102 Jameson 2007, p. 163. In this, he is simply reiterating Aristotle who defined tragedy as an
     'imitation of action' which is 'complete' [*teleios*] (2000, 1449b).

however, is that because the narrative categories of experience have become extinct in capitalist modernity, traditional forms of existential 'closure' such as destiny, fate and fortune are no longer available to the writer. She must thus find a structural substitute from elsewhere. It is here that Jameson's notion of a 'libidinal apparatus', adapted from Lyotard's *dispositif*, comes to the fore. Jameson defines it as 'a structure which, produced by the accidents of a certain history, can be alienated and pressed into the service of a quite different one, reinvested with new and unexpected content'.[103] Such structures must be envisaged as formal abstractions from really existing objects, systems, or spaces. In *Tarr*, for instance, Wyndham Lewis draws on what Jameson calls 'national allegory', 'the diplomatic system of pre-War nation-states';[104] this system was the product of the political history of pre-1914 Europe, but Lewis abstracts its form and re-functions it to develop a characterological system of psychic allegories (Kreisler as Germany, Soltyk as Poland, and so on).[105] The typical modernist text is thus a configuration of two opposed levels which have become autonomous: the level of the sentence or 'style' and the level of the narrative structure. At the extreme, the story that ultimately gets told is the merest pretext for the writing of sentences. In this respect, high fiction comes to resemble the reified social reality it represents: pristine surfaces with all traces of praxis and production concealed. Style becomes a linguistic mode of reification.

4.4   *The Utopian Vocation of Style*

No description of Jameson's theory of style would be complete, however, without registering the *pleasure* it produces in writer and reader alike. Thus far the Jamesonian theory of style I have reconstructed sounds like nothing so much

---

103   Jameson 1979, p. 10.

104   Jameson 1979, p. 11.

105   Jameson even goes so far as to show that non-fictional theories such as Freud's presupposed the same logic of figuration. The psychoanalytic models he developed were allegorical and presupposed the topography of the city and the dynamics of the political state; without the objective structures offered to him by his historical moment, Freud could not have figured the mind in the way he did (cf. Jameson 1979, p. 96). It should be observed, however, that, in Freud's case, the function of the objective structures was different from those of the modernist novel: in the latter they recontain the potentially unlimited molecular-level sentence-production. Another example is Joyce's use of Homer's *Odyssey* and of what Jameson (misleadingly) calls the 'classical city' of Dublin as informing structures which recontain the potentially infinite sentence-production of *Ulysses* (Jameson 2007, pp. 137–51).

as a panegyric to the lost narrative *Gemeinschaft*. There is certainly something of the 'Romantic anti-capitalist' about Jameson, but no bleary-eyed nostalgic is he. In an essay on Conrad, for example, Jameson reads the writer's style as simultaneously ideological and Utopian: it is Utopian because, against the drab greyness to which capitalist rationalisation and reification have subjected the human sensorium, it offers a revitalisation of our sense of sight – 'before all, to make you *see*' –[106] via an almost limitless impressionistic sentence-production; at the same time, however, it is ideological in that, by transforming this desiccated perceptual world into pockets of vibrant colour, it reifies the world in its own way, by wrenching 'the living raw material of life ... from the historical situation in which alone change is meaningful, to preserve it, beyond time, in the imaginary'.[107] In other words, Conrad dereifies the world only to denarrativise it in a different way. Nonetheless, the affective intensity of style, its 'Utopian vocation' as Jameson has it,[108] must not be forgotten amidst the keening for the storytellers of old.

Such, then, is Jameson's theory of style. It is a predominantly modernist linguistic practice, unique to the bourgeois monadic subject who has lost all organic links to his or her public, a borderline physiological phenomenon, involving a detailed elaboration of individual sentences which develop autonomously in contradistinction to the organic unity of the literary work. Its causes are variously *political*, arising from the passive revolution of the bourgeoisie from 1848 onwards; *economic*, with the shift from feudalism to capitalism effecting the demise of traditional narrative categories of storytelling, and the situation of incomplete modernisation producing temporal and spatial disjunctions; and *social*, with the sapping of the collective vitality of language itself and the decline of public meeting places which used to provide the raw material for the production of anecdotes and tales. The development of style was subject to national variations, depending on the relative presence or absence of these political, economic and social factors. If a situation were to occur in which this particular triangulation of forces were to alter in some way, style could potentially disappear. It is just such an alteration that Jameson claims occurred in postmodernity.

---

106   From Conrad's preface to *The Nigger of the Narcissus* (cited in Jameson 1981, p. 232).
107   Jameson 1981, p. 238.
108   Jameson 1981, p. 230.

5   Postmodernity and the End of Style

In his work on postmodernism Jameson tends to emphasise only one of the factors which enabled modernist style, adding a second which never actually features in his writings on modernism per se. Initially, he stresses that style was bound up with the monadic bourgeois individual, the demise of which through the so-called 'death of the subject' spelt the end of style:

> What we must now stress ... is the degree to which the high-modernist conception of a unique *style*, along with the accompanying collective ideals of an artistic or political vanguard or avant-garde, themselves stand or fall along with that older notion (or experience) of the so-called centered subject ... The end of the bourgeois ego, or monad, no doubt brings with it the end of the psychopathologies of that ego ... [B]ut it means the end of much more – the end, for example, of style.[109]

This is coupled with a second factor: pastiche, an emasculated form of parody – 'amputated of the satiric impulse, devoid of laughter and of any conviction that alongside the abnormal tongue you have momentarily borrowed, some healthy linguistic normality still exists'.[110] What caused the rise of pastiche? Jameson suggests it was the 'linguistic fragmentation of social life itself to the point where the norm itself is eclipsed: reduced to a neutral and reified media speech'.[111] A more promising line of approach comes when he claims that '[f]aceless masters continue to inflect the economic strategies which constrain our existences, but they no longer need to impose their speech (or are henceforth unable to)'.[112] It is as if in the age of the image and the simulacrum, the word loses its power to effect political obedience.[113] All that is left to the writer is 'the imitation of dead styles'.[114] In a more recent text, Jameson tempers the extremity of his argument somewhat: 'Nobody thinks that writers like David Foster Wallace are styleless, but rather that the production of the individual or personal style ... is no longer of the same order as modernist style'.[115]

---

109   Jameson 1991, p. 15.
110   Jameson 1991, p. 17.
111   Ibid.
112   Ibid.
113   I shall pursue this notion in Part 3, where I offer an alternative account of the underlying modern and postmodern linguistic situations.
114   Jameson 1991, p. 18.
115   Interview in Buchanan 2006, p. 124.

It is as if the ideology of modernism has become so dominant that the reader experiences postmodern texts as stylised, even if style in Jameson's sense never featured in their actual production.

In an astonishing essay, 'Modernism and Imperialism', Jameson will even go as far as to suggest that the writing of Joyce himself – the modernist *par excellence* – is *styleless* in just this postmodern sense: a suggestion certainly designed to provoke. Thanks to the British occupation, Dublin was prevented from undergoing the rapid expansion and rationalisation that the imperial metropolises experienced in the late nineteenth and early twentieth centuries. It meant that those collective meeting places and resources of anecdote and gossip were kept intact in Ireland for far longer than in Britain. Encounters in Joyce's Dublin, unlike their equivalents in Forster and Woolf, are primarily linguistic. *Ulysses* thus combines pre-modern collective linguistic vitality with the most cutting-edge novelistic techniques appropriated from the more advanced metropolises: 'Joyce leaps over the stage of the modern into full post-modernism. The pastiche of styles in the Oxen of the Sun not merely discredits the category of style as such, but presents an enumeration of English styles, of the styles of the imperial occupying armies'.[116] We might read this passage as employing a logic of combined and uneven development, an important feature of Jameson's work, which goes some way to mitigating the potentially static nature of his periodising schema.

To summarise, then, with the completion of capitalist modernisation in the stage of 'late capitalism', the demise of the bourgeois individual subject and the disappearance of linguistic norms, style withered away. All that remains, says Jameson, is pastiche.

6   Jameson's Theory of Style: A Balance-Sheet

It will not have gone unnoticed that this theory of style rests upon certain major – and problematic – historico-literary claims. Before articulating these problems and suggesting potential solutions, however, we must first consider its virtues. Firstly, Jameson's theory of style makes a fascinating attempt to account historically and materially for the gradual autonomisation of the individual sentence within the history of literature. He does so by demonstrating what Ricoeur's reformulation of Aristotle's *Poetics* simply could not accept: that human experience undergoes profound mutations throughout the course of

---

116   Jameson 2007, p. 166.

history, and that these mutations are the effect of the changing ways in which humans collectively organise and carry out their social and material reproduction.[117] He traces these mutations into the heart of shifts in literary forms, and in doing so provides an account of their genesis which Ricoeur's formalism prevented. Secondly, Jameson's theory provides an implicit understanding of the changing nature of language beyond the ken of Ricoeur's threefold mimesis. He posits a direct link between the sapping of the collective vitality of language – effected by the disappearance of pre-modern collective meeting places, the extinction of the narrative categories of experience, and the replacement of oratorical aristocratic forms with written bourgeois equivalents – and the rise of individually sculpted private styles. Finally, Jameson captures the sheer *ambivalence* of style, the fact that it arises out of a certain breakdown in social relationships but that it nonetheless attests to a pleasurable Utopian prefiguration; likewise, if style is an index of social and literary plotlessness, it nonetheless compensates for this in its laborious, self-conscious elaboration of individual sentences. Taken together, these three strengths offer a suggestive foundation for the elaboration of a Marxist theory of style.

Yet one cannot help but feel that Jameson's theory fails precisely on the two fronts where, on his logic, it should most succeed: interpretive semantic richness and politicisation.[118] Despite all the caveats Jameson makes about his system of periodisation and his theory of the modes of production as being non-reductive, and despite his argument that any text can be reconstructed on three levels, each with its own historical scope (from political history, to the social, to human history as such),[119] and despite – finally – his conception of a literary work as a 'response' to a (Sartrean) 'situation' or symbolic 'resolution' of a historical contradiction, could it not be said that Jameson's theory of style is too static, simple and stagist to be of any great semantic or political interest? The stages are: market capitalism-realism-rhetoric, monopoly capitalism-modernism-style, late capitalism-postmodernism-stylelessness. This criticism can even be articulated in Jameson's own terms. For he writes that History, like Time, can only be made to appear when, in objective reality, its multiple temporalities suddenly intersect in the explosion of an Event that

---

117   '[Ricoeur is] apparently unwilling to entertain any possibility that human time has in late capitalism undergone a kind of structural mutation' (Jameson 2009, p. 494).

118   'I will here argue the priority of a Marxian interpretive framework in terms of semantic richness' (Jameson 1981, 10); 'The only effective liberation [from the grip of Necessity] begins with the recognition that there is nothing that is not social and historical – indeed, that everything is "in the last analysis" political' (ibid., p. 20).

119   Jameson 1981, p. 75 ff.

momentarily ignites lived experience.[120] In those periods of political defeat, it is the task of a Marxist poetics mimetically to configure those temporalities so as to provide an artificial substitute for the Event and to function as a reminder that History is indeed the product of collective human acts. Yet by reducing all practices with their unique temporalities to the epic purview of the mode of production, does one not lack the uneven and intersecting mediations required to make History as Event appear? Jameson's caveat that if we see every social formation as consisting of '*several* modes of production' then 'the temptation to classify texts according to the appropriate mode of production is thereby removed' is rarely brought to bear on his actual analyses of literary texts;[121] instead, we are left with ingenious critical elaborations of individual works on the one hand and magnificent generalisations about the various epic-scale periods on the other. What he lacks are those multiple mediating categories which were such a vital strength to Raymond Williams's critical *and* political analyses: formation, structure of feeling, and residual-dominant-emergent. Moreover, I say this in full knowledge of Jameson's explicit calls for mediation or 'transcoding';[122] as it happens, Jameson will only ever use *one* category of mediation to triangulate between the cultural and the economic spheres, and it is almost always reification. To adopt a different terminology, then, one might say that Jameson's stories lack *sub-plots*: the combined and uneven strands which master story-tellers weave into powerful catharsis-inducing narratives. Without them, it is not only semantic richness which falls by the wayside, but *the political as such*.

For politics is the time of strategy, the time 'full of knots and wombs pregnant with events'.[123] Eagleton noted long ago that Jameson's style lacks two elements typical of the revolutionary: satire and polemic. We have already seen, in Williams's response to a similar accusation, that the politics of style is not nearly as simple as all that. Nonetheless, it is certainly true that Jameson's expansiveness of vision comes at the price of a viewpoint practically *beyond* History. Take, for example, his total repudiation of ethics as an individualist mystification of what are properly collective political affairs.[124] In his earlier work this takes the guise of repeated proclamations that the Marxist dialectic is 'beyond good and evil' because of its capacity to think progress and destruction as the identity

---

120   Jameson 2009, pp. 475–612.

121   Jameson 1981, p. 95.

122   Jameson 1981, pp. 39–43.

123   Bensaïd 2007, p. 151.

124   E.g., Jameson 1981, pp. 234–5.

of opposites. It was for this reason that he came to see *every* example of ideology as simultaneously a prefiguration of Utopia. In his later work, starting with *Brecht and Method*,[125] this has transformed into a far more passive, possibly even ahistorical optimism: 'the true dialectician ... will always wish patiently to wait for the stirrings of historical evolution even within defeat'.[126] Likewise, he writes elsewhere that in order to perceive the successes dialectically inherent to failures, one's '[p]oint of view must be an elevated and a distant, even a glacial one, in order for these all-too-human categories of success and failure to become indifferent in their own opposition'.[127] The question that invites itself is: indifferent to whom? Such passages could even be read as a return of the repressed. The Marxist storyteller whose life-project has been to 'tell the tale of the tribe', to renarrativise a reified social reality and, in doing so, to explode contemplation and make collective political action possible again; this Marxist advocates nothing so much as a collective form of waiting, in which readers are advised to sit, contemplate, and let the dialectic do its work. There is no doubt, of course, that in times of political defeat such words are a wise and radical call for patience and endurance. But it is nonetheless difficult to dismiss the sense of a disjunction between the overt drive for praxis and narrative, and this increasingly prominent advocacy of contemplation – that very contemplation of which style was said to be the chief linguistic mode.

---

125   Jameson 1998.
126   Jameson 1998, p. 23.
127   Jameson 2009, p. 554.

Coda: New Styles for New Social Relations

One of the principal tasks of Part 2 of this book has been the demonstration of the various ways in which literary styles are constitutively social and political. We saw in Chapter 5 that this has two senses: not only that literary styles embody and mediate social relations, but that styles themselves are immanent constituents of these modes of relationality. I have tended to stress the former at the expense the latter, but no conception of style within the context of a Marxist poetics would be complete without some recognition of the capacity for *new* styles to embody new social relations. After all, it will be recalled from Chapter 2 that Trotsky saw the development of new journalistic styles as a key component of the production of a new, post-capitalist humanity.

Of the three thinkers studied in this book, Raymond Williams was the one most concerned with the creation of new styles as components of new social relations. In the final chapter of *Marxism and Literature*, entitled 'Creative Practice', Williams outlines his conception of literary creativity. He begins by arguing that 'creation' is, strictly speaking, very rare. It cannot simply be equated with the 'arts' and the 'aesthetic' per se, since most of what these things achieve is, technically speaking, the 'detailed and substantial *performance of a known model*'.[1] The vast majority of literary works are active reproductions of pre-existing modes, genres, types and forms. At most, they exhibit minor variations on the known model. Creation in the strict sense, Williams argues, must be aligned with the 'emergent' – the proleptic mode of practical consciousness. Creation occurs via the 'introduction of different notations and conventions' which are themselves immanent aspects of changes in the social formation.[2] These changes are not, however, reducible to institutional change since the 'social area excluded by certain practical hegemonies is often one of their sources', meaning that – in what we might call an Althusserian insistence – there is always a potential temporal and practical disjunction between the social formation in its totality and the practice of writing in particular. Literary production is creative 'in the material social sense of a specific practice of self-making, which is in this sense socially neutral: self-composition'.[3] Creation is that rare practice of 'mak[ing] latencies actual'.[4]

---

1 Williams 1977, p. 209; emphasis in the original.
2 Ibid.
3 Williams 1977, p. 210.
4 Ibid.

The modes this creative practice may assume are variable. Firstly, it may simply consist in 'the long and difficult remaking of an inherited (determined) practical consciousness ... a struggle at the roots of the mind ... confronting a hegemony in the fibres of the self'.[5] It can also be 'the embodiment and performance of known but excluded and subordinated experiences and relationships'.[6] Finally, it may consist of the truly 'creative' in the strict sense of 'the articulation and formation of latent, momentary, and newly possible consciousness'.[7] The point here is that each of these modes of creative practice is an immanent and constitutive aspect of human self-composition: by producing new styles we produce new possible modes of relating to and understanding one another.

There is no better proof of Williams's conviction in this regard than his work in the WEA. Sharing that association's traditional objection to 'Public Speaking' – 'it produces a mechanical voice Style [*sic*], in the manner of an average RADA actress'[8] – he invented a course called 'Public Expression'. Rather than the superficial beautification of speech proposed by traditional public speaking courses, his own syllabus was designed specifically to '[equip] members of working-class movements for the discharge of actual public responsibilities'.[9] The course was intended as a way of releasing latent social relations and of giving linguistic body to working-class consciousness: 'Does one impose on a social class that is growing in power the syllabus of an older culture; or does one seek means of releasing and enriching the life-experience which that rising class brings with it?'[10] Rather than *incorporating* the working-class students into written and spoken styles whose origins lay in the social consciousness of the hegemonic class and its selective tradition, Williams sought to work with his students to enable them to produce styles which would be adequate to their unique social experience and would release their emergent practical consciousness. One might even describe it as a counter-hegemonic linguistic practice.

He took a similar approach in the policy proposals put forth in *Communications* (1966). There he identified a dual problem with the traditional methods of teaching writing: students were taught to write in old-fashioned styles and the forms they learned bore little relation to the practical realities of every-

---

5   Williams 1977, p. 212. He argues this point at length in Williams 1989, pp. 77–95.
6   Ibid.
7   Ibid.
8   Williams 1952b, p. 181.
9   Ibid.
10   Ibid.

day life.[11] Rather than being taught debating or the three-minute speech, forms which, as he saw it, play little part in social life, he suggested that they 'need to practise ... such forms as the committee discussion, the verbal report, or the detailed questioning of a speech'.[12] Again, he is trying to connect the critical pedagogy of writing to contemporary everyday activities as well as emergent forms of social consciousness. More significantly, having described the social tone of official forms as one of 'licensed bullying',[13] he goes on to argue that '[i]t would be something if we could learn to write to each other, on official or business occasions, in ways compatible with a self-respecting democratic society'.[14] For Williams, then, there simply will not be a self-respecting democratic society until the linguistic modes of social relation immanent to class society are transformed.

Of course, these examples are not primarily literary in nature. Nonetheless, we saw in Chapters 4 and 5 that the same principles apply: literary styles are immanent components of social relations and until we produce styles capable of inculcating relations beyond domination and exploitation, we shall continue to reproduce the social relations of capitalist production. In tandem with this creative production of literary styles, the very status of literature as such would have to be transformed: no longer set aside as a mere form of 'leisure' or 'play', but reintegrated into the heart of a wider conception of 'society' which goes beyond 'economics and administration'.[15] None of this is to argue, however, that new literary styles are *alone* capable of fundamentally transforming social reality (the ridiculousness of such a proposition is self-evident); but it is certainly to suggest that, without them, the modes of consciousness innate to a class society will persevere. The production of new literary styles is thus a production of new ways of being and acting together, the two elements – *poiēsis* and *praxis* – forming a dialectical unity.

---

11   Williams 1976, p. 142.
12   Ibid.
13   Williams 1976, p. 143.
14   Ibid.
15   Ibid.

PART 3

Style in Marxist Poetics

∴

A General Marxist Theory of Style

The aim of the final part of this book is to develop a set of concepts which, taken together, constitute an overarching theory of literary style as conceived within the framework of a Marxist poetics. It also attempts to provide the Marxist recalibration of Ricoeur's threefold mimesis promised in Chapter 3, and whose formulation was hinted at in subsequent chapters. In many ways the system developed here emerges out of Part 2 in that it tries to incorporate the strengths of Williams's, Eagleton's and Jameson's work respectively, whilst attempting to make up for some of their weaknesses.

Despite the fact that Part 3 is an organic development of Part 2, however, it should nonetheless be seen as an independent theory of literary style in its own right – one which differs from the exegetical mode pursued in the previous four chapters. It is divided into the three moments of Ricoeur's threefold mimesis: prefiguration (mimesis$_1$), configuration (mimesis$_2$) and refiguration (mimesis$_3$). I go beyond Ricoeur's conception by reformulating his insights in a Marxist idiom and by combining them with a new set of concepts designed specifically to enable the analysis, explanation and interpretation of the whole gamut of literary styles. I should state at the outset that I do not believe it necessary for every critical analysis of style to adopt each and every single concept developed here. I do hold, however, that an *exhaustive* stylistic analysis would have to draw on *most* of them.

I begin with mimesis$_1$, or prefiguration, which consists of what I call the 'linguistic situation', 'linguistic ideology' and 'experience'.

1   Mimesis$_1$

1.1   *Linguistic Situation*

Literary style, at its most basic, is the artistic shaping of a pre-existent common language. This common language consists of multiple linguistic practices – including past styles – structured and striated by the divisions and contradictions of the social formation, of which it is an immanent, relatively autonomous element. When a writer sits down to write, she inhabits and confronts a language consisting of a multiplicity of socially determinate elements. One central aspect of the writing process is thus the operation by which the writer's (pre-, semi-, or self-conscious) artistic project comes to determine (or fails to determine) these social determinations. A Marxist poetics will thus require some way of accounting for the origins, types and effects of these resistances inherent to language. Consequently, I propose the following concept: the linguistic situation.

The linguistic situation is a hypothetical reconstruction of the state of language as a writer or set of writers would have experienced it, including its inner tensions and social stratifications. It is the strictly verbal element of mimesis₁ (prefiguration) – that element which was identified in Chapter 3 as an aporia in Ricoeur's plot-centred theory of narration. I use the term 'situation' in full consciousness of its Sartrean connotations: rather than designating an indifferent, static linguistic background, it denotes rather the objective linguistic field which informs and limits one's projects of literary production.[1] It is a field of linguistic possibilities and constraints, blockages and resources. These latter are both *produced* in and through the social practices of which they are the practical consciousness and *defined* relationally in accordance with one's poetic freedom as a writer. (Thus, in Williams's reading of Thomas Hardy, as seen in Chapter 4, the stratification of the English language into educated and customary modes of speech was *produced* by various processes of urbanisation and capitalist expansion, but this was *defined* as an obstacle to be overcome by lexical configuration only because Hardy desired, as part of his project of literary configuration, to unite the two discourses: his freedom defined the obstacles to his freedom). Moreover, unlike Jameson's singularisation and overexpansion of Sartre's concept of the 'situation' (that is, his emphasis on the 'situation' as *one* situation, as opposed to a multiplicity thereof, and his conflation of the 'situation' with the 'period' as such), the fundamental linguistic situation consists of several sub-situations.[2] These range,

---

1   Though our terminology differs, I take 'linguistic situation' to be synonymous with what Jean-Jacques Lecercle has named the 'linguistic conjuncture' or 'linguistic formation' (Lecercle 2006, pp. 103–4, 156). I am grateful to him for drawing my attention to these terms, and to the risk I run of inheriting Sartre's methodological individualism by retaining the term 'situation'. I recognise this risk, but have opted to retain 'situation' in the hope that its place within the totality of my theory will denude it of any residual individualism, and also because of the dramatic potential of the term: it invites the critic to dramatise a writer's or set of writers' confrontation with the obstacle-field of their linguistic context, thereby enabling her to frame literary production as an *act* and, in the process, to avoid simplistic 'reflection' theories of literature.

2   Unlike Sartre (cf. Priest 2001, pp. 177–8), I do not insist on their hierarchical ordering; I stress simply that any linguistic situation is, in reality, an overlapping multiplicity of several linguistic situations, experienced as a unity.

at the broadest, from the Jamesonian 'stagist' conception of cultural shifts (market capitalism-realism-rhetoric, monopoly capitalism-modernism-style, late capitalism-postmodernism-stylelessness), which I shall rewrite from the perspective of a geopolitics of language, all the way to a reconstruction of the strictly limited range of linguistic phenomena (vocabulary, idioms, sociolects, jargon, etc.) which a writer is likely to encounter, given her biographical trajectory. In general, we can divide the linguistic sub-situations into those which deal with the *scope* and *structuring tensions* of a writer's verbal raw material and those dealing with its *semantic* or *ideological content.*

I shall now attempt to demonstrate how, as a first move (but *only* as a first move), the underlying linguistic situation of relatively large periods and spatial expanses might be sketched out. To do so, I shall draw on Perry Anderson's accounts of modernism and postmodernism respectively. What I claim to offer here is not only an example of how such a hypothetical reconstruction might work in practice, but also a more coherent theory of the shift in fundamental linguistic situation from modernism to postmodernism than Jameson himself is able to offer.

Anderson locates the origins of modernism within a force field triangulated by three coordinates:

> an economy and society still only semi-industrial, in which the ruling order still remained to a significant extent agrarian or aristocratic; a technology of dramatic inventions whose impact was still fresh or incipient; and an open political horizon, in which revolutionary upheavals of one kind or another against the prevailing order were widely expected or feared.[3]

The first coordinate meant a 'codification of a highly formalized *academicism* in the visual and other arts, which itself was institutionalized within official regimes of states and society still massively pervaded, often dominated, by aristocratic or landowning classes'.[4] This gave writers and artists something official against which to rebel and to measure themselves: a set of taboos to be broken. The second coordinate meant that technology was still open to appropriation by groups across the political spectrum: it was not yet fully integrated into a diverse and expanded capitalist economy. There was still an excitement which could be exploited by all the arts. Likewise, the third

---

3   Anderson 1998, p. 81. This is a summary of his earlier article, Anderson 1984.
4   Anderson 1984, p. 104.

coordinate signalled a social world constantly on the verge of some epic shift, the political ground trembling beneath one's feet. European modernism 'thus flowered in the space between a still usable classical past, a still indeterminate technical present, and a still unpredictable political future. Or, put another way, it arose at the intersection between a semi-aristocratic ruling order, a semi-industrialized capitalist economy, and a semi-emergent or -insurgent, labour movement'.[5]

Postmodernism was the name that came to be ascribed to social and cultural phenomena once those three coordinates disappeared. By the end of the Second World War the aristocratic tradition 'received its quietus' across continental Europe.[6] Another 20 years later and 'the bourgeoisie too – in any strict sense, as a class possessed of self-consciousness and morale – was all but extinct'.[7] This coincided with the process of so-called *embourgeoisement* of the working class in the West and, in the 1990s, with what Anderson refers to as 'a general *encanaillement* of the possessing classes ...: starlet princesses and sleazeball presidents, beds for rent in the official residence and bribes for killer ads, disneyfication of protocols and tarantinization of practices'.[8] Taken together, this spelled the end of the academicist establishment, along with the official, moribund morality of the bourgeois age; at a time when hedonism has become enthroned as the chief collective virtue – when the superego screams 'Enjoy!' instead of 'No!' –[9] there is no one left to outrage and no taboos to be broken. These major shifts in class composition were accompanied by the routinisation of technological innovation – its total subsumption under the rule of capital. By far the greatest technological event of the postmodern era was the arrival of the colour television: this sealed the hegemony of the visual and the spoken over the written word. Finally, in terms of the third coordinate (social revolution), the onset of the Cold War 'chilled all insurgent hopes in Europe' whilst the labour movement in America was 'neutered' and the left 'hounded'.[10] Beyond the West there remained acts of political hope, especially in the form of decolonisation movements. But in the West itself, except for the social explo-

---

5   Anderson 1984, p. 105.

6   Anderson 1998, p. 84.

7   Anderson 1998, p. 85. In place of the old bourgeoisie arose 'an aquarium of floating, evanescent forms – the projectors and managers, auditors and janitors, administrators and speculators of contemporary capital: functions of the monetary universe that knows no social fixities or stable identities' (ibid.).

8   Anderson 1998, p. 86.

9   Cf. Žižek 1999.

10   Anderson 1998, p. 89.

sion of 1968–74,[11] a long period of political defeat set in, reaching its peak in the 1980s. In conclusion: 'postmodernism emerged from the constellation of a *déclassé* ruling order, a mediatized technology and a monochrome politics'.[12] The underlying cause of these great shifts was, of course, the new historical phase which emerged from the end of the postwar economic boom.

What does any of this have to do with language? I claim that by drawing on Anderson's overviews of the historical coordinates of modernism and postmodernism we can chart the transformations of the broadest linguistic situations of English more accurately and more coherently than Jameson himself. The major difference between so-called modernism (roughly 1848–45) and postmodernism (roughly 1945-present) is the predominance of language relative to the image, and vice versa. In the period of modernism, language itself was one of the central means and fields of class rule: literacy rates were rising rapidly, newspapers were growing, radio spread the word of rulers across the vast expanses of the nation. In such a situation, language itself was overdetermined, not only by its association with the lies and wiles of power, but also by its insinuation into the fabric of official mores. For those nations like Britain which ruled large formal empires, there was an extra tension at work: the need to distinguish quite sharply between a 'proper' use of the mother tongue and its diluted, adulterated use by one's colonial subjects.[13] In such situations, the Sartrean 'Look' assumed a decidedly linguistic hue. Thus, in the West, during the period of modernism the extreme conservatism of social mores and the use of language as a tool of everyday class and imperial rule produced a linguistic situation structured by hidden linguistic laws which possessed all the force of the primitive taboo. To experiment with language in such a situation was, necessarily, in no matter how minor a manner, to question the social and political structure of the day.

In postmodernism this changed. As far as the English language was concerned, there were three large shifts. The most significant of these was the rise of the visual. Where the word had once been the principal instrument of rule, overdetermining the linguistic formation of any writer in that modernist period, the image became both the new instrument of power and the central principle of what Peter Osborne has called 'photo-capitalism'.[14] Television was a major factor in both the demise of formal oratory as a means of

11 The fact that these tumultuous years – not to mention the entire wave of decolonisation – do not feature prominently in Anderson's account should alert us to its limitations.
12 Anderson 1998, p. 92.
13 Cf. Bhabha 1994, pp. 85–92.
14 Osborne 2013, p. 118.

Peter Osborne: "photo-capitalism"

political control – the Age of Churchill – and the rise of the era of the image and the soundbite (for which Ronald Reagan, Tony Blair and Silvio Berlusconi stand as the degraded epitomes). This rise of the photographic as the cultural and political dominant went hand in hand with a profound geopolitical shift: the emergence of the US as the new global hegemon following the Second World War. Peter Osborne has argued that '[t]he photographic image is ... the dominant visual form of the American Empire'.[15] The rise of this new hegemon involved a transition from a predominantly formal British empire, with its many instances of direct military occupation and administration of subaltern lands, and hence with its existentially felt need to demarcate clear borders between its own proper use of the English tongue and that version of it used by its subjects, to a predominantly informal US empire, where rule was carried out by a US proxy, usually a 'local strongman' who spoke the indigenous tongue.[16] American English had always enjoyed a certain freedom from the stuffy, rule-bound constraints of its British overlords; it was an English rich with the spoken *argots* of everyday life. But now, as the de facto global linguistic hegemon, ruling by economic and (later) financial interventions rather than direct formal rule, it became an English surprisingly apposite for a linguistically lax televisual era.

The third, complementary component of this postmodern linguistic situation was the abovementioned 'general *encanaillement* of the possessing classes'. The moralistic proprieties of the bourgeoisie, especially after the cultural shifts of the 1960s, gave way to rule by ostentatious glitz (in Britain this was coeval with the neoliberalisation process actively imposed by Thatcher, one which produced a social reconfiguration in which the Old Boys of the military and the judiciary gave way to brash entrepreneurs and culturally crass *nouveaux riches*).[17] The linguistic upshot of this was a general 'casualisation' of the

---

15   Ibid.
16   'The answer was to find a local strongman ... and to provide economic and military assistance to him and his family and immediate allies so that they could repress or buy off opposition and accumulate considerable wealth and power for themselves. In return they would always keep their country open to the operations of US capital and support, and if necessary promote US interests, both in the country and in the region ... as a whole' (Harvey 2005, p. 27). This is not to suggest that the British were averse to this tactic; on the contrary, the historical record shows that 'Britain's informal or free trade empire, in Latin America, the middle east or east Asia, was more extensive and often more profitable than its formal one, and statesmen generally preferred it, resorting to the expense and danger of formal conquest only when forced to do so' (Howe 2003).
17   Cf. Harvey 2005, p. 31.

spoken and written word. By the time of the rise of the so-called 'social media' in the first decade of the twenty-first century, it was now perfectly normal to find computer software addressing one in the most familiar and informal terms: 'Thanks for being cool and confirming your registration. What's next? You can invite your friends to Vimeo, because everything is better with pals'.[18] It is in this precise context that Jameson's basic insight into postmodernity is correct: 'My sense is that this is essentially a visual culture, wired for sound – but one where the linguistic element ... is slack and flabby, and not to be made interesting without ingenuity, daring, and keen motivation'.[19] The linguistic situation of postmodernity is thus one decidedly *lacking* those innate taboo-like forces and implicit social laws with which the modern period was replete. It is a linguistic culture in which, broadly speaking, anything goes. And when anything goes, language becomes 'flabby'. Is it surprising that literary groups like Oulipo ended up *imposing* linguistic limitations on themselves? When taboos no longer exist, they must be invented.

Of course, this international aspect of the linguistic situation is merely the underlying one, the ground on and through which the contradictions of the individual *national* linguistic situations play themselves out. At this level, it is worth remembering that any mention of 'the' national language presupposes the achieved and continuing hegemony of one prestigious dialect, or what Bourdieu calls a 'legitimate language'.[20] For the sake of brevity, I shall focus here on the legitimate language of Britain: Standard English. Unlike continental Europe, where the great nationalist movements of the nineteenth century invented official national tongues almost overnight – usually based on a formal literary language that the vast majority of the population did not speak – Standard English was, if no less an exercise in political unification, a typically more gradualist affair.[21] It has five essential characteristics: it is a variety of English with a distinctive combination of linguistic features, but – crucially – with no local base; it is primarily a matter of grammar, vocabulary and orthography, but is not always necessarily coupled with Received Pronunciation; it is the variety of English which carries the most social prestige or, in Bourdieu's terms, symbolic capital; it is enforced, disseminated and reproduced as the legitimate language via the education system, the media, the courts, and other ideological

---

18   This was the style that greeted one in June 2013 on signing up to the video content website, vimeo.com.

19   Jameson 1991, p. 299.

20   Bourdieu 1991, pp. 43–65.

21   Cf. Hobsbawm 1992, pp. 51–63.

state apparatuses;[22] and, perhaps most significantly, almost no one actually
uses it in everyday speech.[23] Thus, any writer active in Britain today will sense
a curious tension between the formality of the 'legitimate language' and the
increasing *in*formality of English in general within postmodernity. Moreover,
writers active at any point in Britain in the modern era will then experience
the further tension between the dialects and idioms of the various (regional)
linguistic communities to which they belong (each, it must be added, function-
ing as a unique cognitive and affective assemblage) and the codified power
of Standard English which is taught in schools and universities and which is
omnipresent in the media. Everything they write will then necessarily entail a
negotiation between these variants, a negotiation which is political in the very
precise sense that it implies a set of linguistic allegiances (whether real, unconscious or tactical) to specific collectives within the social formation.
     To become *conscious* of this negotiation, however, would require that a
writer has internally experienced and formed existential attachments to a variant of English other than Standard English. More specifically, it would mean
that she has formed attachments to a variant of English which is *widely diver-
gent* from Standard English (it being presupposed that those who speak with
Received Pronunciation, whilst not guaranteeing their use of Standard English,
will be more likely to feel an affinity with its structure of feeling than those who
have lived their entire lives speaking a 'non-prestigious' dialect). Here, then,
biographical factors come into play. For it will surely be possible to produce a
hypothetical reconstruction of the variants of English with which a writer has a)
come into contact and b) formed an existential attachment. It is precisely here
that what, in Chapter 5, I called Williams's 'sociological perspectivism' could
be further developed. If nothing else, such a reconstruction would remind us
of the simple fact that not all authors can imitate all voices – and *especially*
not with the empathy of those who have lived them from the inside. Authors'
life trajectories expose them only to a limited range of the effectively infinite
variants of spoken and written language, and of this range they will learn to
speak, write and understand themselves in even fewer.[24] Nonetheless, to imitate idioms beyond the range of those variants to which writers have formed

---

22   Cf. Lecercle 2015 on 'linguistic interpellation' by the ideological state apparatuses of the
      family and the education system.
23   Crystal 2004, p. 110. I have occasionally supplemented Crystal's useful characterisation of
      Standard English with a Marxist vocabulary.
24   This is obviously not to suggest that conventions for the written representation of speech
      are always empirically accurate; on the contrary, they have often played a large part in
      *mis*representing historically verifiable modes of speech.

existential attachments will force them into either studying the idiom in sufficient depth so as to be able sensitively to reproduce it (as in Joseph O'Connor's
gloriously polyphonic novels, *Star of the Sea* and *Redemption Falls*), or to resort
to linguistic stereotypes almost always overdetermined by derogatory connotations (as in T.S. Eliot's attempt to reproduce bar-room speech in *The Waste Land*
or Martin Amis's travesty of working-class speech in his recent novel, *Lionel
Asbo*). Thus, the act of verbal mimesis is only partly a matter of verbal craft
(though it is certainly this); it is equally a matter of the geographical and social
borders a given writer has been able to cross in both reality and imagination.[25]

All of this, of course, presupposes that one's relation to the English language
is that of a native speaker. Yet there is one situation in particular in which that
is obviously not the case: immigrant or émigré writers. This expands the relevance of the national and international sub-situations in several ways. The social
and geographical journeys mentioned above assume a further depth in that it
is not only a range of dialects that the writer experiences, but also of actual
languages as well; their existential attachments may well not be to the language in which they write, but rather to the mother tongue spoken in the home,
hence freeing them from the innate doxas of the state language's clichéd formulations. It was precisely for this reason that Raymond Williams was dubious
of modernist linguistic experimentation: it was at once one of the most profound periods of stylistic development in the history of western literature and
an index of émigré writers' alienation from a communally embedded language.
Peter Quartermain and Charles Bernstein have gone so far as to suggest – quite
rightly – that the revolution in twentieth-century poetics arose precisely from
such a configuration of circumstances: '[Gertrude] Stein, William Carlos Williams, and Louis Zukofsky – three poets who created the ground for twentieth-
century poetry – all learned English as a second language'.[26] This enabled them
to develop what Bernstein calls an 'associational' rather than an 'etymological'
English, the difference being that '[e]tymological writing is symbolic and connotative, while associational writing involves a lateral glissade into *mis*hearing,

---

25   The exception to this, of course, is that whole range of omnipresent, anonymous, collect-
      ive jargon which forms the daily tissue of our linguistic lives in postmodernity: managerial
      cant, user manual plainness, advertising slogans, bureaucratic sophistry, legalese, com-
      puter software vox pop, and so on. These postmodern *argots* are so ubiquitous as to be
      practically impossible *not* to encounter; thus, an author's use of them – often for purposes
      of parody – is much less dependent on her geographical and social trajectory.

26   Bernstein 1992, p. 108. Bernstein is drawing on Quartermain's work in this section. That
      Stein herself was well aware of this unusual state of affairs is attested to in her brilliant
      lecture, 'What is English Literature' (Stein 1988, pp. 11–55).

sound rather than root connections, dialect, "speech" in [William Carlos] Williams' sense'.[27] Where native speakers are bound by the reality principle of the mother tongue, the émigré is free to indulge the pleasure principle, even if in doing so she linguistically alienates herself from the community. Hence why the revolutionary stylistic gestures of the great (post)moderns always run the risk of becoming politically impotent pyrotechnics: the radicalism of their verbal exploits is difficult to connect to or to reintegrate into the dominant modes of speaking and writing of the larger community. It is at once a glorious linguistic liberation and a potentially Pyrrhic victory.

The final linguistic sub-situation is formally similar to that of the émigré, in that the writer lives in and through two or more languages; the difference is its enforced nature: this is the situation of the (ex-)colonial subject. It is this brand of 'politics of style' with which contemporary theory is most at home, since it is so *overtly* political. The mere choice of writing in the language of the coloniser rather than in the mother tongue (be it a tribal, national or some other collective dialect) entails a whole series of political implications for which the writer will be held to account. Whilst there is no way of doing justice to this immensely complex issue in the framework of this book, by focusing on one example it will be possible to discern the types of issues at stake.[28] In his 1965 essay, 'English and the African Writer', Chinua Achebe takes on the African writers who claim that those who have chosen to write in English or French are 'unpatriotic smart alecs, with an eye on the main chance outside their countries'.[29] Instead, whilst he recognises that English is the 'world language that history has forced down our throats',[30] he calls for 'serious' (p. 348) writers to submit that language to many different kinds of use. In a manner which prefigures Deleuze and Guattari's notions of 'minor literature' and of 'style' as that which makes language stutter [*bégayer*] from the inside,[31] Achebe envisions a situation in which the half dozen Nigerian languages will 'develop as tributaries to feed the one central language enjoying nationwide currency [i.e., English]',[32] and in the process

---

27   Bernstein 1992, p. 109.
28   A more detailed account of this issue would have to begin with Ngũgĩ wa Thiong'o's *Decolonising the Mind* (1986). It would also have to take into account the creation of a common but highly artificial transatlantic idiom for literary translations, developing some of the ideas contained in Pascale Casanova's *La République mondiale des lettres* (1999). See Lecercle 2015 for an excellent overview of – and intervention into – these debates.
29   Achebe 1997, p. 344.
30   Achebe 1997, p. 346.
31   Deleuze 1998, pp. 107–14.
32   Achebe 1997, p. 345.

modifying it to fit their particular experiences and desires. Achebe thus fuses a certain stoic pragmatism (English is, for better or worse, the Nigerian national tongue) with a political desire to alienate it from its ancestral proprietors and make it fit Nigerian writers' needs. Crucially, at no point does he rule out the possibility that political struggle could well result in the introduction of a differ-ent language as the new national tongue: 'This "reality" [of present-day Africa] may change as a result of deliberate, i.e., political, action. If it does, an entirely new situation will arise, and there will be plenty of time to examine it'.[33] This is just one complex example of the profound political difficulties a (post)colonial writer must negotiate.

Taken together, these are the multiple sub-situations which constitute the *scope* and the *structuring tensions* of the linguistic situation as a writer sits down to write.[34] This must then be combined with a very general recogni-tion of the *semantic and ideological content* of the language available to her. If language is, as Raymond Williams believed, nothing less than practical con-sciousness,[35] and words are immanent, determinate aspects of the practical political struggles in which they feature, then the language on which writers go to work must be seen as a web of overdetermined significations and resid-ual intentions, marked by traces of prior use. Simply to denote is inevitably to connote, Barthesian mythologies surreptitiously conjuring themselves behind a writer's back. Each sociolect has its own immanent range of socially determ-inate meanings, both affective and cognitive. Every word is shadowed by a set of culturally specific associations and suggestions. There hovers in the political unconscious a constantly shifting web of clichés and *idées reçues*, each vying for perpetuation, or awaiting new life inspired by the fire of parody. As old his-torical conjunctures give way to new ones, as new hegemons rise and old ones fall, the semantic and ideological content of language shifts and alters, but it remains nonetheless *determinate*. It cannot be used in just any way the writer pleases; if she is to make it conform to her literary project, she will have no choice but to recognise its resistance to her will. To rub against the grain of language is to accept that it does indeed have a grain in the first place.

1.2   *Linguistic Ideology*

Linguistic ideology, the second element of mimesis₁, is the linguistic situation as thought. It consists of two basic levels: a spontaneous and a reflexive one.

33   Achebe 1997, p. 344.
34   Obviously, not all sub-situations apply to all writers.
35   See Chapter 5, section 1.2.

Linguistic ideology in the first sense designates the prevailing general under-standing of what language is and how it works; it consists of a set of non-codified linguistic norms. It is always articulated with the general ruling ideo-logy, even if it does not always cohere with it at every point. For example, today in Britain and America the ruling linguistic common sense arguably implies that language is: non-divine, an indifferent conduit for human communica-tion, and a neutral medium that we all share (what Bourdieu calls 'the illusion of linguistic communism');[36] it also presupposes that it is always at least theor-etically possible to say exactly what you mean (the only legitimate exception being lack of vocabulary or some other potentially alterable deficiency). In other words, this prevailing conception conceals the fact that language is a way of being together, structured by the same class, racial and sexual conflicts as the society at large, and hence equally a field of struggle. Moreover, language in Britain and America is structured by a set of linguistic norms which arise partially from the state-enforced standard language (as outlined above) but which are overdetermined by other axes such as race and sexuality. Thus, both British and American English are centred around a heteronormative concep-tion of language in which certain 'deviations' are classed as homosexual (e.g., the use of 'flowery' language instead of 'plain' prose – the latter being the lin-guistic manifestation of a patriarchal, functionalist ideology); one critic, in an important work on style and sexuality,[37] has gone so far as to suggest that the detection of the very *presence* of a style has often been read as an index of that writer's implicit homosexuality, his refusal to conform to the patriarchal, no-nonsense norm of business-like exactitude constituting the index of his sexual deviation. The force of linguistic ideology is such that it aids the reproduction of the social relations of production, reaffirming the dominant values of the ruling class, including patriarchy, heteronormativity and white supremacy, and inducing subjects to understand themselves in its terms.

The second level of linguistic ideology arises when people (usually intellec-tuals or politicians) self-consciously formulate the question of what language is and how it should function. This comprises all attempts to standardise a language at the level of the state, and all academic and scholarly theories of language. We saw in Chapter 5 that Raymond Williams took structuralism to be just such a self-conscious linguistic ideology: its origins lay in the coloniser's studies of the colonised, the relation of domination subsequently masked in the neutralised parlance of *langue* and *parole*. This prevented any sense of lan-

36   Bourdieu 1991, p. 43.
37   Pierre 2008.

guage as 'actively and presently constitutive'.[38] Such theories of language are *ideologies* to the extent that they systematically mask the fault-lines of conflict and contradiction within language as such and national languages in particular.

Inevitably, the linguistic situation, along with its concomitant and potentially legitimating ideology, is a necessarily hypothetical reconstruction, but it offers crucial insights into the determinate and determining limits of the verbal material on which the literary configurer goes to work. Often, stylistic peculiarities or limitations can be traced back to the scope, tensions and content of the linguistic situation from which the writer set out, though they can never be reduced to it. As we shall see, the poetic act of stylisation transforms this material, sometimes beyond recognition.

1.3   *Experience*

Before we do so, however, we must add a final element to the level of prefiguration. This is that most difficult zone of everyday life to describe: experience itself.[39] Of course, it goes without saying that both the linguistic situation and linguistic ideology are constitutive and indissoluble elements of everyday experience. Nonetheless, Raymond Williams, in his concept of the 'structure of feeling', is right to take into account that realm of transindividual subjectivity which has not yet achieved, or which is currently on the verge of achieving, formalised articulation. It emerges from that permeable membrane of everyday life where the moment-to-moment affective shifts of subjectivity are fused with the historically variable rhythms of social life. It is the liminal, micro-logical point of ever-renewed dialectic between the inner life of the socialised individual and the experiential substance of society. It finds its way into style, not necessarily via self-conscious volition on the part of the author (though it may well become that), but via a process which Helen Vendler has described as 'a cloning of the kinesthetic perceptions of [the] poet'.[40] The socially mediated, affective rhythms of a writer's daily life (to variable degrees) *insinuate* themselves into the very fibres of their styles.

Williams writes of Dickens's style that 'we can recognize behind the distinctive energy of Dickens's new rhythms a common pressure: restless, crowded, vivid: a social world of a radically different kind from that which was still there, and still important, as a basis for the composed, quiet and connected prose

---

38   Williams 1977, p. 26.

39   For a history and philosophical survey of this difficult term, see Jay 2005. For an account of the emergence and scope of the concept of the 'everyday', see Lefebvre 2008.

40   Vendler 1995, p. 4.

of the formally educated tradition'.[41] Dickens's experience of the new, mass
city – its restlessness, bustle and manic activity – insinuated itself into the
very rhythms of his prose. He broke with the mannered, controlled gestures
hitherto predominant in the English novel (which Williams seems to align with
a *habitus* proper to the leisurely strolls of the manor house), thereby bringing to articulation a new structure of feeling. Likewise, when Keats wrote of
Milton that 'Life to him would be death to me',[42] he was implying that the stylistic negotiations of Miltonic verse – ones which were, on the current logic,
mimetic elaborations of Milton's 'kinesthetic perceptions' – were simply not
apt for Keats's own experience. Here, of course, Keats is aware of the break, but
in reality this awareness is often the end product of a period of trial and error in
which the rhythms of a previous writer or group of writers are tested for their
capacity to embody the rhythms of the writer's living present.

Taken together, then, mimesis$_1$ consists of the linguistic situation, linguistic
ideology and the writer's experience (her biographically variable, historically
and geographically local, structure of feeling). We shall now turn to the poetic
act of stylisation – that process by which the writer determines these determinate elements – and to the rationales which inform it.

2   Mimesis$_2$

2.1   *Poetic Shaping*

The sedimented ideological meanings embedded in the language and structured by the tensions of the linguistic situation do not simply persist unadulter-
ated into the literary work. Literary composition is a productive and transformative *poietical* act (of which stylisation is the predominantly verbal component).[43] Consequently, the political significance of an act of stylisation cannot
be reduced to the pre-formed significance of the material that is stylised. The
politics – at this level – is inherent *to the literary act itself, to its product and to the
artistic choices – conscious, semi-conscious and unconscious – that it implies.* Lit-

---

41   Williams 1969, p. 34.

42   Keats 2002, p. 379.

43   Henceforth I shall write 'poietical' as 'poetical'. The abnormal orthography was intended
      simply to remind the reader of the dynamic operation of *poiēsis*; for ease of reading, I
      shall employ the more conventional spelling. The reader should nonetheless bear in mind
      the difference in meaning between my own usage and the now common version, 'poetic',
      which is overdetermined by Romantic associations.

erary production has its own ideological efficacy; it is not simply a 'reflection' or a 'symbolic resolution' of social contradictions (though it is often these things as well), but a constitutive and determinate aspect of them. Bakhtin and Medvedev were thus right when they argued that 'the artist only asserts himself in the process of the artistic selection and shaping of the ideological material. And this artistic assertion is no less social and ideological than epistemological, ethical, political, etc. assertions are'.[44]

We can start to grasp this poetical shaping by turning to Richard Walsh's typically incisive chapter on reader involvement. Against those theories which argue that emotional significance presupposes belief in the actuality of an object or a fictional state of affairs, Walsh claims that:

> Evaluation does not have to be subordinated to representation ... Affective responses to discourse need not wait for narrative; in fact, they may be brought into play by a single word in isolation ... The emotional power of narrative lies in its ability to draw out and particularize the affective charge of words (or images), but that charge is first generated in semiotic rather than narrative terms ... It is inherent in one of the most basic tasks of interpreting a text, which is the naturalization of its language – the evaluative placing of its language – in terms of the discursive contexts available to any given reader.[45]

Walsh recognises that words come loaded with 'emotional freight' (what I have called semantic and ideological content) and that the narrativisation of these words (for he is referring specifically to narrative) is not the pristine *invention* of meanings, but the particularisation and artistic guidance of pre-existing meanings. Words and phrases are stylised, their meanings, tones and timbres put to work within the purview of the author's organised artistic totality. Voloshinov's claim that 'every utterance in the business of life is an objective

---

44   Bakhtin and Medvedev 1978, p. 20. What they omitted is that whilst this is true as far as the literary act itself is concerned, certain writers also act in the capacity of public intellectuals or as members of powerful formations, thus extending the domain in which the artist 'asserts' herself well beyond the strictly literary. One need only think of the formation several years back which included Martin Amis, Ian McEwan and Christopher Hitchens, all of whom made politically dubious pronouncements on the Iraq War, Islam and religion in general – ones whose widespread dissemination was certainly premised upon the cultural capital of their being successful writers but bore no actual relation to literature.

45   Walsh 2007, p. 157.

social enthymeme' can then be reworked to develop Walsh's crucial insight.[46] On the one hand, individual words and concepts, as we saw in Chapter 5, are multiaccentual loci of ongoing political struggles. Yet, for them to mean anything at all presupposes an at least minimally homogeneous and hegemonic structure of social evaluation which constitutes the set of assumptions undergirding the utterance. Walsh gives the example of the concept of 'innocence' as attached to Little Nell in Dickens's *The Old Curiosity Shop*: readers and writer shared an enthymemic understanding of innocence and this was the basis of their emotional involvement. Yet, 'innocence' in Little Nell is not innocence in the abstract: it is a *particular, artistically shaped* mid-nineteenth-century construction of innocence, informed and enhanced by its role within the overall structure of the novel. On the other hand, we can add to this an enthymemic understanding of linguistic tones, timbres and textures: a patrician drawl comes laden with connotations of opulence and conservatism, whereas Cockney rhyming slang – for obvious ideological reasons – implies the ethical range of the huckster. Such socially objective enthymemes are the material which the writer imitates and orchestrates, shaping the various textures into an ordered stylistic totality – and in doing so potentially transforming their ideological valence. (Parody is the most extreme form of this transformation: an idiom is implicitly contradicted by its animating intention, style as idiom at odds with style as instance).[47] The verbal material present in the linguistic situation is thus artistically shaped along two enthymemic axes: ideological or semantic content and textural or tonal connotation.[48] The act of stylisation shapes these enthymemes into new configurations, all the while relying on their ideological acuity as the source of its own artistic vitality.

The range and quality of this operation of shaping is informed and internally limited by several factors, some of which were outlined in the definition of prose style in Chapter 4 or, alternatively, have already been mentioned here: the linguistic situation with its unique conjunctures of scope, structured tensions and historically specific ideological content; the level of formal or informal education of the writer; the quasi-biological factors of writing; and the anticipated reader or audience. I want now, building on Part 2 of this book, to supplement these factors with other aspects which inform and internally limit the opera-

46   Voloshinov 1976, p. 101.
47   This is what Bakhtin refers to as 'double-voiced discourse', which includes 'unidirectional' and 'vari-directional' modes. See Bakhtin 1984, p. 199.
48   Of course, were we not limiting ourselves to style, we would extend the notion of the enthymeme back to the original rhetorical-poetical level of *inventio*: the vast collective warehouse of plots and stereotypes which constitute the raw material of most narratives.

tion of stylistic configuration. These are: stylistic ideology; directionality; and modes, types, genres and forms.[49]

2.2   Stylistic Ideology

By 'stylistic ideology' I mean the specifically literary region of linguistic ideology. Like linguistic ideology, it is a spectrum which ranges from spontaneous to self-reflexive. In terms of the former end of the spectrum, the norms of good writing will be determined largely by the codified and non-codified norms of the linguistic ideology in general. For example, the taboo on 'flowery' language within a heteronormative linguistic ideology extends into the domain of literary style, exerting a form of stylistic censorship (and hence the possibility of transgression) internal to the act of stylisation itself.[50] Moreover, elements of *both* the general and linguistic ideologies often find their way into self-consciously formulated stylistic ideologies. We saw in Chapter 2 that the social and political presuppositions of the classical Greek *polis* determined Aristotle's strictures on *lexis*, and that Buffon's and Fichte's pronouncements on style were premised upon the individualist and proprietorial tendencies of modern capitalist societies. In more recent times, such well-known writers as George Orwell and Stephen King have propagated the doctrine of 'plain style', one which presupposes an immediacy of experience and directness of communication which belies the deeply mediated social and linguistic relations in which writing and reading occur. This is the linguistic branch of an undialectical empiricism which, in various guises (the most developed of which being positivism), has been an integral part of ruling Anglo-American ideology for quite some time.[51] At a greater degree of abstraction, it is also at this level that we must locate the effect of such structural features of the mode of production as the constant innovation required by the commodity form. We saw in Chapters 1 and 5 that the modernist battle cry of 'Make it new!' was partly an effect of the incessant revolutionisation of production which occurs specifically under the capitalist mode of production. This is then in polar opposition to those less frantic pre-modern modes of production in which style was regulated by the overtly politically determined *Stiltrennung* of low, middle and high styles.

---

49   I mention genre and form in the definition of style in prose fiction in Chapter 4, but I want here to draw on the more detailed explanation of those terms developed in Chapter 5.

50   For an overview of the connection between gender relations and stylistic ideology, see the chapter entitled 'Sexual Linguistics: Women's Sentence, Men's Sentencing' in Gilbert and Gubar 1988, p. 227 ff. For a clear example, see Fran Brearton's analysis of Seamus Heaney's sexualised stylistic ideology (Brearton 2009).

51   For a detailed account of the British empiricist tradition, see Easthope 1999, pp. 61–113.

At a more refined level of stylistic ideology are all those self-conscious styl-istic *projects* which writers develop and (to varying degrees of fidelity) put into practice, along with their accompanying theoretical justifications. Obvi-ous examples include Wordsworth and Coleridge's *Lyrical Ballads* (with its prefatory apologia), Ezra Pound's revolutionary poetics, Robbe-Grillet and the *nouveau roman*, and Charles Olson's development of projective verse. Signific-antly, what all such stylistic ideologies have in common is, firstly, an aware-ness of their position within literary history such as they conceive it, and, secondly, an explicitly political desire to overcome modes of writing which they associate with social and artistic conservatism, obsolescence, or outright degradation. Thus, Robbe-Grillet's literary experiments in such novels as *La jalousie* employ self-consciously new styles whose aim is not simply to regen-erate the novel, but proactively to demystify the bourgeois conception of real-ity which he saw as enshrined in the very forms of the classical realist novel itself. Yet, one can only *partially* detect this desire within the texture of his prose (via a cognitive and affective jarring of the reader's sensorium, itself argu-ably informed by the hegemonic styles of classical realism). Close reading or 'practical criticism' thus offers only limited critical guidance when determin-ing the larger stylistic *project* of a writer. It must be supplemented with an analysis of an author's overt paratextual and critical theorisations. The recon-struction of a writer's stylistic ideology thus involves a combination of the-oretical extrapolation from the literary style itself and an interpretation of the terms in which the writer justifies that style; the former is largely text-based, whereas the latter involves an ideological analysis of authorial para-texts, essays and manifestos. Crucially, such a combination enables a literary-critical 'hermeneutics of suspicion', whilst simultaneously allowing for those degrees of authorial self-reflexivity that Williams occasionally underestim-ated.

Furthermore, an author's implicit or explicit stylistic ideology is always articulated with two further regions of ideology: authorial and aesthetic. Terry Eagleton has defined 'authorial ideology' as 'the effect of the author's specific mode of biographical insertion into [the general ideology], a mode of insertion overdetermined by a series of distinct factors: social class, sex, nationality, religion, geographical region, and so on'.[52] Aesthetic ideology, by contrast, is that region of the general ideology which deals with the arts and literature; it includes an 'ideology of the aesthetic' which determines the function, meaning and value of the 'aesthetic' as such within a particular social formation.[53] The most important point to stress here is that *there is no necessary homology between authorial ideology, aesthetic ideology, stylistic ideology, and style.* It is quite possible for an author's own political stance to be at odds with the implicit politics of either her stylistic ideology or her empirical stylistic practice.[54] Take Pound, for example: he combined an authorial ideology which was broadly fascistic with an avant-garde stylistic ideology, produced in the context of an aesthetic ideology which had downgraded poetry to a position of borderline irrelevance within the total social formation. On the other hand, of course, there are cases where an author's political stance is avowedly radical but her stylistic ideology largely conforms to the status quo of aesthetic ideology. The work of a writer like Rachel Kushner then constitutes a curious borderline case: her novel *The Flamethrowers* (2013) appears superficially to conform to the stylistic dominant of contemporary realist prose, yet its content, like the author's overt political pronouncements, is avowedly radical. Moreover, one of the themes of the novel, and something upon which the author has elaborated in interviews,[55] is the very radicalism inherent to a narratorial idiom which refuses to draw attention to itself. Thus, what at first sight appears to be a case of stylistic conformity becomes, on closer inspection, an attempt to tap the subversive potential of stylistic anonymity.

Ultimately, then, unless one upholds a minimally Althusserian emphasis on the differential temporality and determinateness of the various levels that enter into literary production (or, in Althusser's case, that constitute the social formation), one risks a politics of style which reduces stylistic ideology to authorial ideology, reproducing in one fell swoop the indifference to form of the socialist realists or the over-estimation of it by such postmodern American poets as Charles Bernstein.[56] One must postulate a political effectivity inherent to lit-

---

53 Eagleton 1976, p. 60.

54 For a detailed example of this disjunction in the work of George Saunders, see Hartley 2015.

55 E.g., Kushner et al 2015.

56 Whilst Bernstein's poetics constitute a truly impressive body of work, he nonetheless has a strong tendency to equate formal and stylistic avant-garde experimentation with political radicalism as such. See, for example, Bernstein 1992. The two principal works which discuss and challenge this tendency in postmodern American poetics are Blasing (1995), who argues – wrongly, in my view – that politics never inheres in form but is, rather, determined by the specific rhetorical context of utterance, and Caplan (2005), who demonstrates convincingly that a return to apparently conservative verse forms is not in and of itself politically retrograde.

erary styles, which intersects with and potentially disrupts the self-conscious political affiliations of the author, whilst being determined in its own right by authorial, aesthetic and contextual factors.

2.3 Directionality

The second element that informs stylistic configuration is what I shall call 'directionality'. This concept concerns an age-old problem: how truly difficult it is to say precisely what you mean. Indexical deixis is condemned to the vicissitudes of contextual variation.[57] What feels like a simple referential relationship between I, here, now, speaking of this thing in front of me, there, is always triangulated by two invisible forces: the immediate context and the language in which I speak. The former, the principal ground and limitation of deixis, is spatially and temporally contingent, whilst the latter – which, after all, did not originate with me – has a tendency to make me say things I did not *mean* to say. When an individual speaker or writer *feels* as if she is referring directly, centrifugally out of and away from herself towards the world, this outwardly directional act is always intersected by a lateral directionality beyond her volition: context and semiosis. It is crucial to bear this in mind because the incredibly powerful generic dominance of realism as a literary mode has come to enforce upon us an unspoken dogma regarding the directionality of literary language: it is always assumed to be a direct, centrifugal emanation towards the world. Even when we are aware of the fictionality of a particular work, we are nonetheless inclined to assume that the relation between the text and the world it depicts is one of *reference*. And reference itself has come to be understood as a centrifugal, uni-directional movement.

This assumption of centrifugal directionality is usually coupled with a disregard for the two central forces of lateral directionality within the act of poetic shaping: conventional and generic expectations.[58] 'When Milton sat down to write a poem about Edward King', writes Northrop Frye, 'he did not ask himself: "What can I find to say about King?" but "How does poetry require that such a subject should be treated?"'[59] The reigning literary conventions, which are nothing less than historically variable structures of propriety (each linked to the ideological formation of its day), exert a selective and shaping force of their own within the act of stylisation. When an author writes, she does so at

---

57 Cf. Hegel 1977, pp. 58–66.
58 Frye calls this disregard of convention and overestimation of original invention a 'low mimetic prejudice' (Frye 1957, p. 102).
59 Frye 1957, p. 97.

the intersection of two verbal force fields. On the one hand, there is the lex-ical material innate to her unique linguistic situation; in a xylemic movement, she draws up the riches and resistances of the linguistic soil like ink into her pen. On the other hand, however, her awareness of the particular code of pro-priety required by a particular form, occasion or genre will act, at a minimum, as a shaping force internal to her verbal selection and stylisation, or, at a max-imum, as a *substitution* for the language of the linguistic situation. Conventions contain the force of a linguistic propriety which has the filtering power to neg-ate, inform or enhance the verbal resources which are available to a writer. It is quite possible to live in the centre of London, read formal prose in the e-broadsheet, puerile puns in the gutter press, hear Jamaican or cockney dialect on the Underground, the Queen's English as one passes a five-star hotel, not to mention a great number of foreign languages, and yet when one sits down to write a sonnet, one's conception of that form be so stereotypical and superficial that one writes in a diction that Tennyson himself would have found archaic – as if the preceding two and a half centuries of literary innovation had never occurred. In short, the verbal resources of the linguistic situation do not *neces-sarily* enter the work, though they will certainly affect its reception since they constitute the everyday linguistic environment of its readers (thereby making it a virtual norm).

Overall, then, it would perhaps be best to assume that the average direction-ality of a literary work is that of Leopold Bloom's parodic ascension: 'And they beheld Him even Him, ben Bloom Elijah, amid clouds of angels ascend to the glory of the brightness at an angle of fortyfive degrees over Donohoe's in Little Green Street like a shot off a shovel'.[60] Forty-five degrees is midway between heaven and earth, neither entirely centripetal nor fully centrifugal, drawing at once on the 'low mimetic' idioms of Little Green Street and the formal linguistic pieties of the Bible. It is the angle at which the sublime and the sublunary inter-sect on the trajectory of the hypothetical.

2.4   Modes, Types, Genres, Forms

The third element informing poetic shaping is the mode, type, genre and form of the literary work being produced – more specifically, of each of these levels' stylistic proprieties. Obviously, there is no point repeating here my explication of each level individually,[61] so I shall simply suggest the effect of the mutual determination of formal literary elements, before going on to

---

60   Joyce 1993, p. 330.
61   See Chapter 5.

discuss the central differences of stylistic orientation amongst two of the three principal literary modes: lyric and drama (prose fiction having been covered in depth in Chapter 4).

In the *Poetics*, Aristotle divides tragedy into plot, character, thought, diction, melody and spectacle – i.e., into its constituents. What is less commonly recognised, however, is that, despite his naturalist conception of formal teleology,[62] he is very much aware of two crucial facts: that each element of a given form has its own unique social origins which affect its subsequent development, and that each element has a determinate influence on the others.[63] It will be recalled from Chapter 7 that one of the major causes of the autonomisation of style at the level of the individual sentence was the relative demise of pre-modern modes of narrative. As we saw, Jameson claims this was brought about by the extinction of the narrative categories of experience, the demise of collective meeting places which offer the raw materials and situation of storytelling, and the spatial and temporal rifts between individual experience and the overall social structure within modernity. Prior to these epochal shifts in human experience, he claims, the individual sentence in prose fiction had always been subordinate to the overarching narrative representation. But now, in line with the coeval shift in stylistic ideology from use-value to labour value (i.e., the newfound championing of the agonies of the search for *le mot juste*), the sentence had won its autonomy and writers were able to invest their literary prowess in elaborating potentially standalone, stylistically sculpted periods. Thus, we can rearticulate Aristotle's insights and apply them to this particular case. Each formal element of a literary work has its origins in a specific social formation (in this case, narrative and (modern) style); consequently, as that social formation undergoes major shifts in its mode of production (or the mode of production's stage of development), ruling ideology, or political configuration, each element is (potentially) transformed.[64] Moreover, precisely because literary works are nothing but the systemic interactions of their elements as guided by the author's poetic shaping (informed and limited by mimesis$_1$), a socially determined change in *one* aspect (in this case, narrative form) can dramatically alter *another* aspect (here, *style*). Style is thus a *relational* concept, not only in the sense of its being a linguistic mode of social relation, nor even in the sense of its being the totality of the interrelations of sub-styles (instance,

---

62   Cf. Halliwell 1998, pp. 92–6.
63   See especially sections 1448b–1449b of the *Poetics* which discuss the origins and development of poetry (Aristotle 2000). Here Aristotle combines naturalist and historico-cultural explanations of formal elements.
64   The more epochal the shift, the more likely is this transformation.

idiom and interpellation), but because it stands in a dialectical relationship with the other constituents of a literary work. They are a determinate aspect of the possibilities and limitations of style, and are themselves directly and indirectly affected by the specific historical and social conditions of which they are an immanent part. I take this to be a rejection of all formalist theories of literary history which posit a purely intra-systemic interaction of literary elements and their evolution through time, unaffected by social history.

Thus, the operation of stylistic shaping which occurs in mimesis$_2$, and which determines the already determinate verbal materials of mimesis$_1$, is always informed and internally limited by: stylistic ideology, directionality, and the effectivity of the various formal elements with which style enters into relationship. In what follows, to avoid needless repetition, I am presupposing the presence and effect of these elements. Having already dealt with the peculiarities of prose fiction in Chapter 4, I want now to turn briefly to the unique stylistic challenges and limitations a writer faces when composing in the modes of lyric and drama.

2.5   Lyric

The theory of style developed in this book has been a tendentially narratological one. Nonetheless, there is a strong case to be made for the claim that the mode which lends itself most readily to a historical materialist conception of style is poetry – not least the lyric.[65] For the lyric is that type of literary discourse which is necessarily self-conscious of the material basis of language; it foregrounds the materiality of non-sense at the heart of all sense, just as Marx in his early writings stressed the non-sublatable remainder of natural matter which no *Geist* can subsume – most evidently in the fact of our mortality.[66] The lyric condenses into a highly concentrated form all the elements of stylistic configuration here outlined. It demonstrates far more clearly than the average novel ever could that signification is never a simple matter of neutral informational exchange: on the contrary, the lyric is that literary mode which dramatises the noncoincidence between the symbolic system of referential language and the material system of scriptural and acoustic notations, each of which has its own set of historically accumulated connotations. Mutlu Konuk Blasing, in a magisterial work on the lyric, develops this point: 'The excessiveness of each system to the other necessitates a constant negotiation, a constant choosing

65   There has been something of a turn in recent Marxist work on literature towards the relation between capitalism and poetry, away from narrative – some of it pitched consciously against Jameson's grand narrative desires. See Clover 2011, Nealon 2011 and Jennison 2012.

66   Marx 1975, pp. 379–400.

and intentionalising not only of sounds and words but also – and herein lies the difference of poetry – of words as sounds. Each system is made to intentionalise the other's automatisms'.[67] The lyric 'I' simply *is* the gap between the systems, the 'intentionalizing, delimiting figure ... [which] is a requirement of the meaning function',[68] neither wholly the historical individual nor entirely a generic entity. Moreover, the lyric 'I' is simultaneously the cause and effect of the poem's meaning: the cause, because it forces materiality to mean by intentionally organising it, but the effect because the lyric as a mode draws attention to the materiality of the sign which allows it to mean in the first place. The lyric 'I' is the fusion of the generic and historical individual in its operation of organising the material of non-sense into meaning.

Unique to the lyric, moreover, is the essential insight of the Marxist approach to style that has been stressed time and again throughout this book: 'this "I" who "chooses the words he lives by" is also chosen by the language he lives in'.[69] Blasing then employs a very useful conceptual distinction between the 'microrhetoric' of the linguistic code (the unchosen materiality and sociality of the words and their connotations) and the 'macrorhetoric', which is analogous to what I have called the poetic shaping force of the poet, to denote the two stylistic forces at work within the lyric.[70] The *differentia specifica* of poetry as opposed to pure rhetoric lies in that the lyric subject must, as well as simply speaking the words, *be spoken* by them: 'For what individuates her is not what she says but the particular ways in which she makes audible the shape, the "beautiful necessities", of the language'.[71] For Blasing, the lyric appears to be the art of speaking (of) oneself by making language speak (of) itself: in this mode, to do one of these things simply *is* to do the other. Style in the lyric is then first and foremost a matter of the *specific manner* in which one brings language to speak (of) itself. It is the locus where the poet's name, the lyric 'I' and the hidden commitments produced by the linguistic situation are articulated – via the act of *poiēsis* – into so many unique constellations. And it is also – as in Williams's connection of style with the 'structure of feeling' – the locus of that hidden relay system of pleasures and pains, attractions and disgust, erotics and trauma, which punctuate the poet's connection to the mother tongue and, by extension, to her social present and collective history.

---

67   Blasing 2007, p. 29.
68   Blasing 2007, p. 30.
69   Blasing 2007, p. 34.
70   She is building on the work of Renato Barilli who first introduced the term 'microrhetoric'. See Blasing 2007, p. 41, n. 16.
71   Blasing 2007, p. 35.

2.6   *Drama*

Drama, unlike the lyric, is a narrative in which the playwright does not speak in her own voice except in stage directions;[72] it may or may not be performed. Dramas are narratives, not in the sense that they are verbally narrated by a teller figure – Franz Stanzel was mistaken to reduce narrative to mediacy alone –,[73] but because they share with epic the fact of having a plot (*muthos*),[74] and because they possess the double temporality of story (*fabula*) and discourse (*syuzhet*) common to all narratives.[75] Consequently, it is possible to adapt the tripartite definition of style I initially developed in relation to prose fiction (see Chapter 4) and apply it to drama. There are, however, three key differences. Firstly, whilst diegesis in the sense of the real-world representational act of the author under the regime of fictionality is common to both drama and prose fiction, the presence of a verbal, narrative diegesis is generally absent. There is as a rule no so-called 'impersonal' or 'authorial' narration in drama.[76] It consists solely of mimesis, the writer speaking through her characters. But here the second key difference arises. It would be tempting to argue that drama consists primarily of style as idiom (as explained in Chapter 4); but the key feature of idiom according to Walsh's argumentation is that it constructs a distinct subject by virtue of its objectification, and its objectification is nothing but its difference from the narrative diegesis. If that diegesis is absent, there is technically speaking no objectificiation and hence no 'voice as idiom' in

---

 72   Whether or not stage directions are to be read under the regime of fictionality is contextually dependent. As a rule, they are not; they are real-world, practical instructions. The prime exception to this rule are those plays (like Ibsen's *Peer Gynt*) which were not written to be performed, and which thus invite a style of stage direction less bound by the necessity of practical actualisation.

73   Stanzel 1984. Or, rather, he was mistaken to reduce the sense of mediacy to verbal mediacy alone. I agree with Richard Walsh when he writes that 'mediacy is a property of media; ... the distinction between, for instance, fiction and drama is not a distinction between indirect and direct form, but between different semiotic means of representation: in one case symbolic (language), in the other iconic (mise en scène, performance, etc.)' (Walsh 2010, p. 46).

74   As well as character, thought and diction [*lexis*].

75   The criterion of double temporality I take from Chatman 1990, pp. 6–21. For an important critique of the story-discourse distinction, see Walsh 2007, pp. 52–68.

76   I am, of course, aware of the obvious fact that many dramas represent on-stage acts of narration in the narrow sense of diegetic reporting (for a list of the various types – ranging from the chorus to messenger reports – see Nünning and Sommer 2008, section 4), but I wish to distance myself from the position which reduces the narrativity of drama to these exceptional moments alone.

Walsh's specific sense of that word. Drama does, of course, consist principally
of mimesis in the Platonic sense of the poet speaking through the voices of his
characters; it is simply that they are not subordinated to an encompassing narrative diegesis (though they *are* subordinated to the diegetic, representational
act of the author). The final difference between style in prose fiction and style
in drama is that the latter is not purely verbal; it includes spectacle, gesture, set
design, spatial arrangements, costume, lighting, sound-effects, and so on. Nonetheless, for the sake of this book, I am choosing to focus on the verbal element
of dramatic style alone.[77]

   Given that drama belongs to the narrative genus despite lacking narrative
diegesis, much of the communicational burden of narration is shifted onto gesture, spectacle and the characters themselves. Certain events can be literally
enacted onstage and others implied by gestures, thus circumventing the necessity for verbal diegesis. The more relevant aspect for our purposes, however,
is the effect that a lack of narrative diegesis has on characters' speech. For
characters in drama have two functions: a character function and a telling
function.[78] Their character function consists of their role in the events of the
narrative and of their ethical or personal attributes.[79] Their telling function,
by contrast, is as a teller of the narrative. Thus, as a rule, one of the generic
peculiarities of drama is that the stylistic elaborations of the playwright are
always internally limited by the need simultaneously to *characterise* her characters – to give them linguistic tics, ethical attributes and to allow them morally
to develop – whilst using their dialogues to *narrate* past, present, and possible events (onstage or offstage) to the audience. Her stylistic elaborations
thus occur at the cross-roads of two operations: characterisation via idiom and
diegesis (which is, effectively, the dramatic equivalent of style as idiom and
instance in prose fiction).[80] As a result, moments of what Phelan calls 'redund-

---

77   Of course, since not all dramas are written to be performed, this focus on verbal style is
      not entirely misguided, though one should always bear in mind the vast gulf that separates
      writing for reading and writing for speech.
78   I am here adapting and extending the very useful distinction developed by James Phelan
      (2001). Although he is primarily concerned with character narration in non-dramatic texts,
      his insights can be usefully extended to drama.
79   Phelan assigns only the first of these to character function. I am choosing to add the
      element of subjective expressivity that was entailed by Walsh's notion of idiom.
80   Whilst 'idiom' is technically inapplicable to character discourse in drama (because there
      is no narrative diegesis from which it differs), the element of Walsh's definition of 'idiom'
      linked to the expression of a character's subjectivity still very much applies.

ant telling' often occur:[81] 'when a narrator [in our case, a character-teller] gives an unmotivated report of information to a narratee [in our case, another character] that the narratee already possesses'.[82] Skilled dramatists are those who seek out mimetically credible motivations for intra-dramatic diegesis, such that the telling function apparently merges with the character function, preserving the illusion of pure mimesis.[83] We must then add to this a third stylistic element of drama which is the mode of elaboration, verisimilitude, poeticity and so on which arise as a result of: a) the dramatist's skill, b) conventional expectations (e.g., in the naturalist habit one expects 'realistic' everyday speech) and c) the dramatist's stylistic ideology. The overall verbal style of the drama is the totality of relations between these subordinate linguistic operations, unidentifiable with any single one of them, and can be subdivided (just as in level 3 of the definition in Chapter 4) into style as lexical configuration and style as (general) interpellation. Moreover, the narrative *meaning* of any of these three elements of dramatic style (or of their totality) is, as with poetic shaping generally, strongly determined by the particular story of which they are a part.

Let us turn to an example to clarify this abstract terminology. By the end of the first act of *Othello*, Shakespeare requires the audience to have learned the backstory of Othello and Desdemona's courtship. He thus has to find some mimetically convincing motivation for its inclusion. As is typical of Shakespeare, his solution is to incorporate the exposition into the dynamic of the framing mimesis; in this case, the tale of the courtship constitutes Othello's self-defence in the spontaneous *ad hoc* trial called for by Brabantio who has accused Othello of 'charming' and stealing his daughter.[84] Othello's story serves both to provide necessary background knowledge for the audience and to spur on the play itself; it is *doubly* dramatic – internally, as an exciting tale in its own right, and externally via its function within the dynamics of the play.

Othello is carrying out his character and telling functions simultaneously. The tale itself is composed in blank verse which, given that Othello has in-

---

81   Phelan 2001.

82   Phelan 2001, p. 210. The example Phelan gives is from Browning's 'My Last Duchess'. When Browning writes 'the Count your master's' (l. 49), his interlocutor would already have been well aware that his master was indeed the Count; the point is that we, the readers, are not, and thus Browning has to find a way of communicating this to us without breaking the mimetic convention to which the rest of the text conforms.

83   Unless, of course, like Brecht, their stylistic ideology entails an intentional alienation of naturalist, mimetic conventions.

84   1.3.

formed us he is '[r]ude in speech',[85] is significant in itself. It is the formal mode of parlance conventionally adopted for fictional representations of the nobility, one which – via what I have called the idiomatic enthymemic axis – reinforces the impression of Othello as the 'valiant Moor' (and works against Iago's racist portrait from the opening scene). Yet, despite its formality, the 'story of [his] life',[86] by recounting which – he tells us – he wooed Desdemona, would have seemed surprisingly clichéd to its original audience:

> ... I spake of most disastrous chances,
> Of moving accidents by flood and field;
> Of hairbreadth scapes i' th' imminent deadly breach;
> Of being taken by the insolent foe
> And sold to slavery ...
> And of the Cannibals that each other eat,
> The Anthropophagi, and men whose heads
> Do grow beneath their shoulders.[87]

The clumsy anaphora ('Of ... Of ... Of ...') and breathless pace is an implicit mockery of the bombastic style of contemporary travellers' tales, an impression reinforced by the sensationalist mentions of cannibalism. Consequently, the veracity of Othello's life-story is thrown into doubt. That Desdemona 'with a greedy ear/ Devour[ed] up my discourse' (a hint at her own form of cannibalism) and that 'She lov'd me for the dangers I had pass'd;/ And I lov'd her that she did pity them', suggests, not the birth of true love, but the vision of 'two narcissistic readers, each exchanging the other's reading of their own projected role'.[88] As Cohen rightly claims, his '"story" shows Othello, above all, to be less man of action than a *bovaryste*, an imitative reader of adventure romances, an African Quixote in a Venice that is, for him, fabled and commodified'.[89] It is as if Othello is imitating the conventional idiom of the Venetian nobles in order, simultaneously, to present himself as an exotic stereotype; he combines the mystique of the latter with the (assumed) grace of the former.

Thus, if the tale has a diegetic function, it also has a characterological function. We learn, through the telling, that Othello is trapped at the intersection of

---

85   1.3.81.
86   1.3.129.
87   1.3.134–8, 143–5.
88   Cohen 1994, p. 21.
89   Ibid.

stereotype and mimicry, aping *the idea* of a white man's speech (thereby undo-
ing the very proprietorial conception of style) and yet simultaneously conform-
ing to and confounding this latter's Orientalist prejudices. Via Shakespeare's
poetic cunning, Othello's rhetorically brilliant speech speaks partly against
him. Though it does so only to us, the audience; his interlocutors – indeed, perhaps even he himself – are *charmed* by his discourse (cf. the Duke: 'I think this
tale would win my daughter too'),[90] a dramatic irony which Shakespeare reaf-
firms with Othello's final flourish: 'This only is the witchcraft I have us'd'.[91] The
theme of authenticity introduced by Iago in the opening scene is thereby revisited: it is, at this point, strictly undecidable whether Othello is merely *playing*
the part of the exotic warrior or whether he has indeed internalised the stereotypes such that he can only understand himself through them. This is the
point at which the telling and character functions (style as instance and style
as idiom, shaped by Shakespeare into an overarching artistic unity) are totally
inseparable, for in recounting his own self ('the story of my life') he *is* himself, poetics and ethics momentarily indistinguishable. This is then a prime
example of the way in which drama imposes unique limitations on stylistic
elaboration, but ones which, in the hands of great writers, become the source
of artistic possibilities.

2.7 The Pain and Joy of Writing
Having now outlined the major factors which inform the act of poetic shaping
in mimesis₂, no theory of stylistic configuration would be complete without
some recognition of two of the principal affective modes of writing: pain and
joy. We have already referred several times to Flaubert's agonised search for
le mot juste, just as we have drawn on Barthes' explanation of it as an emergent ideological justification for the institution of Literature which, after 1848,
lacked self-evident legitimation (the value of toil thus coming to constitute
social worth). But there are various types of writerly pain, and they are historically and affectively variable. The most significant examples are arguably those
which arise from a mismatch between an emergent structure of feeling and the
pre-existing styles and forms which embody dominant or residual structures
of feeling. Williams has written that 'the effort to respond adequately while the
new experience is still disorganized and disturbing ... is biologically identical
with what we call "physical pain". The creative agony, sometimes thought of

90   1.3.171.
91   1.3.169.

[handwritten: mismatch between structure of feeling and existing forms]

as hyperbole, is literally true'.[92] In such circumstances, the agony of writing simply *is* the experience of attempted and failed articulation of the socially new; pre-existent styles repel the desired emergence, forcing the writer back to the previous forms or making her settle for uneven results. Those rare break-throughs to new styles, however, can often bring with them an outpouring of joy – which is precisely the *experience* of the transindividual structure of feeling achieving its inaugural adequate articulation.[93]

Yet this is only one variant of writerly joy. We saw in Chapters 6 and 7 that style in modernity could arguably be seen as a utopian act in its own right. Eagleton has even gone so far as to call fine writing an 'image of non-alienated labour',[94] combining as it does the sensuousness of the particular with the abstraction of the general via the material labour of composition. My own inter-pretation is somewhat different. Firstly, as I suggested in Chapter 6, the precise quality and valence of this joy is historically determinate. In the context of a classical or neo-classical framework, the joy of writing may be dependent upon a writer's attainment of what she takes to be a 'natural' stylistic law, whereas in post-Romantic composition part of the joy of writing arises from a sense of *escaping* linguistic norms, transcending them just as the pleasure principle momentarily lets slip the mundane limits of the reality principle. But there is also a second, narcissistic element: that libidinal frisson one experiences as the words that shoot from the tip of the pen come laden with the affective traits and psychopathologies of the individual's navigation of the mother tongue. This second aspect also includes a certain libidinal delight in the corporeal elements of language: alliteration, onomatopoeia, assonance, and anaphora all becom-ing traces of a linguistic *jouissance* that runs from the mouth that speaks the

---

92   Williams 1965, pp. 42–3.

93   One thinks, for example, of Saul Bellow's delighted discovery of the slick, supple, yet chatty prose of *The Adventures of Augie March*: 'When I began to write *Augie March* I took off many of these restraints. I think I took off too many, and went too far, but I was feeling the excitement of discovery. I had just increased my freedom, and like any emancipated plebeian I abused it at once ... My first two books are well made. I wrote the first quickly but took great pains with it. I labored with the second and tried to make it letter-perfect. In writing *The Victim* I accepted a Flaubertian standard. Not a bad standard, to be sure, but one which, in the end, I found repressive – repressive because of the circumstances of my life and because of my upbringing in Chicago as the son of immigrants. I could not, with such an instrument as I developed in the first two books, express a variety of things I knew intimately. Those books, though useful, did not give me a form in which I felt comfortable. A writer should be able to express himself easily, naturally, copiously in a form that frees his mind, his energies' (Bellow and Harper 1966).

94   Eagleton 2009, p. 128.

words aloud to the finger tips that type them. Finally, and perhaps most significantly, if we accept that language is a way of being together, but one which
is internally stratified and divided according to broader economic and political divisions, then writing is a way of both revelling in our sociality and, via
the act of stylisation, of symbolically healing the rifts which divide humanity
from itself. Even satire, which aims to exacerbate those rifts, ultimately does so
in order to overcome them. Literary writing thus partakes in and absorbs the
ferocity and mutual recriminations built into the language, our way of being
together, and – however fleetingly – sublates them into an artistic organisation
which only subsequently becomes a factor in those divisions in its own right.
That brief moment of reconciliation, however, is never lost: it is reactivated on
every reading of the text. It is to that reading, and thus to mimesis$_3$, that we
shall now turn.

3   Mimesis$_3$

Reading is an inherently heterogeneous activity which involves various types of
attention and a range of degrees of literary-critical initiation.[95] Consequently,
in order to provide some modicum of order to the following observations concerning readers' receptions of literary styles, I have chosen, following Fredric
Jameson (though not his schema), to adapt the system of 'phases' developed by
Northrop Frye in *The Anatomy of Criticism*.[96] Before enumerating these phases,
however, it is important to stress that any Marxist reading of a style presupposes an awareness of all the concepts I have already outlined under mimesis$_1$
and mimesis$_2$. That is, a theory of literary reception should always, simultaneously, be a theory of literary production. In this section, I wish to focus specifically upon the multi-levelled nature of the reading process across its range
of untrained and professional forms.
      There are, Frye tells us, five phases, each of which is a context or relationship
in which the whole work of literary art can be placed,[97] and each of which isol-
ates a specific unit of the literary work for critical attention (his generic term
for such units being, precisely, 'symbol').[98] The first two phases are the building
blocks of any act of reading: the 'literal' phase, which focuses upon the mater-

---

95   I take the felicitous phrase 'types of attention' from Jameson 1981, p. 71.
96   Frye 1957, pp. 71–128.
97   Frye 1957, pp. 73.
98   Frye 1957, pp. 71.

iality and texture of the individual words and letters,[99] and the 'descriptive' phase whose focus is less the words themselves than that which they represent. Frye calls the literal symbol a 'motif' and its descriptive equivalent a 'sign'.[100] The third, 'formal' phase is a dialectical sublation of the first two.[101] It is the overall totality of the individual literary work, understood from the point of view of style and content simultaneously. At this level, the symbol is an 'image' whose relation to reality is potential and hypothetical (poetry being – Frye here inheriting Aristotle – more philosophical than history but more historical than philosophy).

The fourth, 'mythical' phase spells the broadening of the reader's attention to the social collective; here, the symbol is an 'archetype', a communicable unit, usually a typical or recurring image. It is the phase in which we begin, via our experience of other texts (and hence via intertextuality), to notice generic or conventional similarities between works of literature. It is in regard to archetypes that Frye makes the bold (and mistaken) claim to which we drew attention in Chapter 3: 'Poetry can only be made out of other poems'.[102] Nonetheless, this is to some extent redeemed by his refreshing emphasis on literature as a social fact which he describes as 'one of the techniques of civilization',[103] and which 'has the function of expressing, as a verbal hypothesis, a vision of the goal of work and the forms of desire'.[104] The archetypal critic, says Frye, studies narrative as 'a recurrent act of symbolic communication: in other words a ritual',[105] one whose 'significant content' (Frye's version of *dianoia*) is 'the conflict of desire and reality which has for its basis the work of the dream'.[106] It is the unification of ritual and dream in a form of verbal communication that, for Frye, constitutes myth.

---

99   This is not to be confused with the now conventional meaning of 'literal' as non-metaphorical.

100   Being the compulsive classifier that he was (a flaw for which I have a certain sympathy), Frye also attributed to each phase a type of literature and a type of criticism. Thus, the literal phase is affiliated with symbolist poetry and New Criticism, whilst the descriptive phase is aligned with realism and historical or philological criticism.

101   '[We shall] try to resolve the antithesis in a third phase of symbolism' (Frye 1957, p. 82).

102   Frye 1957, pp. 97. His total formalism is reconfirmed a few pages later when he writes: 'Poetry organizes the content of the world as it passes before the poet, but the forms in which that content is organized come out of the structure of poetry itself' (Frye 1957, p. 102).

103   Frye 1957, pp. 99.

104   Frye 1957, pp. 106.

105   Frye 1957, pp. 105.

106   Ibid.

In the fifth and final phase, the 'anagogic', 'literature imitates the total dream of man, and so imitates the thought of a human mind which is at the circumference and not the center of its reality'.[107] Here, the symbol is called a 'monad', since it identifies each individual literary work's immediate connection to the 'single infinite and eternal verbal symbol which is, as *dianoia*, the Logos, and, as *mythos*, total creative act'.[108] It is a genuinely bizarre conception in which literature as a total system seems to absorb all of nature into itself – a literary parody of Hegel's 'absolute spirit'. There is, at this level, no longer any distinction between a natural reality 'out there' and the dreams and desires contained by literature 'in here'; nature now *conforms* to literature in what strikes one as an odd combination of Blake's home-spun theology with the bourgeois conception of eternal Progress. It is not difficult to see why Jameson chose to jettison this level from his own adaptation of Frye (though I myself will choose to keep it, but alter its function significantly).

For my purposes, I shall rewrite these five phases as the five types of attention that can be paid to literary style. If in one sense I am simply exploiting Frye's framework as a useful structure through which to organise the various levels of stylistic reception, in another I am consciously adopting a five-fold schema to allow for more levels of mediation between the individual sentence and the total mode of production than a political hermeneutics like Jameson's would permit (ironically, since we both base our hermeneutic systems on Frye's). Moreover, I understand each phase as being structured by an internal scale ranging from a reader with basic literacy skills to professional readers such as literary critics: the difference between these levels of sophistication is not qualitative but quantitative, the latter possessing a greater degree of training and practice than the former. For example, *any* reader on reading the first line of Milton's *Paradise Lost* – 'Of man's first disobedience, and the fruit' – will have some inkling, even if pre-conscious, that it possesses some minimal rhythm and intra-linear alliteration between 'first' and 'fruit'; the professional reader, however, will be able to *name* the rhythm (iambic pentameter) and technique (alliteration), explain their poetic history and significance, and make a case for the word 'disobedience' as being itself disobedient in that it is ambiguous as to whether it conforms to iambic pentameter at all. The professional reader is simply a refined naïve reader. Consequently, each phase applies to all readers but to varying degrees.

---

107   Frye 1957, pp. 119.
108   Frye 1957, pp. 121.

3.1   *Literal Phase: Micro-Structures of Feeling*

The first phase is a type of attention broadly similar to that of close reading. In literary terms, its object is the verbal texture, tone and shape of the individual sentences. This is the locus of those small-scale shifts in transindividual subjectivity which I shall call *micro-structures of feeling.* It is the phase which requires the most well-honed ear and alert, verbal sensorium on the part of the critic (though even the naïve reader will experience the effects of such stylistic elements). A precise example of such attention can be found in Theodor W. Adorno's reading of Anatole France's prose: 'While a thought in terms of its content may oppose the irresistibly rising tide of horror, the nerves, the sensitive feelers of historical consciousness, detect in its form ... a trace of connivance at the world'.[109] At the level of content Anatole France is very much the 'last advocate of human dignity', but there is something about his style, his way of writing, which suggests that, perhaps unbeknownst to himself, there lurks a 'latent contempt for mankind'.[110] His writing is structured around a contradiction between what it says and how it says it, the latter itself now part of some larger, less immediate message offered by the text. To detect such an internal contradiction requires on the part of the reader, not only an abstract rationality capable of arguing against a text's explicit propositions, but also a *bodily* form of rationality ('the nerves, the sensitive feelers') capable of somatically intuiting the hidden content of 'visible' arguments. Moreover, the reader must then be able linguistically to articulate this bodily intuition of contradiction: 'the contemplative leisureliness, the sermonizing, however sporadic, the indulgently raised forefinger' is an exemplary Adornian *précis*.[111] The literal phase thus requires: a recognition of the existence of mismatches between form and content, a bodily reason capable of intuiting them, and a linguistic dexterity sufficient to their expression.

It is a type of attention that seeks out the slightest transformations of consciousness in the shape of a sub-clause, the faintest hint of pretension in the diffidence of a cadence, or the covert cynicism that lurks beneath the tone of the worldly-wise. It is also the level at which those difficulties of articulation and diction about which Williams wrote so well in relation to Thomas Hardy are detected. The critic here scans the ocean-bed of the text, mapping out its sudden dips and ridges, its unexpected fractures, in order to prepare it for a more structurally comprehensive analysis.

---

109   Adorno 2005, p. 99.
110   Ibid.
111   Ibid.

"a bodily form of rationality"

3.2   *Identification Phase: Instance, Idiom, Interpellation*

The second phase, which replaces Frye's 'descriptive', is the identification of what in Chapter 4 I called sub-styles. These, it will be recalled, constitute the vocalic tripartition clarified by Richard Walsh: instance, idiom and interpellation. By 'identification' I mean the singling out – pre-conscious, incomplete and automatic in the leisure reader,[112] intentional on the part of the critic – of the various stylistic strands which interweave to form a text. The identification of *style as idiom*, which is almost inevitably the burden of this phase, involves a type of attention attuned to all those moments in which the narrating instance objectifies another's discourse. These range from character dialogue all the way to governed indirect speech (or, in Genette's terms, from reported to transposed speech).[113] More broadly, however, it also includes idiom in the sense of the stylistic quality of the narrative diegesis.[114] The identification of idiom is then inseparable from the process of interpretation and evaluation which simply *is* reading: the ethical evaluation of characters, narrators and linguistic enthymemes based on their transliteration into written styles. Importantly, the extrapolation of the 'politics' of a style at this level should not be reduced to seeking out a sympathetic and faithful rendering of the idioms of socially and politically oppressed groups; as Genette long ago rightly pointed out, in strongly mimetic renderings, a character is always in danger of 'blending with, to the point of *amounting to*, his language'.[115] Thus, the faithful mimetic reproduction of a particular sociolect is not in and of itself a politically progressive act. Depending on the generic conventions within which the author is writing, it may be more politically suggestive for the author to decrease the distance between the narratorial and character idioms, and by drawing the Other into the Same to increase her depth of character by other means.

The identification of *style as interpellation* is, at this level, limited to the singling out of acts of focalisation and an assessment of their specific valence for particular moments in the text (as opposed to the text in its totality, which is the function of the next phase). In practice, of course, the identification of style as interpellation (here, focalisation) is inseparable from that of style as idiom. Take the following example, from Eleanor Catton's recent novel, *The Luminaries*

---

112   Except, of course, in those instances where the abduction (in Peirce's sense) of who is speaking and who is seeing is integral to the interpretation of the text itself.

113   Genette 1980, pp. 171–2. In terms of Brian McHale's useful seven-grade scale of mimeticism in the representation of speech, I am referring to grades 4 to 7, summarised in Genette 1988, p. 56.

114   That is, it encompasses the 'how' of voice considered in Aczel 1998.

115   Genette 1980, pp. 171–2; emphasis added.

(2013). It is 1866, inside the Hokitika Gaol, located at a New Zealand goldfield at the edge of the known world. Until this point, the book as a whole has been characterised by a mixture of zero focalisation (narratorial omniscience) and internal focalisation (restricted to the perspective of a single character). The present chapter focuses on Cowell Devlin, a newly arrived chaplain, but because of Catton's choice of zero focalisation we see him both internally and externally (i.e., the narrator tells us things about him which he does not know about himself). Devlin is sat speaking with the inmates of the gaol about Saint Paul when Ellis Drake enters with 'a woman in his arms':

> Shepard [the gaoler] opened the door wider and invited the sergeant to step inside. Drake was a greasy, nasal fellow of limited intelligence; hearing his name, one was put in mind not of the naval hero but of the common duck, a species he closely resembled. He conveyed his captive into the gaol-house by the vulgar method of the fireman's hold, and deposited her with little ceremony upon the floor. He then reported, nasally, that the whore had either committed a crime against society or a crime against God; she had been found in a posture of such abject insentience that a distinction between gross intoxication and wilful harm could not be made, but he hoped (tipping his hat) that some hours in the gaol-house might serve to clarify the matter. He nudged her senseless body with the tip of his boot, as if to reiterate his point, and added that the instrument of her crime was likely opium. The whore was enslaved to the drug, and had often been seen under its effects.[116]

The focalisation of this passage is unclear. In a particularly acute case of the ambiguity between zero and internal focalisation which has characterised the book heretofore, it hovers between the perspective of Devlin (whose internal focalisation frames the preceding paragraph) and that of the omniscient narrator. When Drake is described as a 'greasy, nasal fellow', the perspective is most likely Devlin's but the judgment is the narrator's. Further proof of this authorial commandeering of a particular focalisation comes in the comic use of what Brian McHale would call the 'indirect content-paraphrase' of the sentence beginning 'He then reported …'. For, having been informed that Drake is a 'greasy, nasal fellow of limited intelligence' we do not expect him to be able to use such formal vocabulary as 'posture of such abject insentience', 'gross intoxication' or 'clarify the matter'; indeed, the humour arises precisely from the gap

---

116   Catton 2013, pp. 88–9.

separating the reader's mental projection of what such a character might 'really' have said and what the narrator *reports* him as saying. Catton thus uses a mixture of enthymemic physical description ('greasy' and 'nasal' being physical signs of immorality in the melodramatic tradition), shifting focalisation, and a commitment to a single narratorial idiom (i.e., one which does not accommodate itself to the probable speech-styles of its characters in passages of free indirect discourse) to produce a carefully crafted comic scene which warms us to Devlin and Anna Wetherell (the 'whore') as it turns us against Drake. That, of course, is the achieved valence of this particular scene; its meaning in the overall narrative may well prove to be different.

A further point can then be made regarding the narratorial style taken as idiom in its own right. For if we have said that the verbal diegesis is the author's style under the regime of fictionality, it must also be said that this style is not necessarily the author *in propria persona*. Walsh was right to warn against the equation of authorial style with the subjective expressivity of the biographical author. In the above passage, we see why: Eleanor Catton's style is a pastiche of the nineteenth-century omniscient narrator. Arguably, the motivations for this are twofold: firstly, because it allows her to write a certain type of formal, verbose sentence that has tended to fall by the wayside in the mainstream contemporary novel (and which is indirectly related to the problem of speech in naturalism discussed in Chapter 5); secondly, because shifts between zero and internal focalisation – typical of the classical realist novel – enable her to maintain at the level of style a type of control which mirrors the overall conceptual structure of *The Luminaries* as such: a character system and chapter-organisation based on the twelve signs of the zodiac.[117] The focalisation is thus partly determined by the need at once to hone in on each of the character-star-signs and to map their shifting mutual trajectories across the night skies of Hokitika – fortune and destiny united in a single narrative strategy. This, in turn, feeds back into the idiom of Catton's style, allowing her to hover over characters' gestures and ethical blindspots whilst never collapsing into pseudo-Jamesian contemplation: the zodiac interconnectedness, reproduced at the level of focalisation, drives the mystery plot forwards, acting as a foil for the production of verbally elaborate sentences. Such, then, are the types of identification – partly political, partly rhetorical – performed in the second phase of mimesis$_3$.

---

117   It would be interesting to compare the use of such structures in the contemporary novel with those used in the modernist novel, the prime case being Joyce's use of *The Odyssey* as an undergirding structure in *Ulysses*, as discussed in Chapter 7.

3.3   *Formal Phase: From Form to Formation*

In practice, of course, the meanings of these individual stylistic strands accumulate into what Wayne Booth called 'the intuitive apprehension of a completed artistic whole'.[118] Booth even considered referring to the 'core norms and choices' which he would eventually, and fatefully, name the 'implied author' as 'style', but felt that this latter term implied the 'merely verbal' and was thus inadequate to his needs.[119] In our case, this artistic whole is the overall act of stylistic configuration. It has two main aspects, depending on whether the analysis is text-oriented or reader-oriented: instance and interpellation. It is important to reiterate that *style as instance* can never be reduced to the 'narrating instance' alone. It is *both* the narrating instance and what Aczel (after Bakhtin) has called the 'voiceless, textually irretrievable, yet theoretically reconstructible, organizing, arranging, juxtaposing subject'.[120] To risk a Coleridgean terminology, it is imagination's esemplastic power acting through the author:[121] the shaping force immanent to the act of stylistic configuration.

At this level, however, the 'formal' phase of mimesis$_3$, we are concerned less with the actual process of artistic organisation performed by the author (through a whole series of drafts, amendments, additions and deletions) than with its *effects* upon the reader. It will be recalled from Chapter 4 that *style as interpellation* at this level – i.e., beyond that of simple focalisation – signifies the overall ideological subject position implied by any fictional discourse and to which the reader (either consciously or unconsciously) imaginatively aligns herself. This alignment is, of course, a very complex phenomenon, consisting of a range of permutations from total alignment, partial reluctance and outright rejection; moreover, there are also variations in one's level of consciousness of the process of interpellation performed by the text. Finally, even though most works of literature come down on one side or the other of an ethical or political dilemma, the best works are often those which inhabit a zone of political ambiguity.[122]

J.G. Ballard's *Cocaine Nights* (1996), for instance, is structured by just such an ambiguity. It is a story about an exclusive Spanish resort for wealthy, retired British expats in which five people have been murdered in a house fire; the

---

118   Booth 1983, p. 73.
119   Booth 1983, p. 74.
120   Aczel 1998, p. 477.
121   Coleridge 2000, p. 239 ff.
122   This is not a transhistorical law: Dante's *Divine Comedy* comes down firmly on the side of Paradise and is none the worse for it. It is only in Romantic modernity that the interdiction on overt sermonising first arises.

narrator, Charles Prentice, visits the resort to defend his brother, an elite club manager, who has confessed to the murders. The narrative follows Charles's descent into the barbaric underworld lurking beneath the civilised façade of the resort. The novel is a conventional first-person narrative in which the narratorial idiom is unremarkable but for its clean, functional precision. Moreover, the formal English employed by the narrator is of the same lexical range as those of the middle-class characters it objectifies; the socially homogeneous world presented thus results in a fairly monological verbal style. The genre is detective fiction, but unlike most such works the impetus here is not so much to discover the culprit as to determine the social significance of the crime: as Andrzej Gasiorek has observed, the 'detective's work is that of ethnography'.[123] The central ambiguity arises when Charles affiliates himself with the subculture of drugs, sex and violence with a view to exposing it but, in doing so, becomes seduced by it himself. This ambiguity is then part of a larger one between the (post)modern, anodyne comforts of the rich retirees, who live out their days in a state of technologically advanced, post-political *anomie*,[124] and the attempt of Crawford (the Dionysian ringleader) to return them to the supposedly liberating vitality of pre-modern savagery. At the end of the novel, the narrator ends up in precisely the same position as the brother he had come to defend, prepared to take responsibility for a murder he did not commit – this time of Crawford himself:

> Did he [the detective] already know, as he walked towards me, that I would take responsibility for the death? Crawford's mission would endure, and the festivals of the Residencia Costasol would continue to fill the sky with their petals and balloons, as the syndicates of guilt sustained their dream.[125]

In what precise sense, then, can this novel be said to interpellate the reader into an overall ideological subject position? It is not the case here, as in much lesser fiction, in which the heroes and villains, virtues and vices are clearly distinguished and their differences upheld (according to the dominant ideology of the specific historical context). Rather, it is strictly undecidable as to whether Ballard wants us to sympathise with Charles's conversion to Dionysianism or to recognise him as a delinquent pure and simple. The interpellation, then, is

---

123   Gasiorek 2005, p. 171.
124   'Politics is over, Charles, it doesn't touch the public imagination any longer' (Ballard 1996, p. 245).
125   Ballard 1996, p. 329.

less a call to the reader to inhabit one subject position than it is a very precise example of Jameson's notion of symbolic resolution: it overtly acknowledges and accounts for the spiritual desolation of 'civilised', postmodern *anomie* and the seductive power of violence, but resolves the contradiction by sublating them both *into the fabric of the narrative itself.* It sublates them by narrating them, thereby forgoing the need to choose. In doing so it implicates the reader in its implicit historical pessimism, producing in her the impression that such oppositions are *in reality* unalterable. Ballard combines an extreme sensitivity to the lived quality of Western postmodernity with a political pessimism in which the only alternative would be a resort to pre-modern sources of vitality. Yet, it is precisely because of this pessimism and its attraction to violence that his novels throw into relief the clinical alienation of the surfaces of postmodernity, the spattered blood making us freshly aware of the affectless sheen it has sullied. The ideological limits of the novel's interpellation are thus at one with its literary merits.

There is then a further aspect to the 'formal' phase, one adapted from Williams's notion of 'formation'. Williams, it will be recalled from Chapter 5, defines formation as a non-institutional, group self-organisation, with specialising, alternative or openly oppositional external relations to more general organisations and institutions within society at large.[126] I want to maintain this useful emphasis on small-scale group collectives, but, for those cases where a writer does *not* constitute part of such a group, to expand the concept to include its more general sense of the process of 'being formed': 'formation' as I use it, then, includes *both* the senses of *group formation* and *individual formation.* The reason I am stressing its importance at this level is because it provides a crucial mediation between the implied ideological subject position of an individual literary work and the small-scale context of the social groupings out of which it emerged. The relation between form and formation might then be imagined as a *Gestalt* figure-ground relationship, in which the contours of the former are thrown into relief by those of the latter, and vice versa.

Often, there will be a great deal of harmony between the two. In the case of Ballard, there is a clear correlation between his biographical formation and the formal features noted above. His traumatic childhood experiences as a prisoner of war under the Japanese in what was originally a British colonial outpost, the Shanghai International Settlement, contrasted sharply with his post-war relocation to Plymouth and Cambridge, which were socially conservative and ridden with nostalgia for a mythical imperial past of village greens and cathedral

---

126   Williams 1981, pp. 57–86.

closes.[127] If, as Jameson claims, modernist formal experimentation grew partly out of the experience of Western metropolises whose truth lay in the brutality of the colonies beyond the everyday lives of writers, then here is a writer who lived the world at both ends: it is no surprise that his work draws on the estrangement techniques of surrealism and combines them with an exposé of the barbaric violence underlying the polite façades of middle England.

Alternatively, the form to formation relation may highlight political discrepancies. The classic example is surely Pound's *Cantos*. Here is a body of work so formally revolutionary that it would set the bar for the next half century of Anglo-American poetics. 'Pound's great achievement', writes Charles Bernstein, one of his inheritors,

> was to create a work using ideological swatches from many social and historical sectors of his own society and an immense variety of other cultures. This complex, polyvocal textuality was the result of his search ... for deeper truths than could be revealed by more monologically organized poems operating with a single voice and a single perspective.[128]

At the level of his overarching style, then, Pound was as progressive as they come, viewed from the standard postmodern perspective that heteroglossia, difference, and multiplicity are positive ends in themselves. Yet, this is precisely why Marxist poetics is a *social* formalism and not a formalism *tout court*: Raymond Williams well knew that the 'innovatory inclusion [of what Bernstein calls 'ideological swatches'] can be traced to its formation, but the isolated technique is more usually traceable to its agency, in direct or displaced domination'.[129] In this case, Pound was a socially privileged émigré who mixed with similarly uprooted and socially mobile artists who came to form radical avant-gardes of varying political allegiances. Yet Pound's extreme modernism was only possible because of his violent backlash against the abstractions and alienations of modernisation which he came to associate with the figure of the Jew. As Robert Casillo has argued, 'Pound turned to Fascism because he shares not only its deep fear of indeterminacy but also its central desire, which is to banish the indeterminate from social life'.[130] The Jew stands as the figure in Pound's work for all the ills of modernity and its indeterminacies, his fascism

---

127 For an interesting account of Ballard's ambiguous relationship to nostalgia, see Walder 2011, pp. 139–62.
128 Bernstein 1992, p. 123.
129 Williams 2007, p. 79.
130 Casillo 1988, p. 324. Cited in Bernstein 1992, p. 124.

thus constituting a political stance more or less diametrically opposed to the implicit politics of his stylistic revolution. Once again, however, the *extreme and total* character of his poetic-political vision was integral to the extremity of his stylistic experimentation; those who wish to bracket Pound's politics from his poetry as a regrettable side-issue are entirely missing the point.

To conclude, the formal phase designates that level at which the reader is interpellated by the total ideological position of the literary work, but which the critical reader can juxtapose with her knowledge of the writer's formation (group or individual). It can be usefully compared to the first of Jameson's three concentric zones of interpretation: political history in which the individual work is grasped as a symbolic act.[131] However, it should be seen as possessing a greater political effectivity, and thus worthy of more sustained critical attention, than Jameson's epic scope would allow.

3.4   *Generic Phase: Projects and Modes*

Until now, we have stressed the uniqueness of each and every act of poetic shaping and reception. At the 'generic' level (my version of Frye's 'mythic' phase), however, we turn our attention to the shared and collective nature of literary forms, types, genres and modes (categories drawn from Williams's *Culture* (1981) and outlined here in Chapter 5). We noted in an earlier chapter that Williams's crucial move was to reformulate the problem of the relation between an individual literary work and the form or genre in which it was written as a 'problem of the relations between social (collective) modes and individual projects';[132] these modes themselves he understood as 'the common property, to be sure with differences of degree, of writers and audiences or readers, before any communicative composition can occur'.[133] Thus, part of the act of reading involves an awareness of the type of mode that is being activated and of this particular text's relation to other examples of that mode. When one reads a detective novel, for instance, one does so with an at least minimal awareness of the history of that genre from Edgar Allan Poe, through Arthur Conan Doyle and Agatha Christie, Raymond Chandler and Dashiell Hammett and onwards up to its contemporary inheritors. Thus, this is the level at which the professional reader will wish to reconstruct the lines of inheritance of particular works, and of the politically charged functions of the selective traditions which limit the field of possible inheritance (whether

---

131   Jameson 1981, pp. 75–82.
132   Williams 1977, p. 187.
133   Williams 1977, pp. 187–8.

official, in the case of canon-formations, which usually entail questions of national identity, or unofficial, in such traditionally countercultural genres as science fiction or avant-garde poetry, each with its sociologically specific readership).

I have already described the effects of type, genre and mode on the act of stylistic configuration. At the level of mimesis₃, however, the emphasis is somewhat different. For here we are concerned less with the socially significant permutations of instance, idiom and interpellation, than with the ideology of form and the way in which it informs and limits the possibilities of cultural expression and reception more generally. Thus, I here conflate Jameson's second and third levels – the 'social' at which the text is read as an 'ideologeme' and the 'historical' proper at which it is read as the 'ideology of form'.[134] This is in order to avoid the political pitfalls of Jameson's epic scope (outlined in Chapter 7) and to emphasise that any analysis of the ideology of form requires the dialogism that Jameson associates only with the level of the social; all forms, genres, types and modes (on a scale of most to least) are *simultaneously* politically significant in their own right – they act as apparatuses of cognitive and affective distributions, privileging some ideological purviews over others – *and* internal mediators, enablers and obstacles to residual, dominant and emergent structures of feeling.

This is clarified in the following passage by Raymond Williams:

> When I hear people talk about literature, describing what so-and-so did with that form – how did he handle the short novel? – I often think we should reverse the question and ask how did the short novel handle him. Because anyone who has carefully observed his own practice of writing eventually finds that there is a point where, although he is holding the pen or tapping the typewriter, what is being written, while not separate from him, is not only him either, and of course this other force is literary form. Very few if any of us could write at all if certain forms were not available. And then we may be lucky, we may find forms which happen to correspond to our experience. But take the case of the nineteenth-century working-class writers, who wanted to write about their working lives. The most popular form was the novel, but though they had marvelous material that could go into the novel very few of them managed to write good or even any novels. Instead they wrote marvelous autobiographies. Why? Because the form coming down through the religious tradition was

---

134 Jameson 1981, pp. 83–102.

of the witness confessing the story of his life, or there was the defence speech at the trial when the man tells the judge who he is and what he has done, or of course other kinds of speech ... Indeed the forms of working-class consciousness are bound to be different from the literary forms of another class, and it is a long struggle to find new and adequate forms.[135]

The key here is that, unlike Jameson, whose formulation of the politics of literature consists in an either-or choice between its significance as a symbolic act or as the ideology of its form, Williams combines the effectivity of formal ideology (and, by extension, of genre, type and mode) with the problem of the class attachments inherent to specific forms. For him, forms are *doubly* political: once, along the axis of their implicit mode of presentation of the world, and once in their attachment to the consciousness of a specific class or class fraction – and, by extension, to the selective tradition of canon formation, whereby the social hegemon invites the continuance and reproduction of forms favourable or co-optable to its ruling intentions. I would then want simply to add a *third* element: that the ideology of a form does not remain constant through time; whilst it begins life as a symbolic act within a specific situation, and thus with a specific political implication, over time it can be 'refunctioned' (to use a Brechtian phrase) and become 'sedimented' with fresh ideological significance, depending on the new historical situations in which it is inherited and developed – though it will always to some extent continue to emit, beneath these layers, the political connotations of its origins.[136]

It is now clear, then, that the type of critical reading performed at the generic level of projects and modes involves a retrospective reinterpretation of the previous three levels, focussing on the conjunction of literary-ideological inheritance with the non-synchronous developments of residual, dominant and emergent interests and attachments. Both Williams and Jameson, in their different ways, stress that 'the dialogue of class struggle is one in which two opposing discourses fight it out within the general unity of a shared code'.[137] Given that this is the case, the generic phase of mimesis₃ seeks out shifts and

135 Williams 1989, p. 86.
136 On the ideology of form as a process of sedimentation, see Jameson 1981, pp. 140–41.
137 Jameson 1981, p. 84. Cf. also Williams 1963, p. 310: '... in a society where a particular class and hence a particular use of the common language is dominant a large part of the literature, carrying as it does a body of vital common experience, will be attracted to the dominant language mode. At the same time, a national literature, as English has never ceased to be, will, while containing this relation, contain also elements of the whole culture and language'.

"the dialogue of class struggle is one in which two opposing discourses fight it out within the general unity of a shared code"

changes in those shared collective literary modes and the uses to which they are put, interpreting them as potential indicators (and immanent constituents) of shifts in the structure of feeling – and, ultimately, in the movements of class struggle itself.[138]

Take, for example, China Miéville's recent novel, *The City and the City* (2009). The blurb describes it as an 'existential thriller', but it would be more accurate to say that it combines the structure of the detective novel with the estrangement effects of science fiction.[139] To observe that it uses the structure of the detective novel is already to suggest that it will likely contain several socially significant generic features: a plot which dramatises the narratological relation of *fabula* and *sjuzet* in the relation of crime to investigation; an exploration of urban space, including those areas which most middle-class readers would not, in reality, get to experience; the readerly satisfaction of the solving of a puzzle, and so on. The rise of the detective was at one with the gradual demise of faith in the divine revelation of guilt and the increasing lack of confidence in the reliability of confessions extracted by torture and of testimonies given by witnesses in courts of law.[140] By extension, it was a cultural agent in the shift from a sovereign to a disciplinary regime of power, one bound up with post-Enlightenment rationalism, most evidently embodied in the increasing hegemony of the empirical sciences. It was also a means of imaginatively negotiating the massively growing cities and the human confusion to which they gave rise. The best detective stories combined the sensationalism of Gothic (enabling a free play on the deepest fears embedded in the political unconscious) with a scientific rationality capable of surmounting them; the resolution of crimes was thus simultaneously an act of catharsis effected by the readership, their fears assuaged as their pleasures in logical abduction were indulged.

The genre of detective fiction will thus never be entirely free of this ideological baggage, yet it becomes available for rearticulation according to historically variable fears and contexts. China Miéville, in typically self-conscious guise, will then use this urban genre par excellence ('the urban experience runs deep in crime fiction', says Knight)[141] as a means of reflecting upon contemporary urban experience itself. The basic premise of the novel is that two ostensibly post-Soviet Eastern European cities – Besźel, in post-Fordist decline, and Ul Qoma, riding the neoliberal financial wave – inhabit the same geographical

---

138   These shifts are to be understood as larger in scope than the micro-structures of feeling referred to in the literal phase.
139   The best-known account of the use of estrangement in science fiction is Suvin 1979.
140   Throughout this section I am drawing on Knight 2010.
141   Knight 2010, p. 28.

China Miéville,
The City and the City

space, but that it is illegal for their respective inhabitants to acknowledge the presence of the other city. Their everyday lives are premised upon the 'unseeing' of their urban counterparts. When a murder victim turns up in Besźel, however, the trail leads the detective, Inspector Borlú, to cross over into the other city. As well as being a riveting story in its own right, then, it is in many ways a parable about the neoliberal city and the ways in which structures of existential disavowal – between classes and races – are built into its very fabric.

Most significant, however, is the way in which Miéville exploits the generic traits of detective fiction to question the forms of alienation and solidarity of the urban totality which that genre itself has traditionally taken as its chief domain. As Niall Martin has observed, in adopting the form of the police procedural, in which 'the detective's determination to solve the murder of someone who initially seems beneath the law's contempt ... uncovers a conspiracy which extends upwards to those who consider themselves above its reach',[142] 'an epistemological desire for the solution to a mystery is aligned with a more ethical desire to witness justice being done'.[143] Within the world constructed by the novel, the police procedural is refunctioned in such a way that it comes to foreground the critical theme of seeing and unseeing in the neoliberal city:

> As an inspector he [Borlú] exemplifies the equation of knowledge with visibility: with the task of revealing a truth which is assumed to be hidden. However, as a policeman he is also polis man – a man of the city – and as such, is concerned primarily with enforcing observance of the rules and limits that constitute the society of which he is a part. He is charged, literally, with policing what may and may not be seen. As both an inspector and a policeman, Borlú becomes increasingly aware of a rupture present within the law that he himself embodies.[144]

Thus, in *The City and the City* 'truth is precisely that which everybody knows, yet nobody can acknowledge'[145] and is in this respect an allegory of the so-called 'post-ideological' condition of postmodernity, which, according to Žižek, is summarised by the formula 'they know it and still do it':[146] ideology is no

---

142 Martin 2013, p. 4.
143 Ibid.
144 Martin 2013, p. 5.
145 Ibid.
146 Cited in Martin 2013, p. 6.

longer *epistemological* but *practical*.[147] The ultimate cost incurred by Borlú in acknowledging the unacknowledged is not closure but, as Martin has it, 'the discovery of exile from home'.[148] Miéville thus takes up the decidedly geographically *rootless* quality of the classical detective and transforms it into the fate of *any* figure who chooses consistently and committedly to acknowledge the unacknowledged in the postmodern, neoliberal cityscape: 'the discovery of the truth of exile'.[149] In doing so, he exploits the generic resources of detective fiction in order to make a critical literary intervention into the current historical and political conjuncture.

It is only by reconstructing these lines of inheritance and situating individual works within the modes, genres and types from which they emerge that the broader political significance of a literary work comes into focus. The critical reader retroactively reframes the first three phases – including unique patterns of idiom, formal disjunctions, stylistic peculiarities, and so on – from this new perspective: as the writer's project to break new ground within a mode or genre which may or may not – because of its ideological affiliations – be congenial to her.

3.5   Utopian Phase

It is only at the fifth, utopian phase that we reach the universal significance of literary styles. As we have seen, Frye describes his 'anagogic' phase as that in which 'literature imitates the total dream of man, and so imitates the thought of a human mind which is at the circumference and not at the center of its reality'.[150] It is that phase at which 'nature becomes, not the container, but the thing contained'[151] and where 'the *dianoia* of art is no longer a *mimesis logou*, but the Logos, the shaping word which is both reason and, as Goethe's Faust speculated, *praxis* or creative act'.[152] Given such idealist desires for the ultimate absorption of material life into the spirit of Literature, it is no surprise that Jameson rejected Frye's reconfiguration of medieval allegory.[153] Yet I hold that it is worth retaining, so long as we redefine it as follows: the Utopian phase is the analogue in mimesis$_3$ of the joy of writing in mimesis$_2$; it denotes the potential connection of men and women throughout human history via their written

---

147   Whether ideology was ever a purely epistemological issue is another question entirely.
148   Martin 2013, p. 6.
149   Martin 2013, pp. 6–7.
150   Frye 1957, p. 119.
151   Ibid.
152   Frye 1957, p. 120.
153   Jameson 1981, pp. 72–4.

"'ideology is no longer epistemological but practical'"

products and acts of translation, raising them up (*anagogic* from *anagein*, 'to lift up') to the experience of a possible future in which the economic, political, social and cultural divisions that have structured all hitherto existing languages will have been overcome. It is the level at which the political dream of collective human self-emancipation makes itself available to readers by enabling them to catch glimpses of the language of reconciliation of which all authentic stylisation is but a dim foreshadowing. Like Alain Badiou's notion of the generic,[154] which inscribes itself into the historical multiplicity of being, yet exceeds it towards the universal, or Walter Benjamin's notion of a 'pure language' at which all translation secretly aims,[155] the utopian phase is the experience, not of the *elimination* of the fallen and scarred matter of language, but of its *transfiguration* into what Williams calls – with a modesty which masks its world-historical significance – a 'common culture'.[156]

4   *Poiēsis* and *Praxis*

Having now set out a systematic theory of style, we are in a position to ree-mphasise the logical core of Marxist poetics. It has been observed that Marx 'removed one of philosophy's most ancient taboos: the radical distinction be-tween *praxis* and *poiēsis*';[157] where *praxis* had been the 'free' activity of citizens of the *polis* to transform themselves by seeking their own (autotelic) perfection, *poiēsis* was necessary action which sought only the (external) perfection of its product, not the man producing. Marx, in a revolutionary move, identified the two:

> ... *praxis* constantly passes over into *poiēsis* and vice versa. There is never any effective freedom which is not also a material transformation, which is not registered historically in *exteriority*. But nor is there any work which is not a transformation of self, as though human beings could change their conditions of existence while maintaining an invariant 'essence'.[158]

Praxis and *poiēsis* thus constitute a mutually mediating unity. This is the source of the two fundamental insights of a Marxist poetics. The first has been traced

---

154   E.g., Badiou 2005.
155   Benjamin 1973, p. 74.
156   Williams 1963, pp. 318–23.
157   Balibar 2007, p. 40.
158   Balibar 2007, p. 41.

at length throughout this entire book: literary styles are acts of poetic shaping which take the internally divided and pre-structured language which is an indissoluble element of human *praxis* as their raw material and configure it, via *poiesis*, into a unique, meaningful literary work which has multiple political valences. The second insight, unique to Marxist poetics, is that praxis itself alters the material structure of human experience, the modes of human communication and intersubjectivity and, thereby, the raw materials of *poiēsis*. Both *praxis* and *poiēsis* are immanent modes of literary production.

In their different ways, Georg Lukács and Raymond Williams paved the way for this insight. The work of the former, as we have seen, allows the interpretation that the proletariat was the solution to the problem that the novel was born to fail to solve, capable of transforming in reality, via its *praxis*, those alienating conditions of modernity which the novel itself merely configured through *poiēsis*. The proletariat – on my reading of Lukács's text – was thus called upon to become a collective epic poet, composing reality and literature in a single, revolutionary process. Williams, on the other hand, argued that the 'collective democratic institution' (e.g., trade unions, the political party) was the culture produced by the working class.[159] He thus extended the concept of *poiēsis* (a term he himself never actually uses) beyond the narrow, bourgeois sense of 'cultural' or 'literary' to the results of political *praxis* as such. Both of these critics pointed towards the logical conclusion of a Marxist poetics: the writer can forge her styles from the prefigured linguistic terrain she inherits, or she can attempt to *alter the raw materials of literary production itself via political organisation*. Both approaches, from a Marxist perspective, are equally 'creative', in that they both inform the process of literary composition, albeit in more and less immediate ways. The point, however, is that *poiēsis* and *praxis* are immanent to and mutually constitutive of one another. The poet and political activist inhabit the same plane of immanence. It is the task of Marxist poetics constantly to reveal this hidden plane and to elaborate its political and literary ramifications: revolutionaries are the unacknowledged poets of the world.

---

159 Williams 1963, p. 313.

Conclusion

This book began by delineating the conceptual and historical preconditions for the coming into being of a 'politics of style'. It traced the history of a sub-terranean current of stylistics within the Marxist tradition and identified the strengths and weaknesses of Paul Ricoeur's paradigm of the 'threefold mimesis'. The second part of the book undertook a series of critical reconstructions of the implicit and explicit theories of style in the oeuvres of Raymond Williams, Terry Eagleton and Fredric Jameson. Out of an immanent critique of their work – and a historicisation of Ricoeur's threefold mimesis – the final part of the book developed a set of concepts for the critical analysis of literary styles. We are now in a position to summarise the main features of these reconstructions and of the new theory of style here developed.

Williams's implicit theory of style showed him to be a thinker for whom immanence is a central principle. This principle is at the heart of his political vision and runs through every aspect of his work, especially those related to style: keywords, language, forms, techniques, and what was named his 'sociolo-gical perspectivism'. Williams's writings on naturalist drama formed the basis of his broader reflections on language and of his immanent critique of the then-dominant Marxist theories of literature and culture. His theory of style is also inseparable from his development of the concept of the 'structure of feeling' – indeed, the two are often taken by him to be synonymous. Finally, Williams's conception of historical temporality, which arose out of his keen interest in the notion of inheritance, was described as an immanent, self-conscious tra-ditionality, consciously positioned against the ideology of modernism and the conservative organicism of F.R. Leavis and the *Scrutiny* formation.

Terry Eagleton's work, meanwhile, is informed by a political theology of style. The central problematic of Eagleton's lifework is to aestheticise and somatise emancipatory discourse whilst leaving enough of a rational subject intact so as to enable political agency. Central to this problematic are his recent metaphysical (re)turn and his calls for a renewal of close reading, both of which find their origins in his early works of political theology. His attempt to fuse an overtly Catholic theory of language with Marxist literary criticism unsurprisingly produces certain contradictions; these contradictions persist in his writings to this day. Eagleton's calls for attention to the stylistic texture of literary works is integral to the theory of style developed in Part 3 of this book, but his general understanding of style suffers from an overemphasis on monological and singular elements of literary works, as opposed to dialogical and relational ones. Nonetheless, the sheer scope and grandeur of his ethico-political vision of 'tragic humanism' outweighs any limitations of this localised element of his work.

Finally, if one were to extend the logic of Lukács's *Theory of the Novel*, which claims that the novel is the epic of modernity, then Fredric Jameson could be understood as the epic poet of *post*modernity. This is a double-edged blade insofar as it encompasses at once his capacity for producing large-scale historical syntheses and his consequent tendency to downplay the political import of individual literary works. The first half of Chapter 7 suggested that Jameson tends to underestimate the importance of politics in favour of economics and its equivalent in the realm of historical temporality – stagist periodisation. The second half of the chapter then systematically reconstructed his theory of style as a predominantly modernist linguistic practice. Jameson sees style as unique to the bourgeois monadic subject who has lost all organic links to his or her public, a borderline physiological phenomenon, and involving a detailed elaboration of individual sentences which develop autonomously in contradistinction to the organic unity of the literary work.

Out of this process of immanent critique, it became possible to develop an independent theory of style. It should now be clear that style is an inherently relational concept in at least three senses:

1. It is a linguistic mode of social relation between writer and potential reader (informed and internally limited by the factors listed in sub-chapter 4.3).
2. It is the poetically shaped interrelation of the three linguistic operations featured in fictional narratives: instance, idiom and interpellation.
3. Its textual autonomy is informed and limited by its relation to other formal elements of a given literary work (most notably to plot and action).

This relationality becomes actualised through the operation of configuration. Prior to this, however, there exists a linguistic situation structured and striated by the same divisions and contradictions as the social formation itself, of which it is an immanent element. To think this linguistic situation is to produce a linguistic ideology, inevitably influenced by the general ideology of the ruling class.[1] Together with the writer's historically specific social experience, the linguistic situation and linguistic ideology constitute the verbal horizon of all writing.

---

[1] Those attempts to produce a Marxist philosophy of language – e.g., Voloshinov, Gramsci or Lecercle – are exceptional to the extent that they aim precisely to counteract linguistic ideologies.

The various strands of relationality inherent to style are then produced, informed and held in unity via the operation of configuration or poetic shaping. This operation is transformative and *productive* (hence its centrality to a Marxist *poetics*). It takes the raw material of the linguistic situation, including its words, phrases, jargons, and verbal stereotypes, and sculpts them into an artistic totality which transforms the political valence of the ideological content, all the while relying on this latter's vitality for its verbal vigour. This operation of poetic shaping is internally limited by the following factors: stylistic ideology, which is the specifically literary region of linguistic ideology, and which accounts for those self-conscious stylistic projects that writers often develop; directionality, which denotes the fact that when an individual writer feels as if she is referring directly, centrifugally out of and away from herself towards the world, this outwardly directional act is always intersected by a lateral directionality beyond her volition (context and pre-existing language); and the modes, types, genres and forms in and through which the writer is working and which she activates as a means of social relation with the potential reader. This operation of lexical configuration is often accompanied by the historically variable pains, pleasures and cathexes experienced during the process of literary composition.

The moment of reading, or of refiguration in Ricoeur's vocabulary, consists of five phases or types of attention. These phases each range from spontaneous interpretation to self-conscious critical analysis.

1. The literal phase is equivalent to what is known as 'close reading': its object is the verbal texture, tone and shape of the individual sentences. This is the locus of those small-scale shifts in transindividual subjectivity that I have called micro-structures of feeling.

2. The identification phase involves the singling out of the various stylistic strands which interweave to form a text: style as instance, style as idiom, style as interpellation.

3. The formal phase focuses on the effects of the overall stylistic configuration on the reader, and the relation between this overall unity and the *formation* – individual or group – out of which it emerged.

4. The generic phase has as its object the shared and collective nature of literary forms, types, genres and modes – especially the ways in which they embody ideologies, become ideologically refunctioned, and are inherited.

5. Finally, the utopian phase denotes the potential connection of men and women throughout human history via their written products and acts of translation, raising them up to the experience of a possible future in which

the economic, political, social and cultural divisions that have structured all
hitherto existing languages will have been overcome.

Taken together, this book offers a theory of style which is simultaneously a
Marxist rearticulation of Paul Ricoeur's threefold mimesis.

Ultimately, the preceding chapters have identified the following ways in
which style is political:

1. Theories of style inevitably involve conceptions of language as such, that is,
   linguistic ideologies. Since, as Williams constantly reminds us, a definition
   of language is always, implicitly or explicitly, a definition of human beings
   in the world, the understanding of language implied by a theory of style
   involves political evaluations.
2. Any theory of style implicitly includes a politics of time, since it must explain
   the endurance of old styles, the advent of stylistic novelty, and breaks with
   past conventions. Attitudes towards stylistic innovation thus necessarily
   involve, at the level of language, attitudes towards the past, present and
   future.
3. The politics of a style does not inhere in the mode(s) of verbal phrasing
   alone, nor solely – in the case of heteroglossia – in their mutual internal relations. It resides in the articulation of the style with the intentions, purposes
   and social formations through which the style achieves its efficacy. In other
   words, the politics of style is never purely intra-textual.
4. Styles are at once expressions and embodiments of transindividual subjectivity, and are especially important as indices of newly emergent social
   subjectivity. In embodying the linguistic ways – past, present, and emergent – in which humans relate to one another, styles are necessarily immanent to politics, in that this latter, along with the economic organisation of
   social reproduction, influences the modes that human interrelationality will
   assume. In reproducing certain styles, we simultaneously reproduce the specific social relations they embody.
5. Styles imply specific attitudes towards, and evaluations of, the world they
   represent. Inherited styles are thus, in a minimal sense, *already committed*.
   Because of this, the politics of a style is never reducible to the politics
   of its author; rather, 'politics' here applies to the *conjunction* of authorial
   ideology, aesthetic ideology, stylistic ideology, and stylistic practice – with
   no presumed relation of homology between them.
6. The composition of styles involves the social use of the material means of
   communication, which are also means of production. It has as its presupposition a learned technology of writing mediated predominantly by the ruling
   class via the education system.

7. Styles can be proleptic symptoms of affects or relations which are currently historically unrealisable. They point towards an imagined future of political, economic, social and linguistic reconciliation.

It is in all these *multiple* ways, then, that style is political.

This book was also intended as one aspect of a potentially larger 'Marxist poetics' that would aim to reconceptualise a range of literary concepts. Building on recent work by Franco Moretti on prose,[2] John Frow on genre and character,[3] Caroline Levine on form,[4] Fredric Jameson on realism,[5] and Alex Woloch on character systems,[6] a 'Marxist poetics' would constitute an expansive literary-critical research programme that seeks simultaneously to contribute to the contemporary renewal of the Marxist tradition. Like Williams's 'cultural materialism', it would deploy the insights of historical materialism not only to identify the limitations of non-Marxist discourses, but also – crucially – to overcome Marxism's *own* residual idealisms. Such a programme would also seek to trace forgotten lines of inheritance within the Marxist tradition itself: those subterranean currents of Marxist poetics that have been a consistent, if overlooked, element of Marxism from its earliest beginnings. Ultimately, Marxist poetics comprises a philological investigation of what Marxism truly was, an attempted remaking of what it is, and a resource of hope for what it will become.

2   Moretti 2013.
3   Frow 2006 and 2014.
4   Levine 2015.
5   Jameson 2013.
6   Woloch 2003.

Bibliography

Abrams, M.H. 1953, *The Mirror and the Lamp: Romantic Theory and the Critical Tradition*, New York: Oxford University Press.

Achebe, Chinua 1997, 'English and the African Writer', *Transition*, 75/76: 342–9.

Aczel, Richard 1998, 'Hearing Voices in Narrative Texts', *New Literary History*, 29, 3: 467–500.

Adorno, Theodor W. 2005 [1951], *Minima Moralia: Reflections on Damaged Life*, translated by E.F.N. Jephcott, London: Verso.

Alderson, David 2004, *Terry Eagleton*, New York: Palgrave Macmillan.

Althusser, Louis 2005 [1965], *For Marx*, translated by Ben Brewster, London: Verso.

Anderson, Perry 1964, 'Origins of the Present Crisis', *New Left Review*, I, 23: 26–53.

————— 1968, 'Components of the National Culture', *New Left Review*, I, 50: 3–57.

————— 1976a, 'The Antinomies of Antonio Gramsci', *New Left Review*, 100: 5–78.

————— 1976b, *Considerations on Western Marxism*, London: NLB.

————— 1983, *In the Tracks of Historical Materialism*, London: Verso.

————— 1984, 'Modernity and Revolution', *New Left Review*, 144: 96–113.

————— 1998, *The Origins of Postmodernity*, London: Verso.

Aquilina, Mario 2014, *The Event of Style in Literature*, Basingstoke: Palgrave Macmillan.

Aristotle 1934, *The Nichomachean Ethics*, translated by H. Rackham, Cambridge, Mass.: Harvard University Press.

————— 2000, *Poetics*, in *Classical Literary Criticism*, edited by T.S. Dorsch and Penelope Murray, London: Penguin.

————— 2007 [1991], *On Rhetoric*, translated by George A. Kennedy, New York: Oxford University Press.

Auerbach, Erich 2003 [1946], *Mimesis: The Representation of Reality in Western Literature*, translated by Willard R. Trask, Princeton, 50th anniversary ed., N.J.: Princeton University Press.

Badiou, Alain 2005 [1988], *Being and Event*, translated by Oliver Feltham, London: Continuum.

Bakhtin, Mikhail M. 1981, *The Dialogic Imagination: Four Essays*, translated by Vadim Liapunov and Kenneth Brostrom, Austin: University of Texas Press.

————— 1984, *Problems of Dostoevsky's Poetics*, translated by Caryl Emerson. Minneapolis: University of Minnesota Press.

Bakhtin, Mikhaik M. and Pavel N. Medvedev 1978 [1928], *The Formal Method in Literary Scholarship: A Critical Introduction to Sociological Poetics*, Baltimore: Johns Hopkins University Press.

Balibar, Étienne 2007 [1993], *The Philosophy of Marx*, translated by Chris Turner, London: Verso.

Ballard, J.G. 1996, *Cocaine Nights*, London: Flamingo.

Barthes, Roland 1953, *Le degré zéro de l'écriture*, Paris: Éditions du Seuil.

———— 1957, *Mythologies*, Paris: Éditions du Seuil.

Bellow, Saul and Gordon Lloyd Harper 1966, 'Saul Bellow, the Art of Fiction, No. 37', *The Paris Review*, 36.

Benjamin, Walter 1973 [1955], *Illuminations*, translated by Harry Zohn, London: Fontana.

Bennett, Tony 2003, *Formalism and Marxism*, London: Routledge.

Bensaïd, Daniel 2007, 'Leaps! Leaps! Leaps!', in *Lenin Reloaded: Towards a Politics of Truth*, edited by Sebastian Budgen, Stathis Kouvelakis and Slavoj Žižek, Durham: Duke University Press.

Bernstein, Charles 1992, *A Poetics*, Cambridge, Mass.: Harvard University Press.

Bernstein, J.M. 1984, *The Philosophy of the Novel: Lukács, Marxism and the Dialectics of Form*, Minneapolis: University of Minnesota Press.

Berthier, Philippe and É. Bordas 2005, *Stendhal et le style*, Paris: Presses Sorbonne Nouvelle.

Bhabha, Homi K. 1994, *The Location of Culture*, London: Routledge.

Bidet, Jacques 2008, 'Falling Short of Marx: Habermas', in *Critical Companion to Contemporary Marxism*, edited by Jacques Bidet, Eustache Kouvelakis and Stathis Kouvelakis, Leiden: Brill.

Blasing, Mutlu Konuk 1995, *Politics and Form in Postmodern Poetry: O'Hara, Bishop, Ashbery and Merrill*, Cambridge: Cambridge University Press.

———— 2007, *Lyric Poetry: The Pain and the Pleasure of Words*, Princeton, N.J.: Princeton University Press.

Boer, Roland 2007, *Criticism of Heaven: On Marxism and Theology*, Leiden: Brill.

Booth, Wayne C. 1983, *The Rhetoric of Fiction*, Chicago: University of Chicago Press.

Bosteels, Bruno 2011, *The Actuality of Communism*, London: Verso.

Bourdieu, Pierre 1991, *Language and Symbolic Power*, translated by Gino Raymond and Matthew Adamson, Cambridge: Polity.

Boxall, Peter 2015, *The Value of the Novel*, New York: Cambridge University Press.

Brearton, Fran 2009, 'Heaney and the Feminine', in *The Cambridge Companion to Seamus Heaney*, edited by Bernard O'Donoghue, Cambridge: Cambridge University Press.

Brouillette, Sarah 2013, 'Academic Labor, the Aesthetics of Management, and the Promise of Autonomous Work', available at: http://nonsite.org/article/academic-labor-the-aesthetics-of-management-and-the-promise-of-autonomous-work.

Buchanan, Ian 2006, *Fredric Jameson: Live Theory*, New York: Continuum.

Buffon, Georges Louis Leclerc de 1853, *Oeuvres Complètes De Buffon (Avec La Nomenclature Linnéenne Et La Classification De Cuvier)*, Volume 12, Paris: Garnier frères.

Bühler, Karl 2011 [1934], *Theory of Language: The Representational Function of Language*, translated by Donald Fraser Goodwin, Philadelphia: John Benjamins Pub. Co.

Burke, Kenneth 1966, *Language as Symbolic Action: Essays on Life, Literature and Method*, Berkeley: University of California Press.

Caplan, David 2005, *Questions of Possibility: Contemporary Poetry and Poetic Form*, Oxford: Oxford University Press.

Casanova, Pascale 1999, *La république mondiale des lettres*, Paris: Editions du Seuil.

Casillo, Robert 1988, *The Genealogy of Demons: Anti-Semitism, Fascism, and the Myths of Ezra Pound*, Evanston, Ill.: Northwestern University Press.

Catton, Eleanor 2013, *The Luminaries: A Novel*, London: Granta.

Chatman, Seymour 1978, *Story and Discourse: Narrative Structure in Fiction and Film*, Ithaca, N.Y.: Cornell University Press.

Chatman, Seymour 1990, *Coming to Terms: The Rhetoric of Narrative in Fiction and Film*, Ithaca, N.Y.: Cornell University Press.

Chitty, Andrew 1998, 'Recognition and the Social Relations of Production', *Historical Materialism*, 2, 1: 57–98.

———— 2009, 'Species-Being and Capital', in *Karl Marx and Contemporary Philosophy*, edited by Andrew Chitty, London: Palgrave.

———— 2011, 'Hegel and Marx', in *A Companion to Hegel*, edited by Stephen Houlgate and Michael Baur, Oxford: Wiley-Blackwell.

Clover, Joshua 2011, 'Autumn of the System: Poetry and Financial Capital', *Journal of Narrative Theory*, 41, 1: 34–52.

Cohen, Tom 1994, *Anti-Mimesis from Plato to Hitchcock*, Cambridge: Cambridge University Press.

Coleridge, Samuel Taylor 2000, *Samuel Taylor Coleridge: The Major Works*, Oxford: Oxford University Press.

Collini, Stefan 2006, *Absent Minds: Intellectuals in Britain*, Oxford: Oxford University Press.

Connor, Steven 1997, 'Raymond Williams's Time', in *Raymond Williams Now: Knowledge, Limits and the Future*, edited by Jeff Wallace, Rod Jones and Sophie Nield. New York: St Martin's Press.

Corredor, Eva L. 1997, *Lukács after Communism: Interviews with Contemporary Intellectuals*, Durham, NC: Duke University Press.

Crystal, David 2004, *The Cambridge Encyclopedia of the English Language*, Cambridge: Cambridge University Press.

Curtius, Ernst Rober 1990 [1948], *European Literature and the Latin Middle Ages*, translated by Willard R. Trask, Princeton, N.J.: Princeton University Press.

Deleuze, Gilles 1998 [1993], *Essays Critical and Clinical*, translated by Daniel W. Smith and Michael A. Greco, London: Verso.

———— 2008 [1964], *Proust and Signs: The Complete Text*, London: Continuum.

Deleuze, Gilles and Félix Guattari 1983 [1972], *Anti-Oedipus: Capitalism and Schizophrenia*, translated by Robert Hurley, Mark Seem and Helen R. Lane, Minneapolis: University of Minnesota Press.

Derrida, Jacques 2008, 'Marx & Sons', in *Ghostly Demarcations: A Symposium on Jacques Derrida's Specters of Marx*, edited by Michael Sprinker, London: Verso.

Derrida, Jacques and Stefano Agosti 1978, *Spurs: Nietzsche's Styles = Eperons: Les Styles De Nietzsche*, Chicago: University of Chicago Press.

Eagleton, Terry 1970, *The Body as Language: Outline of a 'New Left' Theology*, London: Sheed & Ward.

————— 1973, 'William Hazlitt: An Empiricist Radical', *New Blackfriars*, 54, 634: 108–17.

————— 1975, *Myths of Power: A Marxist Study of the Brontës*, London: Macmillan.

————— 1976, *Criticism and Ideology: A Study in Marxist Literary Theory*, London: NLB.

————— 1981a, 'The Idealism of American Criticism', *New Left Review*, I, 127: 53–65.

————— 1981b, *Walter Benjamin, or, Towards a Revolutionary Criticism*, London: NLB.

————— 1982, 'Fredric Jameson: The Politics of Style', *Diacritics*, 12, 3: 14–22.

————— 1985, 'Brecht and Rhetoric', *New Literary History*, 16, 3: 633–38.

————— 1986, *Against the Grain: Essays 1975–1985*, London: Verso.

————— 1990, *The Ideology of the Aesthetic*, Oxford: Blackwell.

————— 1996a, 'Introduction', in *Marxist Literary Theory: A Reader*, edited by Terry Eagleton and Drew Milne, Oxford: Blackwell.

————— 1996b [1983], *Literary Theory: An Introduction*, Oxford: Blackwell.

————— 2000a, 'The Crack of Bloom', *The Guardian*, 20 August.

————— 2000b, *The Idea of Culture*, Oxford: Blackwell.

————— 2001, *The Gatekeeper: A Memoir*, London: Allen Lane.

————— 2002, *Sweet Violence: A Study of the Tragic*, Oxford: Blackwell.

————— 2003, *After Theory*, London: Allen Lane.

————— 2005a, *The English Novel*, Oxford: Blackwell.

————— 2005b [1984], *The Function of Criticism*, London: Verso.

————— 2005c, *Holy Terror*, Oxford: Oxford University Press.

————— 2007a, *How to Read a Poem*, Oxford: Blackwell.

————— 2007b, 'Jesus: Messiah or Bolshevik?' *The Guardian*, Tuesday, 4 December.

————— 2007c, *The Meaning of Life*, Oxford: Oxford University Press.

————— 2007d, 'Stars and Swipes', *The Guardian*, Saturday 5 May.

————— 2009a, 'Jameson and Form', *New Left Review*, 59: 123–37.

————— 2009b, *Reason, Faith, and Revolution: Reflections on the God Debate*, New Haven: Yale University Press.

————— 2012, 'Terry Eagleton on the Event of Literature (Part 2)', available at: http://www.youtube.com/watch?v=xDbne1t2oxs.

————— 2013, *How to Read Literature*, New Haven, CT: Yale University Press.

Eagleton, Terry, Alexander Barker and Alex Niven 2012, 'An Interview with Terry Eagleton', *The Oxonian Review*, no. 19, 4, available at: http://www.oxonianreview.org/wp/an-interview-with-terry-eagleton/

Eagleton, Terry and Matthew Beaumont 2009, *The Task of the Critic: Terry Eagleton in Dialogue*, London: Verso.

Easthope, Antony 1999, *Englishness and National Culture*, London: Routledge.

Eliot, T.S. 1972, *Selected Essays*, London: Faber.

Feuerbach, Ludwig 1989 [1841], *The Essence of Christianity*, translated by George Eliot, New York: Prometheus.

Finch, Alison 2004, 'The Stylistic Achievements of Flaubert's Fiction', in *The Cambridge Companion to Flaubert*, edited by Timothy Unwin, Cambridge: Cambridge University Press.

Fludernik, Monika 1996, *Towards a 'Natural' Narratology*, London: Routledge.

Frow, John 2006, *Genre*, London: Routledge.

———— 2014, *Character and Person*, Oxford: Oxford University Press.

Frye, Northrop 1957, *Anatomy of Criticism: Four Essays*, Princeton, N.J.: Princeton University Press.

Gaipa, Mark 1995, 'Culture, Anarchy, and the Politics of Modernist Style in Joyce's "Oxen of the Sun"', *Modern Fiction Studies*, 41, 2: 195–217.

Gąsiorek, Andrzej 2005, *J.G. Ballard*, Manchester: Manchester University Press.

Gauger, Hans-Martin 1995, *Über Sprache und Stil*, Munich: C.H. Beck.

Genette, Gérard 1980, *Narrative Discourse: An Essay in Method*, translated by Jane E. Lewin, Ithaca, N.Y.: Cornell University Press.

———— 1988, *Narrative Discourse Revisited*, translated by Jane E. Lewin, Ithaca, N.Y.: Cornell University Press.

Gibson, Andrew 1996, *Towards a Postmodern Theory of Narrative*, Edinburgh: Edinburgh University Press.

Giddens, Anthony 1972, *Politics and Sociology in the Thought of Max Weber*, London: Macmillan.

Gilbert, Sandra M. and Susan Gubar 1988, *No Man's Land: The Place of the Woman Writer in the Twentieth Century*, Volume 1, New Haven: Yale University Press.

Goldsmith, Kenneth 2011, *Uncreative Writing: Managing Language in the Digital Age*, New York: Columbia University Press.

Grossberg, Lawrence 2010, 'Raymond Williams and the Absent Modernity', in *About Raymond Williams*, edited by Monika Seidl, Roman Horak and Lawrence Grossberg, London: Routledge.

Gumbrecht, Hans Ulrich, Karl Ludwig Pfeiffer and Armin Biermann 1986, *Stil: Geschichten und Funktionen eines kulturwissenschaftlichen Diskurselements*, Frankfurt am Main: Suhrkamp.

Halliwell, Stephen 1998 [1986], *Aristotle's Poetics*, Chicago: University of Chicago Press.

———— 2012, 'Diegesis – Mimesis', *The Living Handbook of Narratology*, available at: http://wikis.sub.uni-hamburg.de/lhn/index.php/Diegesis_-_Mimesis

Hamon, Philippe 2004, 'What is a Description?', in *Narrative Theory: Critical Concepts in Literary and Cultural Studies*, edited by Mieke Bal, London: Routledge.

Hartley, Daniel 2015, 'Style as Structure of Feeling: Emergent Forms of Life in the Theory of Raymond Williams and George Saunders's *Tenth of December*', in *Emergent Forms of Life in Anglophone Literature: Conceptual Frameworks and Critical Analyses*, edited by Michael Basseler, Daniel Hartley and Ansgar Nünning, Trier: WVT.

—————— forthcoming, 'Combined and Uneven Styles in the Modern World-System: Stylistic Ideology in José de Alencar, Machado de Assis and Thomas Hardy', *European Journal of English Studies*.

Harvey, David 2005, *A Brief History of Neoliberalism*, Oxford: Oxford University Press.

Haug, Wolfgang Fritz 1987, *Pluraler Marxismus*, Volume 2, Berlin: Argument.

Heath, Stephen 1994, 'I.A. Richards, F.R. Leavis and Cambridge English', in *Cambridge Minds*, edited by Richard Mason, Cambridge: Cambridge University Press.

Hegel, Georg Wilhelm Friedrich 1977 [1807], *Phenomenology of Spirit*, translated by A.V. Miller, Oxford: Clarendon Press.

Helmling, Steven 2001, *The Success and Failure of Fredric Jameson: Writing, the Sublime, and the Dialectic of Critique*, Albany: State University of New York Press.

Herman, David 2008, *Basic Elements of Narrative*, Oxford: Blackwell.

Higgins, John 1999, *Raymond Williams: Literature, Marxism and Cultural Materialism*, London: Routledge.

Hilliard, Christopher 2012, *English as a Vocation: The Scrutiny Movement*, Oxford: Oxford University Press.

Hobsbawm, Eric. J. 1992, *Nations and Nationalism since 1780: Programme, Myth, Reality*, 2nd ed., Cambridge: Cambridge University Press.

Holland, Eugene W. 1999, *Deleuze and Guattari's Anti-Oedipus: Introduction to Schizoanalysis*, London: Routledge.

Howe, Stephen 2003, 'American Empire: History and Future of an Idea', available at: https://www.opendemocracy.net/conflict-americanpower/article_1279.jsp.

Hühn, Peter and Jens Kiefer 2005, *The Narratological Analysis of Lyric Poetry: Studies in English Poetry from the 16th to the 20th Century*, Berlin: Walter de Gruyter.

Innes, Doreen C. 1985, 'Theophrastus and the Theory of Style', in *Theophrastus of Eresus: On His Life and Work*, edited by William W. Fortenbaugh, New Brunswick, N.J.: Transaction Publishers.

Jacoby, Russell 1981, *Dialectic of Defeat: Contours of Western Marxism*, Cambridge: Cambridge University Press.

Jakobson, Roman 1987, *Language in Literature*, Cambridge, Mass.: Belknap Press.

Jameson, Fredric 1971, *Marxism and Form: Twentieth-Century Dialectical Theories of Literature*, Princeton: Princeton University Press.

—————— 1972, *The Prison-House of Language. A Critical Account of Structuralism and Russian Formalism*, Princeton: Princeton University Press.

—————— 1979, *Fables of Aggression: Wyndham Lewis, the Modernist as Fascist*, Berkeley: University of California Press.

———— 1981, *The Political Unconscious: Narrative as a Socially Symbolic Act*, Ithaca, N.Y.: Cornell University Press.

———— 1984 [1961], *Sartre: The Origins of a Style*, 2nd ed., New York; Guildford: Columbia University Press.

———— 1987a, 'A Brief Response', *Social Text*, 19: 26–7.

———— 1987b, 'The State of the Subject (III)', *Critical Quarterly*, 29, 4: 16–25.

———— 1991, *Postmodernism, or, the Cultural Logic of Late Capitalism*, Durham: Duke University Press.

———— 1992, *The Geopolitical Aesthetic: Cinema and Space in the World System*, Bloomington: Indiana University Press.

———— 1998, *Brecht and Method*, London: Verso.

———— 2002, *A Singular Modernity: Essay on the Ontology of the Present*, London: Verso.

———— 2005, *Archaeologies of the Future: The Desire Called Utopia and Other Science Fictions*, London: Verso.

———— 2007a, *Jameson on Jameson: Conversations on Cultural Marxism*, Durham, N.C.: London: Duke University Press.

———— 2007b, *The Modernist Papers*, London: Verso.

———— 2008, *The Ideologies of Theory*, updated ed., London: Verso.

———— 2009, *Valences of the Dialectic*, London: Verso.

———— 2010a, 'Conclusion', in *Aesthetics and Politics*, London: Verso.

———— 2010b, *The Hegel Variations: On the Phenomenology of Spirit*, London: Verso.

———— 2011, *Representing Capital: A Commentary on Volume One*, London: Verso.

———— 2013, *The Antinomies of Realism*, London: Verso.

Jay, Martin 2005, *Songs of Experience: Modern American and European Variations on a Universal Theme*, Berkeley: University of California Press.

Jennison, Ruth 2012, *The Zukofsky Era: Modernity, Margins, and the Avant-Garde*, Hopkins Studies in Modernism, Baltimore: Johns Hopkins University Press.

Jones, Paul 2004, *Raymond Williams's Sociology of Culture: A Critical Reconstruction*, Basingstoke: Palgrave Macmillan.

Joyce, James 1993 [1922], *Ulysses*, Oxford: Oxford University Press.

Keats, John 2002, *Selected Letters of John Keats*, rev. ed., Cambridge, Mass.: Harvard University Press.

Kennedy, George A. 1999, *Classical Rhetoric and its Christian and Secular Tradition from Ancient to Modern Times*, 2nd ed., Chapel Hill: University of North Carolina Press.

Knight, Stephen Thomas 2010, *Crime Fiction since 1800: Detection, Death, Diversity*, 2nd ed., Basingstoke: Palgrave Macmillan.

Knights, L.C. 1936, 'Shakespeare and Profit Inflations', *Scrutiny*, 5, 1: 48–60.

Kushner, Rachel, Matthew Hart and Alexander Rocca 2015, 'An Interview With Rachel Kushner', *Contemporary Literature*, 56, 2: 192–215.

Leavis, F.R. 1932, *New Bearings in English Poetry*, London: Chatto and Windus.

———— 1962 [1948], *The Great Tradition*, Harmondsworth: Penguin.

Lecercle, Jean-Jacques 2007, *A Marxist Philosophy of Language*, translated by Gregory Elliott, Leiden: Brill.

———— 2015, 'Littérateurs de tous les pays, unissez-vous!', available at: http://revueperiode.net/litterateurs-de-tous-les-pays-unissez-vous/#identifier_22_2075.

Lefebvre, Henri 2008, *Critique of Everyday Life*, London: Verso.

Levinas, Emmanuel 1987, *Time and the Other*, Pittsburgh, PA: Duquesne University Press.

Levine, Caroline 2015, *Forms: Whole, Rhythm, Hierarchy, Network*, Princeton: Princeton University Press.

Lukács, Georg 1970, *Writer and Critic and Other Essays*, London: Merlin Press.

———— 1971 [1920], *The Theory of the Novel: A Historico-Philosophical Essay on the Forms of Great Epic Literature*, translated by Anna Bostock, London: Merlin Press.

MacIntyre, Alasdair C. 2002, *A Short History of Ethics: A History of Moral Philosophy from the Homeric Age to the Twentieth Century*, 2nd ed., London: Routledge.

Margolis, Joseph 1992, 'Praxis and Meaning: Marx's Species Being and Aristotle's Political Animal', in *Marx and Aristotle: Nineteenth-Century German Social Theory and Classical Antiquity*, edited by George E. McCarthy, Maryland: Rowman & Littlefield Publishers.

Martin, Niall 2013, 'Unacknowledged Cities: Modernity and Acknowledgement in China Miéville's *The City and the City* and Marc Isaacs' *All White in Barking*', *European Journal of Cultural Studies*, 16, 6: 710–24.

Marx, Karl 1973, *Surveys from Exile*, translated by David Fernbach, London: Penguin Books.

———— 1975a [1842], 'Bemerkungen Über Die Neueste Preußische Zensurinstruktion', in *MEGA*, Volume 1, Berlin: Dietz Verlag.

———— 1975b [1842], 'Comments on the Latest Prussian Censorship Instruction', in Karl Marx and Frederick Engels, *Collected Works*, Volume 1, London: Lawrence and Wishart.

———— 1975c [1843–44], *Early Writings*, translated by Rodney Livingstone and Gregor Benton, Harmondsworth: Penguin.

———— 1990 [1867], *Capital: A Critique of Political Economy*, translated by Ben Fowkes, London: Penguin Classics.

Marx, Karl and Friedrich Engels 1956, *Karl Marx and Frederick Engels: Selected Correspondence*, Moscow: Foreign Languages Pub. House.

———— 1978, *Werke*, Volume 3, *MEW*, Berlin: Dietz Verlag.

Mayeda, Graham 2008, 'Commentary on Fichte's "The Illegality of the Unauthorised Reprinting of Books": An Essay in Intellectual Property During the Age of the Enlightenment', *University of Ottawa Law and Technology Journal*, 5, 1 & 2: 141–98.

McCabe, Herbert 2003 [1968], *Law, Love and Language*, London: Continuum.

McKeon, Michael 2002, *The Origins of the English Novel, 1600–1740*, 15th anniversary ed., Baltimore: John Hopkins University Press.

Moi, Toril 2006, *Henrik Ibsen and the Birth of Modernism: Art, Theater, Philosophy*, Oxford: Oxford University Press.

Mommsen, Wolfgang J. 1989, *The Political and Social Theory of Max Weber: Collected Essays*, Chicago: University of Chicago Press.

Moretti, Franco 2013, *The Bourgeois: Between History and Literature*, London: Verso.

Mulhern, Francis 1979, *The Moment of 'Scrutiny'*, London: NLB.

Nealon, Christopher S. 2011, *The Matter of Capital: Poetry and Crisis in the American Century*, Cambridge, Mass.: Harvard University Press.

Ngũgĩ wa, Thiong'o 1986, *Decolonising the Mind: The Politics of Language in African Literature*, London: Currey.

Nielsen, Henrik Skov 2011, 'Unnatural Narratology, Impersonal Voices, Real Authors, and Non-Communicative Narration', in *Unnatural Narratives – Unnatural Narratology*, edited by Jan Alber and Rüdiger Heinze, Berlin: De Gruyter.

Nietzsche, Friedrich Wilhelm 1997 [1873–6], *Untimely Meditations*, translated by R.J. Hollingdale, Cambridge: Cambridge University Press.

Nünning, Ansgar and Roy Sommer 2008, 'Diegetic and Mimetic Narrativity: Some Further Steps Towards a Narratology of Drama', in *Theorizing Narrativity*, edited by John Pier and José Ángel García Landa, Berlin: De Gruyter.

O'Connor, Alan 1989, *Raymond Williams: Writing, Culture, Politics*, Oxford: Basil Blackwell.

Osborne, Peter 1995, *The Politics of Time: Modernity and Avant-Garde*, London: Verso.

———— 2013, *Anywhere or Not at All: Philosophy of Contemporary Art*, London: Verso.

Phelan, James 2001, 'Redundant Telling, Preserving the Mimetic, and the Functions of Character Narration', *Narrative*, 9, 2: 210–16.

Pierre, Scott J. St. 2008, 'Abnormal Tongues: Style and Sexuality in Modern Literature and Culture' [Ph.D. thesis], University of Michigan.

Postone, Moishe 1993, *Time, Labor, and Social Domination: A Reinterpretation of Marx's Critical Theory*, Cambridge: Cambridge University Press.

Prawer, Siegbert Salomon 1978, *Karl Marx and World Literature*, Oxford: Oxford University Press.

Priest, Stephen 2001, *Sartre: Basic Writings*, London: Routledge.

Proust, Marcel 2003 [1927], *In Search of Lost Time: Finding Time Again*, translated by Ian Patterson, London: Penguin.

Puchner, Martin 2006, *Poetry of the Revolution: Marx, Manifestos, and the Avant-Gardes*, Princeton, N.J.: Princeton University Press.

Quiller-Couch, Arthur 1916, *On the Art of Writing*, available at: http://www.bartleby.com/190/12.html.

Rancière, Jacques 1998, *La parole muette: essai sur les contradictions de la littérature*, Paris: Hachette littératures.

———— 2004, *The Politics of Aesthetics: The Distribution of the Sensible*, translated by Gabriel Rockhill, London: Continuum.

Read, Jason 2003, *The Micro-Politics of Capital: Marx and the Prehistory of the Present*, Albany: State University of New York Press.

Richards, I.A. 2004 [1929], *Practical Criticism: A Study of Literary Judgment*, New Brunswick, N.J.: Transaction.

Ricoeur, Paul 1984a. *Temps et récit*, Volume 2, Paris: Seuil.

———— 1984b, *Time and Narrative*, translated by Kathleen McLaughlin and David Pellauer, Volume 1, Chicago: University of Chicago Press.

———— 1985, *Time and Narrative*, translated by Kathleen McLaughlin and David Pellauer, Volume 2, Chicago: University of Chicago Press.

———— 2003 [1974], *The Rule of Metaphor*, translated by Robert Czerny, Kathleen McLaughlin and S.J. John Costello, Oxford: Routledge.

Robin, Régine 1986, *Le réalisme socialiste: une esthétique impossible*, Paris: Payot.

Rose, Margaret A. 1978, *Reading the Young Marx and Engels: Poetry, Parody, and the Censor*, Totowa, N.J.: Croom Helm/ Rowman and Littlefield.

Sartre, Jean-Paul 1947, *Situations: essais critiques*, Paris: Gallimard.

———— 2001 [1948], *What is Literature?*, translated by Bernard Frechtman, London: Routledge.

Silva, Ludovico 1971, *El Estilo de Marx*, Mexico: Siglo Ventuno.

Simpson, David 1992, 'Raymond Williams: Feeling for Structures, Voicing "History"', *Social Text*, 30, 30: 9–26.

Smith, Dai 2008, *Raymond Williams: A Warrior's Tale*, Cardigan: Parthian.

Smith, James 2008, *Terry Eagleton: A Critical Introduction*, Cambridge: Polity.

Spitzer, Leo 1970, *Études de style*, translated by Eliane Kaufholz, Alain Coulon and Michel Foucault, Paris: Gallimard.

Stanzel, Franz K. 1984 [1979], *A Theory of Narrative*, translated by Charlotte Goedsche, Cambridge: Cambridge University Press.

Stein, Gertrude 1988 [1935], *Lectures in America*, London: Virago.

Suvin, Darko 1979, *Metamorphoses of Science Fiction: On the Poetics and History of a Literary Genre*, New Haven: Yale University Press.

Taylor, Dennis 1993, *Hardy's Literary Language and Victorian Philology*, Oxford: Oxford University Press.

Terdiman, Richard 1994, '1848', in *A New History of French Literature*, edited by Denis Hollier, Cambridge, Mass.: Harvard University Press.

Therborn, Göran 1976, *Science, Class and Society: On the Formation of Sociology and Historical Materialism*, London: New Left Books.

Thomas, Peter D. 2006, 'Modernity as "Passive Revolution": Gramsci and the Fundamental Concepts of Historical Materialism', *Journal of the Canadian Historical Association/ Revue de la Société historique du Canada*, 17, 2: 61–78.

———— 2008, 'Immanence', *Historical Materialism*, 16: 239–43.

———— 2009, *The Gramscian Moment: Philosophy, Hegemony and Marxism*, Leiden: Brill.

Thompson, E.P. 1961a, 'The Long Revolution (Part 1)', *New Left Review*, I, 9: 24–33.

———— 1961b, 'The Long Revolution (Part 2)', *New Left Review*, I, 10: 34–9.

———— 1995 [1978], *The Poverty of Theory, or an Orrery of Errors*, London: Merlin Press.

Trotsky, Leon 2005 [1925], *Literature and Revolution*, translated by Rose Strunsky, Chicago: Haymarket Books.

Turchetto, Maria 2007, 'From "Mass Worker" to "Empire": The Disconcerting Trajectory of Italian *Operaismo*', in *Critical Companion to Contemporary Marxism*, edited by Jacques Bidet and Stathis Kouvelakis, Leiden: Brill.

Vendler, Helen 1995, *The Breaking of Style: Hopkins, Heaney, Graham*, Cambridge, Mass.: Harvard University Press.

Vickers, Brian 1988, *In Defence of Rhetoric*, Oxford: Oxford University Press.

Voloshinov, V.N. 1976, *Freudianism: A Marxist Critique*, translated by I.R. Titunik, New York: Academic Press.

Walder, Dennis 2011, *Postcolonial Nostalgias: Writing, Representation and Memory*, New York: Routledge.

Wallace, Jeff 1993, 'Language, Nature and the Politics of Materialism: Raymond Williams and D.H. Lawrence', in *Raymond Williams: Politics, Education, Letters*, edited by W. John Morgan and Peter Preston, Basingstoke: St. Martin's Press.

Walsh, Richard 2007, *The Rhetoric of Fictionality: Narrative Theory and the Idea of Fiction*, Columbus: Ohio State University Press.

———— 2010, 'Person, Level, Voice: A Rhetorical Reconsideration', in *Postclassical Narratology: Approaches and Analyses*, edited by Jan Alber and Monika Fludernik, Columbus: Ohio State University Press.

Watt, Ian 1957, *The Rise of the Novel: Studies in Defoe, Richardson, and Fielding*, Berkeley: University of California Press.

White, Hayden 1975, *Metahistory: The Historical Imagination in Nineteenth-Century Europe*, Baltimore: John Hopkins University Press.

———— 1987, *The Content of Form: Narrative Discourse and Historical Representation*, Baltimore: Johns Hopkins University Press.

Williams, Raymond 1952a, *Drama from Ibsen to Eliot*, 2nd ed., London: Chatto & Windus.

———— 1952b, 'The Teaching of Public Expression', in *Border Country: Raymond Williams in Adult Education*, edited by John McIlroy and Sallie Westwood, Leicester: NIACE.

———— 1963 [1958], *Culture and Society: 1780–1950*, Harmondsworth: Penguin Books.

———— 1965 [1961], *The Long Revolution*, Harmondsworth: Penguin Books.

———— 1969, *The Pelican Book of English Prose: From 1780 to the Present Day*, Volume 2, Harmondsworth: Penguin.

———— 1970, *The English Novel from Dickens to Lawrence*, London: Chatto & Windus.

———— 1971, *Orwell*, London: Fontana/ Collins.

———— 1973a, *The Country and the City*, New York: Oxford University Press.

———— 1973b [1968], *Drama from Ibsen to Brecht*, 2nd revised ed., Harmondsworth: Penguin Books.

———— 1976 [1962], *Communications*, 3rd ed., Harmondsworth: Penguin Books.

———— 1977a, *Marxism and Literature*, Oxford: Oxford University Press.

———— 1977b, 'Realism, Naturalism and Their Alternatives', *Ciné-Tracts*. 1, 3: 1–8.

———— 1979a [1966], *Modern Tragedy*, revised ed., London: Verso.

———— 1979b, *Politics and Letters: Interviews with 'New Left Review'*, London: NLB.

———— 1981a, *Culture*, London: Fontana.

———— 1981b, 'Marxism, Structuralism and Literary Analysis', *New Left Review*, I, 129: 51–66.

———— 1983a [1976], *Keywords: A Vocabulary of Culture and Society*, revised and expanded ed., London: Fontana.

———— 1983b, *Writing in Society*, London: Verso.

———— 1989a, *Resources of Hope: Culture, Democracy, Socialism*, London: Verso.

———— 1989b, *What I Came to Say*, London: Hutchinson Radius.

———— 1991 [1954], *Drama in Performance*, Milton Keynes: Open University Press.

———— 2007 [1989], *The Politics of Modernism: Against the New Conformists*, London: Verso.

———— 2010 [1980], *Culture and Materialism: Selected Essays*, London: Verso.

Williams, Raymond and Michael Orrom 1954, *Preface to Film*, London: Film Drama.

Woloch, Alex 2003, *The One Vs. the Many: Minor Characters and the Space of the Protagonist in the Novel*, Princeton, N.J.: Princeton University Press.

Woodmansee, Martha 1984, 'The Genius and the Copyright: Economic and Legal Conditions of the Emergence of the "Author"', *Eighteenth-Century Studies*, 17, 4: 425–48.

Žižek, Slavoj 1999, "You May!", *London Review of Books*, 21, 6: 3–6.

Name Index

Subject Index